FAIR AND EFFECTIVE
REPRESENTATION?

Enduring Questions in American Political Life
Series Editor: Wilson Carey McWilliams, Rutgers University

This series explores the political, social, and cultural issues that originated during the founding of the American nation but are still heatedly debated today. Each book offers teachers and students a concise but comprehensive summary of the issue's evolution, along with the crucial documents spanning the range of American history. In addition, *Enduring Questions in American Political Life* provides insightful contemporary perspectives that illuminate the enduring relevance and future prospects of important issues on the American political landscape.

FAIR AND EFFECTIVE REPRESENTATION?

Debating Electoral Reform and Minority Rights

Mark E. Rush
and Richard L. Engstrom

Introduction by Bruce E. Cain

ROWMAN & LITTLEFIELD PUBLISHERS, INC.
Lanham • New York • Boulder • Oxford

ROWMAN & LITTLEFIELD PUBLISHERS, INC.

Published in the United States of America
by Rowman & Littlefield Publishers, Inc.
4720 Boston Way, Lanham, Maryland 20706
www.rowmanlittlefield.com

12 Hid's Copse Road
Cumnor Hill, Oxford OX2 9JJ, England

British Library Cataloguing in Publication Information Available

Library of Congress Cataloging-in-Publication Data

Rush, Mark E.
    Fair and effective representation? : debating electoral reform and minority rights
/ Mark E. Rush and Richard L. Engstrom ; introd. by Bruce E. Cain
        p.   cm. — (Enduring questions in American political life)
    Includes bibliographical references and index.
    ISBN 0-8476-9211-6 (alk. paper). — ISBN 0-8476-9212-4 (pbk. : alk. paper)
    1. Apportionment (Election law)—United States.   2. Election districts—United
States.   3. Gerrymandering—United States.   4. Representative government and
representation—United States.   I. Engstrom, Richard Lee, 1946– II. Series.
JK1341.R89   2001
328.73'07345—dc21   00-059225

Printed in the United States of America

♾ ™ The paper used in this publication meets the minimum requirements of American
National Standard for Information Sciences—Permanence of Paper for Printed Library
Materials, ANSI/NISO Z39.48–1992.

Mark Rush dedicates this to Flor, William, and Alex

Dick Engstrom dedicates this to Louise C. Engstrom
and the late Elmer F. Engstrom

Contents

Acknowledgments

Any book is a group effort. In addition to thanking each other we would like to make special mention of several people who helped make this book possible. First, many thanks to the folks at Rowman & Littlefield for soliciting and supporting our efforts and to Bruce Cain for writing the opening remarks. In addition, we wish to thank Susan Slim and Alex Sedgwick for their many hours of assistance in proofreading, fact checking, and so forth; and Suzyn Smith, who assisted with the index.

Introduction:
Exploring the Last Taboo of U.S. Politics

Bruce E. Cain

Curiously, despite many other fundamental changes in the American political system since its founding, there is an enormous cultural and political resistance to abandoning the single-member plurality (SMP) rules used for electing most state and all congressional representatives. Dozens of other important reforms have been introduced since the nineteenth century, such as the direct election of the Senate, adoption of presidential primaries, expansion of the franchise to women and minorities, limitations on campaign contributions and expenditures, disclosure requirements, registration of lobbyists, and the popular initiative and referendum. But very few states have even tried multi-member districts, let alone alternative voting rules such as limited, cumulative, and preference voting. How odd that a political culture so seemingly open to experimentation and change is so loyal to this particular systemic feature. The mere proposal of relatively minor changes in the electoral rule can be politically damaging, as Lani Guinier discovered in the early 1990s when she openly advocated the adoption of semi-proportional-representation (semi-PR) rules.

In this volume, two highly respected voting rights scholars, Richard Engstrom and Mark Rush, take on the question of proportionality rules, the final taboo of U.S. politics. As Engstrom points out, there are indications at the local level at least that some jurisdictions are willing to adopt alternative electoral systems. As he tells us, "Cumulative voting has been adopted by almost sixty counties, municipalities, and school boards in five states, while limited voting has been adopted by almost forty such units, also in five states." Preference voting has been adopted more infrequently: historically, it has been tried only twenty-two times since the beginning of the twentieth century. Currently, it is used only in Cambridge, Massachusetts, for its city council and school committee and in New York City for its thirty-two community school boards. The exceptions do not seem likely to become the rule. Cambridge and New York City are not strong selling points for the rest of the country. Think of the salsa ad depicting fictional southwestern ranchers who string up their cook when they discover that the sauce they are eating was made in New York City. This conveys pretty accurately how the proportionality cause is "aided" by an association with New York and Cambridge.

So why take up the hitherto unpopular cause of alternative electoral systems? Richard Engstrom argues that the time is right for a reexamination of the rules. He believes that substituting semi-PR rules—that is, cumulative, limited, and preference voting—for the current SMP rules is the most efficacious means of extricating state and local jurisdictions from an increasingly complex and legally tangled political thicket. But still, the reader might ask, why now? The fundamental importance of the choice between majoritarian and proportional rules has been understood and debated for over a century. Some societies—for example, Italy, Israel, the Netherlands—went in the proportional direction, adopting complex formulas that assign seats to parties based on vote shares, while others, the Anglo-American democracies especially, veered in the majoritarian direction, assigning one representative to each seat and electing that person by simple-majority or -plurality rules. As Rush points out, all decisions about political rules are trade-offs. Switching from one system to the other might improve performance in one dimension, such as the fairness of representation for some groups, but at the cost of decreasing performance for others, such as the ability to form a predictable governing majority. So why open an old and seemingly irresolvable controversy?

There are several answers. First, U.S. demography has changed dramatically in the last thirty years owing in large part to the new immigration policies adopted in 1965. With the end of policies that favored white Europeans, legal immigration from Mexico and Asia expanded rapidly, and with it, the nonwhite share of the U.S. population. This has increased the diversity of the American electorate and restored ethnicity to the level of political salience it held in the middle and late nineteenth century. The Voting Rights Act and a more aggressive application of the post–Civil War constitutional amendments (especially the Fourteenth) have helped create the expectation that electoral outcomes should be "fair" to substantially sized nonwhite minority groups.

Even though the Supreme Court has made it clear that there is no explicit group right to proportional representation, the "specter of proportionality" has always haunted the voting rights debate. The language of the Voting Rights Act deftly dances around the issue, guaranteeing only that protected classes of individuals who have historically suffered discrimination have the right "to elect a representative of their own choice." But this vaguely defined formal right evolved over time into an informal goal of roughly proportional descriptive representation, eventually developing critics on both the right and the left.

From the right, drawing districts in order to enhance minority representation looked like yet another affirmative action quota system (Thernstrom 1987). This position, as both Engstrom and Rush explain, was eventually incorporated into the Court's reasoning in the *Shaw* line of cases in which the Court held that drawing lines on primarily racial grounds violated the Fourteenth Amendment.

At the same time, critics arose on the left. Some of them argued that the price of creating minority seats was a significant reduction in white liberal representation, causing nonwhites to win the battle but not the war for progressive policies (Lublin 1997; Grofman and Handley 1998). Indeed, for a while, the cause of greater nonwhite representation was perceived in certain Democratic circles as a Republican plot. Removing African American and Latino voters from white seats only enhanced Republican chances, they argued. The final verdict on this issue is mixed, as Democrats found ingenious ways to accommodate their political needs with the expanded requirements of the Voting Rights Act. But the political ingenuity that saved the Democrats from being bleached into electoral oblivion gave rise to the cartographic monstrosities that eventually caught the Court's attention in the *Shaw* cases (Kousser 1999).

Critics on the left began to contemplate the difficulty of resolving disputes between protected groups when geographic circumstances caused them to lay claim to the same area and revealed the arbitrariness of giving representation to some disadvantaged political identities but not others. Geographic representation by definition advantages geographically concentrated groups. Groups that are less than optimally dispersed cannot be helped even by the most creative districting schemes. For instance, consider the practical difficulty of creating majority-female districts as women persist in their unfortunate habit of living close to men. Representational questions also arise for those who live in a geographically concentrated minority community. It could be said, for example, that the districting process imposes a political identity upon them rather than allowing them to choose one for themselves.

So one very important reason that the old debate about electoral rules has been revived in the new millennium is that circumstances have changed and the question of minority representation is now more salient than it was fifty years ago. In an era in which assimilation to the Anglo-American ideal was the prevailing norm and minorities had fewer legal protections, devices such as at-large majority districts and SMP systems helped blur identities and force people into big-tent coalitions. But the downside of such institutionally induced political assimilation was little or no minority representation. As the United States sought to correct the problem of minority underrepresentation, it moved more to SMP districts and to consciously designing district boundaries to be more fair. As one who has been personally involved in this exercise, I can testify that it is a cumbersome and controversial process. The question raised in this volume is whether there is a better way to adjust the political system to new legal, cultural, and demographic demands.

Another feature of the recent revival of the old debate over electoral rules is that it poses the choice in less extreme terms than previously. There is more interest today in the so-called semi-PR systems than before. These systems can be viewed as a compromise between the at-large PR systems used in European democracies and the Anglo-American SMP rules. The semi-PR options include concentrating multiple votes on one candidate (cumulative voting), limiting votes to a number less than the number of elected offices (limited voting), and expressing an order of preferences so as to make surplus votes count (preference voting). All have the effect of lowering the threshold of representation for minority groups, which is the minimum vote share a group needs to win a seat in the relevant legislative body. Also, none of these systems gives more power to party bosses, a move that would be anathema to most American voters, and all can be adapted to geographical districts if so desired.

A third factor in the revival of this hoary controversy is the growing support from reform groups who detest the competitive stranglehold produced by the current party duopoly system. To pluralists, the two-party system is a big tent under which many groups come together and form broad-based coalitions. To some reformers and legal theorists under the sway of the economic-markets model, rules that favor two parties merely discriminate against minor parties and in the process prevent the healthy emergence of new blood and ideas. According to this view, in both the political and the economic marketplace, more competition is better than less. The role of reform and court intervention is to break up the anticompetitive practices of the two major political parties in the United States and promote a healthier political market. PR and semi-PR rules are potential duopoly-breaking devices that will spur competition and foster the growth of minor parties.

This last argument for proportionality, while potentially important in terms of the future of alternative voting systems in America, is not central to the Engstrom–Rush disagreement. Although Rush touches on these concerns in his essay when he considers the views of various PR advocates, his specific disagreement with Engstrom is over whether these alternative systems solve the problems of fairer racial representation. Rush's essay also reminds the reader that important strands of the debate exist outside the narrower voting rights framework and that the pro-PR political coalition as it exists today is somewhat more diverse than one might think. Antipathy towards the parties and the two-party system is a potentially important motive for changing the rules. The populist strain in the U.S. political culture has greatly influenced the electoral reforms that have been introduced over the last century. Suspicious of mediation by elites and dedicated to the cause of elevating the influence of the individual voter, populists prefer weak to strong parties and pragmatic to ideological approaches. This rules out the strong-party forms of PR and European-style parliamentary legislative structures as serious candidates for widespread adoption. But it is easier to imagine that semi-PR rules, especially limited and cumulative voting with multimember districts, might fill the gap between the present duopoly and highly ideological multipartyism.

Rush's critique of PR generally, and of the Engstrom case specifically, centers on the assumption that the rule changes solve political problems. He argues that while rule changes might solve some problems, they introduce others. A core principle of political science is that all rules present trade-offs between different representational values. Consequently, there is no certain evolution towards a more nearly perfect, fairer system; there is only alternation between systems that favor some values and interests and systems that favor others. In Engstrom's view, an alternative voting system is the route out of the political thicket of racial gerrymandering. In Rush's view, it merely takes you from one thicket to another. The problem of drawing fair boundaries in an SMP district-based system might be solved by moving to a PR or semi-PR system. But designing the new system would involve making new decisions that are equally political. As Rush tells us, "A new electoral system will not eradicate vote dilution; it will simply manifest it differently. . . . While an alternative electoral system will put an end to redistricting-based gerrymandering controversies, it will replace them with quota controversies."

Clearly, Rush's critique raises a profound problem. In an ideal world, perhaps, policies are political and rules are not. People can disagree about government decisions but should agree about how to make those decisions. The problem is that political actors understand that political rules favor some individuals and groups over others and, in the quest for power, seek to get every possible strategic advantage. The decision to move from the status quo position of single member, simple plurality to semi-PR or PR might potentially weaken the political power of certain geographically based groups and give more representation to more dispersed groups. Politicians elected under the old rules may fear the uncertainty that the new rules would introduce. In short, there will be problems associated with every change, and resistance from political actors who can foresee the potential consequences and risks for them.

The technical term for this problem is "rule endogeneity." It simply means that the rules, as much as the policies, are the product of political forces and incentives. At one level, this would seem to be an argument for sticking with the status quo: if all that one is doing by changing the rules is exchanging one set of controversies for another, why bother? Indeed, there is much to say for sticking with the arbitrary system that we know rather than adopting one that we do not know. Predictability is correlated with systemic stability. The process to which voters become accustomed can acquire a legitimacy that new systems lack at the outset. Translated into the language of the voting rights debate, the argument would be the following. Even though some groups do not get fair-share representation under the current rules and the process of making it fairer to them is cumbersome and contentious in all the ways Engstrom describes, it might be better to leave things as they are rather than adopt an unfamiliar system for the sake of benefiting a few groups.

On the other hand, the reader might question the unspoken assumption that there should be only one uniform system of rules in the United States and that the debate is about adopting one or the other. As both authors remind us, the United States has a history of experimenting at the local level with alternative electoral rules. There is no reason to think that one set of rules works best for all conditions in the country nor that rules that work well in one time period will work well in another. An at-large, simple-majority system might work perfectly well when the population is homogeneous but might prove to be systematically unfair when the electorate is divided into a majority and minority along racially polarized lines. A PR or semi-PR system might function well when there are numerous cleavages that must be represented but might seem to inhibit broad coalition building in a homogeneous population.

Ideally, rules would be chosen to suit the prevailing conditions and would facilitate the achievement of a mutually agreed-upon fair division. In the language of political ethics, these rules would be adopted behind the "veil of ignorance," meaning that people would choose the outcome not knowing how they would personally fare under the new rules. The critical design problem, of course, is that political actors are in the business of lifting the veil and peeking at what is behind it. If people choose rules based on self-interested calculation, then the rules that will be adopted will favor the majority unless it is constrained by charters or constitutions requiring supermajority approval of rule change to ensure that the new rules suit at least some of the minority.

Given all this, it is not surprising that many of the recent experiments with alternative electoral rules have been created under the threat of legal intervention. The Supreme Court in essence has tried to rise above the constraints of normal politics and find solutions that compromise between fairness to the majority principle and minority rights. In the easy cases, this does not put too much pressure on the courts, but given the political nature of many court appointments and the importance of electoral approval for many state judges, it is clear that courts cannot by themselves solve the problem of rule endogeneity. Examining the forces that must be overcome to make the changes that are discussed in this volume shows why electoral rule changes are the final taboo of U.S. politics.

The debate between Engstrom and Rush sets out the pros and cons of this debate very clearly. Reading Engstrom's essay, one cannot help but see that the course that we have set ourselves upon is tortuous and perhaps even doomed to failure. Our allegiance to the current district-based system causes us to try to manipulate the system into a fairness that it does not naturally yield. In the process, we must adhere to the Court's insistence that this manipulation not be too self-consciously racial, or else we run afoul of the Fourteenth Amendment.

The next round of redistricting will reveal whether such a complex balancing act can be achieved.

At the same time, reading Rush's essay, one will question whether we are jumping from one political thicket into another. The search for a perfect system is futile, and the political cost of trying to overcome the inertia that favors the current system is considerable. The reader will have to decide whether the outcome is worth the effort. This volume nicely illuminates the issues. Deciding between these options is a collective task for the country.

I

DEBATING ELECTORAL REFORM
AND MINORITY RIGHTS

1

The Political Thicket, Electoral Reform, and Minority Voting Rights

Richard L. Engstrom

During the 1990s state and local governments across the United States engaged in a recurring activity called redistricting, the revision of the boundaries of the geographic districts used to elect members of the U.S. House of Representatives, state legislatures, and many local legislative bodies. Altering these districts has often been a contentious process, but it was particularly conflictive during the 1990s. It provoked a "political melee" in one state (Aguilar 1998, 797) and one of "the most intense, combative, and divisive political battles" in the history of another (Holmes 1998, 191). In a third state, the revision of district lines stimulated "levels of partisan acrimony unparalleled in anyone's memory" (Scher, Mills, and Hotaling 1997, 224). In yet another, it resulted in "a protracted process that was heated, confusing, and controversial" (Sellers, Canon, and Schousen 1998, 270).

Redistricting also stimulated extensive and expensive litigation. People feeling adversely affected by the results took their complaints to court at unprecedented rates (Weber 1995). The redistricting process, which began in 1991 following the release of new population figures from the 1990 census, had not reached closure in some settings as late as 1999. Litigation concerning congressional districts in Florida and North Carolina, state legislative districts in Alabama, Louisiana, and North Carolina, and local election districts in, for example, Lawrence, Massachusetts; Dooly County, Georgia; and Dallas County, Alabama, was still pending late that year.[1] The 1999 councilmanic election in Chicago was held under a new ward map that was revised, under court order, in late 1998 (*Barnett v. City of Chicago* 1998). In some settings the revision of district boundaries became almost a continuous activity, as redistricting was followed by "re-redistricting," sometimes more than once (Kubin 1997, 837 n. 1; see also Engstrom and Kirksey 1998).

Almost all of this litigation concerned allegations of "gerrymandering" in

3

Fig. 1.1 The Massachusetts gerrymander of 1812.
Source: *Boston Globe,* March 26, 1812.

one form or another. Gerrymandering refers to "discriminatory districting which operates unfairly to inflate the political strength of one group and deflate that of another" (Dixon 1971a, 29). The groups at issue in these allegations were usually, but not always, African Americans and/or Latinos, the largest racial and language minority groups in this country. Allegations of gerrymandering against African Americans and Latinos have been common in America's redistricting experience and were again so in the 1990s. But that decade also witnessed a new type of gerrymandering allegation—one maintaining that district lines had been unfairly manipulated to favor, rather than disadvantage, these groups. Numerous districting plans were adopted that contained one or more odd-shaped, contorted districts in which African Americans or Latinos constituted numerical majorities of sufficient size to provide them with opportunities to elect representatives of their choice. The original source of the expression "gerrymander," a convex-shaped state senate district adopted in Massachusetts in 1812 (figure 1.1), looked like a model of compactness compared to many of these new majority-minority districts. The shapes of some of these new districts were said to resemble "four spiders having an orgy" (figure 1.2), "a pair of earmuffs" (figure 1.3), and the mark of Zorro (figure 1.4).[2]

Whites or Anglos challenging majority-minority districts found a receptive audience in the Supreme Court. A majority of that Court has imposed new constraints on the intentional creation of such districts, constraints that do not apply to the creation of districts designed to accomplish other purposes, such as to advantage particular incumbents, a particular political party, or even voters of a particular socioeconomic or European ethnic background. While the

Fig. 1.2 Texas Congressional District 18: "Four Spiders Having an Orgy." Source: *Bush v. Vera* 1996, 988.

precise nature of the new constraints is not yet clear, they no doubt will reduce the number of majority-minority districts adopted by many states and localities in the future. The round of redistricting following the 2000 census of population therefore is expected to result in fewer such districts than did the post-1990 round. Given that majority-minority districts have been the major medium for the election of minority representatives in this country, due to the persistence of racially polarized voting, a reduction in the number of such districts is likewise expected to result in fewer minority representatives on governing bodies across the country.

Much of the conflict associated with the revision of district lines could be avoided, as well as the expensive litigation that so often follows these decisions, by the adoption of other election systems that are as democratic as, if not more democratic than, those currently in place. These alternative election systems can also provide a context in which minority voters have realistic opportunities to elect candidates of their choice without manipulating district lines in the way the Supreme Court has found objectionable. A retrogression in minority electoral opportunities, in short, could be avoided by the adoption of these systems.

This chapter reviews the interests at stake in, and the conflictive nature of, the redistricting process. Special attention is devoted to the new allegations of racial gerrymandering in favor of minorities and the Supreme Court's response to these allegations. The new constraints that the Court has imposed on districts designed to empower minorities are identified and their ambiguity is

Fig. 1.3 Illinois Congressional District 4: "A
Pair of Earmuffs." **Source: 1992, The Washington Post. Reprinted with permission.**

highlighted. Alternative electoral arrangements—in particular limited, cumulative, and preference voting systems—that could eliminate many of the gerrymandering allegations, racial and otherwise, that are inherent in the redistricting process, and thereby reduce greatly the conflict and the expensive
litigation associated with that process, are identified and evaluated. The arguments against these systems advanced by their opponents, or by those who
simply prefer to retain advantages provided them by the current arrangements,
are reviewed and evaluated. The predicted negative consequences of employ-
ing these alternative systems are compared, when possible, with the recent
experience with these systems in this country and are found to be without
empirical support. Finally, I argue that the significant benefits that result from
conducting elections under these arrangements justify much more serious consideration of them in this country. Electoral systems such as limited, cumulative, and preference voting can reduce the political conflict and litigation that
currently result from revising district lines and bring us closer to the goal of
"fair and effective representation" for all people (*Reynolds v. Sims* 1964,
565–66).

Redistricting Conflicts

The redistricting process, often called reapportionment, begins anew after each
decennial census. These revisions are required by U.S. Supreme Court deci-

Fig. 1.4 Louisiana Congressional District 4: "The Mark of Zorro." **Source: 1992, The Washington Post. Reprinted with permission.**

sions, beginning in the 1960s, that held that geographic districts used to elect legislators must comply with the "one person, one vote" rule.[3] This rule, in application, means that the districts used to elect members of a particular legislative body must contain approximately the same number of people.[4] New census figures almost always reveal that districts no longer satisfy this requirement and therefore need to be rearranged. One might think that bringing districts into compliance with such a straightforward rule would be a relatively simple task, but it has not been so. To the contrary, every decennial census since 1960 has stimulated "reapportionment wars" in states and localities across the country (see, e.g., Engstrom 1992b, 4; Kousser 1998, 137; Aguilar 1998, 797). Redistricting following the 2000 census promises to follow the same pattern.

In other democracies with similar election systems—winner-take-all elections, by simple plurality or majority vote, within geographic districts—the revision of district boundaries is typically the responsibility of independent commissions that are under instructions to disregard political considerations when deciding where to place district lines.[5] In the United States, however, the responsibility for revising election districts is almost always placed, at least initially, with an elected legislative body. State legislatures are typically responsible for revising the districts used to elect their own members, as well as those used to elect members of the U.S. House of Representatives from that state. Local legislative bodies, such as county boards, municipal councils, and school boards, are likewise usually responsible for revising the districts used to elect their members. The legislative battles over district lines have been said to be "among the most contentious in American politics" (Silverberg 1996, 913). Indeed, the periodic revision of district boundaries has been identified as "one of the most conflictual forms of regular politics in the United States" (Gelman and King 1996, 207). Studies of the revision of district boundaries employ expressions like "virulent," "acrimonious," and "nasty" to describe the legislative conflicts that result (see Kousser 1998, 207; Holmes 1998, 221; Scher, Mills, and Hotaling 1997, 237). One participant in the process has said, "It is the bitterest, cruelest, most partisan, most divisive issue I've ever run into" (Attlesey 1996, 44A). Redistricting has even been called "the blood sport of politics" in this country (Aleinikoff and Issacharoff 1993, 588).

Conflicts over district boundaries are not contained solely within the legislative bodies that adopt the lines. Those outside legislative halls with an interest in where the lines are placed have themselves engaged in "name calling and finger pointing" (Bybee 1998, 56; see also Scher, Mills, and Hotaling, 1997, 215–18). Nor, as noted above, is the issue always resolved in the legislature. In many instances the districting decisions made by a legislature become a subject for judicial evaluation. The legislative battle, in short, is followed by the "bloody combatants heading off to the courthouse" to continue the fight (Kubin 1997, 855). A round of "expensive and caustic litigation" is now an expected part of the redistricting process in many states and localities (Issacharoff 1995, 68).[6]

Not every redistricting experience is especially divisive, but redesigning districts is always potentially conflictive. While stimulated by the need to bring districts into compliance with the one person, one vote rule, the battles themselves have little to do anymore with concerns that the districts be equipopulous. The conflictive potential relates to who is grouped with whom, rather than how many people are grouped together. Numerous districting plans can be drawn that satisfy the basic one person, one vote requirement but have vastly different electoral consequences, or at least expected consequences. It is these potential consequences that make the process so contentious.

Political Consequences of Redistricting

One of the most immediate consequences of redistricting is the effect that new districts have on the reelection prospects of incumbent legislators. A legislator might find that the partisan complexion of the new district is not as favorable as that of the previous district. A Democratic incumbent could be faced with more voters inclined to support Republicans, or a Republican incumbent faced with more voters inclined to support Democrats. Key constituents, such as campaign workers or contributors, could be removed from a legislator's district. Often worse, from the incumbents' perspective, two or more incumbents could be placed in the same district, forcing them to compete with each other for reelection. Redistricting, in short, can become a matter of political survival. According to a state legislator who has been through the process, redistricting "makes political enemies out of neighbors" (Holmes 1998, 207). Not surprisingly, given these intensely personal consequences, the protection of incumbents is said to be, in many settings, the first de facto rule of redistricting, even though it may not be included in any list of criteria allegedly followed by those drawing the lines (Hanson 1966, 35; see also Silverberg 1996, 930; Kubin 1997, 853 n. 90). And when incumbent protection is acknowledged, it is often done so implicitly, through more euphemistic expressions like "preserving the cores of existing districts" or "minimizing the displacement of constituents" (see Scher, Mills, and Hotaling 1997, 162–63; Silverberg 1996, 938; Cirincione, Darling, and O'Rourke 2000, 201, 206–7; see esp. *Diaz v. Silver* 1997, 104, 122).

Redistricting creates conflict between or among groups of legislators as well. Partisan battles are particularly common. District lines can affect how well political parties might do in legislative elections or, more accurately, how well the votes cast for a party's legislative candidates might translate into seats in a legislative body (Gelman and King 1996). The single-member district system relied upon so heavily in this country makes district lines an especially important factor in how votes convert into seats. No matter how the votes are divided between or among candidates within a particular district, only one candidate is a winner. When district-based outcomes are added together, it is unlikely that political parties win seats in proportion to the votes their candidates receive. Indeed, there is a well-documented tendency within this system for the party whose candidates receive the most votes overall to win a proportion of the seats that significantly exceeds its proportion of the votes. District lines can be manipulated to try to enhance the translation of votes into seats for a party by distributing its supporters more advantageously across the districts than the supporters of another party. Different parties therefore typically prefer different plans, and allegations of gerrymandering are hurled back and forth between party supporters (see, e.g., Scher, Mills, and Hotaling 1997, 235–38; Kousser 1998; Williams 1994).

Although the one person, one vote rule imposes a serious constraint on the partisan manipulation of boundaries (see Gelman and King 1996; Jewett 2000), it does not preclude that practice. While American voters are now less predictable in their support for political parties, and the candidates affiliated with them, than they have been in the past, partisan predispositions still have an important impact on their candidate preferences (see, e.g., Abramson, Aldrich, and Rohde 1999, 167–74, 189–90, 240–42, 290–92; Shea 1999; Bibby and Holbrook 1999, 104). Districting cartographers take these predispositions into account in the line-drawing process. Now that computers are used to help design districts, the creation of an "equipopulous gerrymander" is in fact much easier, in a technical sense, than it used to be (see Eagles, Katz, and Mark 1999). Data recording the past preferences of voters at the precinct level, combined with legislators' knowledge of their local areas, can be used to evaluate the likely partisan consequences of different districting arrangements. Not surprisingly, studies reveal that political parties in control of the redistricting process tend to benefit from the districts that result (see esp. Gelman and King 1996, 210–11). This tendency is no doubt reinforced by the U.S. Supreme Court's apparent lack of interest in policing the partisan manipulation of districts (see, e.g., the commentaries by Scher, Mills, and Hotaling 1997, 129–49; and Williams, 1994, 564–68).

Another frequent source of controversy is the projected consequences that different districting plans have for the representation of racial and linguistic minority groups. As noted above, this was an especially controversial issue in many settings during the 1990s. Owing to group-based divisions in candidate preferences, these consequences usually are much more predictable than the partisan consequences of different plans. There is a clear tendency for African Americans and Latinos to prefer to be represented by members of their own group, and therefore the relative presence of minority group voters within districts is strongly related to the election of minority group members. Almost all African American and Latino legislators have been elected in districts in which minority group members constitute a majority of the electorate.[7]

The federal Voting Rights Act protects African Americans and particular "language minorities"—Latinos, Native Americans, Native Alaskans, and Asian Americans—from districting arrangements that systematically dilute their voting strength (79 Stat. 667). A protected minority's ability to elect representatives of its choice can be impeded by dispersing its voters across districts and/or by overconcentrating them within one or a few districts. Section 2 of the Voting Rights Act contains a nationwide prohibition on dilutive arrangements. Section 5 contains a special "preclearance" provision that requires selected (primarily southern) states and localities to gain permission from either the U.S. attorney general or a federal district court in Washington, D.C., to implement a new districting plan. Permission is to be granted only when there is no discriminatory purpose behind, and no discriminatory effect will result from, the new plan (see Engstrom 1994). Exactly what these protections require has been a matter of debate, but in many settings they were interpreted in the early 1990s to require the creation of as many minority opportunity districts—districts in which minority voters would have a reasonable chance of electing a representative of their choice—as possible. In other settings the adoption of the maximum number of such districts may not have been viewed as required, but it was seen as a way to immunize a new plan from a challenge based on the Voting Rights Act. These considerations usually resulted in an increase in the number of majority-minority districts, which necessitated a greater rearrangement of districts than would otherwise have been the case.[8]

The residential distribution of minority voters is not always conducive to creating minority opportunity districts that are neat in appearance. In many settings such districts could not be created unless the districts had odd or contorted shapes. Tentacle-like extensions had to be appended to districts to capture more minority voters, and/or narrow unpopulated, or lightly populated, "land bridges" were used to connect geographically separate concentrations of minority voters. But residential patterns were not the only factor influencing the shape of the resulting districts. Incumbent protection and partisan concerns also contributed to the shapes of many of the majority-minority districts (see, e.g., *Shaw v. Hunt,* 1996, 907, 920, 936–38, Stevens, J., dissenting; *Bush v. Vera* 1996, 959, 963–66, 973–75). Indeed, the combination of incumbent, partisan, and minority voting rights considerations resulted in this latest round of redistricting being particularly conflictive (see, e.g., Gronke and Wilson 1999, 151, 159; and more generally, Eagles, Katz, and Mark 2000, 136; Webster 2000, 142).

An increase in the number of minority opportunity districts was inevitably threatening to the reelection prospects of some white or Anglo incumbents. The number of legislative seats, and therefore districts, is usually fixed when district boundaries are revised.[9] Any increase in the electoral opportunities of one group consequently must come at the expense of another.

Increasing the number of majority-minority districts has been widely believed to have important partisan consequences as well. No demographic category of voters supports the Democratic Party's candidates more than African Americans (Abramson, Aldrich, and Rohde 1999, 92–93, 101–2, 235–38). Latinos, other than Cuban Americans, also tend to be among the strongest supporters of Democrats (Abramson, Aldrich, and Rohde 1999, 93–96, 235–36; de la Garza et al. 1992, 122, 126–27; DeSipio 1996, 29–31). When voters from these groups constitute majorities within districts, the districts are likely to be "packed" with far more Democratic voters than necessary to elect Democratic candidates, as whites or Anglos likely to vote for Democrats will be captured within them as well (see Weber 2000, 221–23). The adjacent districts, in turn, are said to be "bleached," or overwhelmingly white or Anglo, and therefore fertile territory for Republican candidates. In many settings Republicans became proponents of increasing the number of majority-minority districts. Republicans were regularly accused of favoring these districts, not because the districts would benefit minorities, but because the plans containing them would benefit Republican candidates. This partisan consequence of majority-minority districts was viewed by many as virtually axiomatic—more majority-minority districts would result in the election not only of more minority candidates but also of more Republicans.

There was nothing axiomatic about this, however (Engstrom 1995a). While minority opportunity districts could often be drawn in a way that would give the Republicans an edge in adjacent districts, much depended on who was designing the districts. There are many ways to draw majority-minority districts and also many ways to draw the adjacent white or Anglo districts, not to mention all the other districts within a plan. The partisan bias of plans containing new majority-minority districts therefore varied depending on which party a plan was intended to benefit (see, e.g., Gronke and Wilson 1999, 161–69; see also, concerning state legislative redistricting, Lublin and Voss 2000).

In some of the states in which new majority–African American congressional districts were created, Democratic control of the redistricting process allowed the other districts to be tilted in favor of the Democrats rather than the Republicans. The Democrats, through some very creative line drawing, were able "to finesse the 'bleaching' problem" in these states (Karlan 1998, 742). Even though white Democratic incumbents would lose minority voters from their districts, they retained more of their previous constituent base in their new districts than did the Republican incumbents (Petrocik and Desposato 1998, 625). While these changes would leave some of these white Democratic incumbents in a less secure position, their districts were still viewed as winnable, and therefore the overall arrangements were seen as biased in favor of their party, at least given past, and therefore projected, voting behavior (Petrocik and Desposato, 1998, 616). These plans were, in short, "friendly" to the Democrats (Petrocik and Desposato 1998, 630; see also Engstrom 1995a; Lyons and Galderisi 1995, 867–68; and Lublin 1997, 102, 106–11). This strategy did entail a risk commonly associated with this form of gerrymandering, however. If the electoral support for the party declined, some of the Democratic incumbents could be vulnerable to defeat.

The North Carolina Example

Congressional districting in North Carolina provides an excellent illustration of this finessing strategy and its consequences when a party's electoral fortunes change (see, e.g., Gronke and Wilson 1999, 165–66; also, concerning Louisiana, see Engstrom and Kirksey 1998, 242–46). In 1990 the Democratic candidates received 53.5 percent of the votes cast in North Carolina's eleven congressional districts and won seven districts (63.6 percent). Without the need to comply with the Voting Rights Act, congressional redistricting might not have been very controversial in North Carolina, as population growth reflected in the 1990 census resulted in the state gaining another seat in the U.S. House. The addition of seats usually makes it easier to protect incumbents while bringing districts in line with the one person, one vote rule. North Carolina's population, however, was 22 percent African American, yet none of its congressional districts was a majority–African American district, and no African American had been elected to Congress from that state since 1898. The creation of at least one, if not two, majority–African American districts

Fig. 1.5 North Carolina Congressional District 12. **Source: 1992, The Washington Post. Reprinted with permission.**

within a new twelve-district plan was widely viewed as necessary to comply with the Voting Rights Act.

Democrats controlled the redistricting process in North Carolina. The legislature was responsible for adopting a new plan, and Democrats constituted large majorities in both chambers. The governor, a Republican, did not have the authority to veto a plan. After adopting a plan containing one majority–African American district, which the U.S. Department of Justice refused to preclear, the legislature adopted a second plan with two such districts. Both of the majority–African American districts, district 1 (57.3 percent African American in total population, 53.4 percent in voting-age population) and district 12 (56.6 percent African American in total population, 53.3 percent in voting-age population) (see figure 1.5), were bizarre in appearance. The shapes were directly related to the Democrats' effort to minimize the bleaching problem. Despite the creation of the two new majority–African American districts, each of the six white Democratic incumbents (the seventh, seventy-eight years of age and in failing health, had announced his retirement) was provided with a district in which he still had "a good chance of winning reelection" (Gronke and Wilson 1999, 169, 166–67; see also Sellers, Canon, and Schousen 1998, 278; and Lyons and Galderisi 1995, 867–68). This was accomplished by adopting the risky strategy of "maximizing winnable seats rather than absolutely safe ones" (Gronke and Wilson 1999, 165). The plan, approved by the Justice Department, was so favorable to the Democrats that it reportedly left Republican legislators "apoplectic" (Sellers, Canon, and Schousen 1998, 280). Indeed, Republicans challenged the plan in federal court, alleging that it was a Democratic gerrymander. The Republican plaintiffs argued that the primary purpose of the plan was "to further the interests of white Democratic Congressmen in avoiding competitive elections" (quoted in *Pope v. Blue* 1992, 396).

A federal district court, citing Supreme Court precedents, dismissed the partisan gerrymandering complaint (*Pope v. Blue* 1992). But the Republicans no doubt felt that their gerrymandering allegation was confirmed by the 1992 elections. While the Democratic candidates received only a bare majority, 50.7 percent, of the votes cast in the twelve U.S. House elections, they increased the number of seats they won under the new twelve-seat plan to eight (66.7 percent). African American Democrats were elected in both of the new majority-minority districts while each of the six white Democratic incumbents seeking reelection also won. The Republican plaintiffs' assertion that these incumbents would not face competitive elections in their new districts proved to be false, however. The reason the votes for the Democratic candidates translated into seats so favorably was that five of the Democratic incumbents received less than 60 percent of the votes cast within their new districts. The strategy of creating winnable rather than safe seats for the Democratic incumbents paid off handsomely for the party, at least in 1992.

The federal court that dismissed the partisan gerrymandering complaint may have been better at reading election returns than the Republican plaintiffs, however. The court at least appears to have been very prescient when it stated, at the end of its opinion, "While members of the minority political party in any redistricted state may be apt to bemoan their fate, they can take solace in the fact that even the best laid plans often go astray" (*Pope v. Blue* 1992, 399). What went astray in North Carolina, as in much of the rest of the South, was support for the Democratic Party. In the next congressional elections, in 1994, the vote for Democratic candidates in North Carolina dropped, resulting in a complete reversal in the partisan division in seats. One Republican incumbent won reelection unopposed, while Republican candidates won 54.3 percent of the votes cast in the remaining eleven House elections. This translated into the Republicans now winning seven of the eleven contested seats, and eight overall. Republicans won in four districts that had elected Democrats in 1992, winning less than 60 percent of the vote in each. The marginal nature of some of North Carolina districts was again apparent in the 1996 election, when two of these seats were recaptured by Democratic candidates who received only 52.5 and 54.4 percent of the vote. The Democrats consequently were able to convert 45.2 percent of the votes overall into half (six) of the seats that year.[10]

Another Gerrymandering Challenge

The Republican attack on North Carolina's congressional districts did not exhaust the legal challenges to the new plan. A second lawsuit challenged the constitutionality of the new majority–African American districts. This suit, brought by white voters, alleged that the creation of these districts constituted an impermissible racial gerrymander. In response to this complaint, the Supreme Court legitimized a new type of legal challenge to election district lines, one that focuses on the shapes and other features of specific geographic districts.

The white complainants in North Carolina, although they asserted racial gerrymandering, did not argue that the new plan unfairly diluted the voting strength of the white voters in the state. This was no doubt because whites were still overrepresented in a proportional sense despite the creation of the two majority–African American districts. While whites constituted 76 percent of the state's population and 79 percent of its voting-age population, they were a majority in ten (83 percent) of the districts. They complained instead that the majority–African American districts were created "without regard to any other considerations, such as compactness, contiguousness, geographical boundaries, or political subdivisions" (quoted in *Shaw v. Reno* 1993, 637). Their concept of gerrymandering, in short, was a district-specific notion divorced from any requirement that a set of districts unfairly advantaged one group at the expense of another. They argued that the deliberate creation of these majority–African American districts in and of itself violated their right to "a 'color-blind' electoral process" (*Shaw v. Reno* 1993, 641–42). This novel claim was, like its partisan-gerrymandering cousin, found to be without merit and summarily dismissed by a federal district court (*Shaw v. Barr* 1992).

The Supreme Court, however, resurrected the complaint. Through a 5-4 decision in *Shaw v. Reno* (1993), the Court held that if the plaintiffs were correct that nonracial districting criteria had been disregarded in the creation of these districts, the plan could constitute a violation of the Equal Protection Clause of the Fourteenth Amendment. Justice Sandra Day O'Connor, writing for the majority, acknowledged that the plaintiffs' notion of racial gerrymandering was "analytically distinct" from the traditional gerrymandering allegation that district lines discriminate by unfairly diluting a group's voting strength (*Shaw v. Reno* 1993, 652). But O'Connor found the plaintiffs' district-specific approach to the concept persuasive because, in her words, "*appearances* do matter" when it comes to districting (*Shaw v. Reno* 1993, 647, emphasis added). Indeed, in a statement that makes sense only if one focuses exclusively on form and completely disregards function, O'Connor found that "it is unsettling how closely the North Carolina plan resembles the most egregious racial gerrymanders of the past" (*Shaw v. Reno* 1993, 641).

It was not the appearances per se of districts that concerned the Court, however. Districts with "extremely irregular" or even "bizarre" boundaries (*Shaw v. Reno* 1993, 642, 644) were not found to be problematic unless those features appeared to be related to race. O'Connor argued that race-based districting "threatens special harms," even when it is intended to be benign (*Shaw v. Reno* 1993, 649–50). Specifically, reapportionment legislation that cannot be understood as anything other than an effort to classify and separate voters by race injures voters in other ways. It reinforces racial stereotypes and threatens to undermine our system of representative democracy by signaling to elected officials that they represent a particular racial group rather than their constituency as a whole. (*Shaw v. Reno* 1993, 650)

The gerrymandering claim recognized in *Shaw* requires judges to perform a "different analysis" than they would in a vote-dilution case (*Shaw v. Reno* 1993,650). One major difference is that the plaintiffs in *Shaw*-type cases are not required to prove that they actually have been harmed. Plaintiffs alleging dilutive gerrymandering, whether racial or partisan, must convince judges that they are harmed by a set of districts in that their group's opportunity to elect candidates of its choice is negatively affected by the district boundaries (see *Thornburg v. Gingles* 1986; *Growe v. Emison* 1993; *Johnson v. DeGrandy* 1994; *Davis v. Bandemer* 1986). In cases proceeding under *Shaw,* however, plaintiffs alleging racial gerrymandering do not need to convince judges that the "special harms" identified in O'Connor's opinion in fact occur. Just the threat that such harms might occur is sufficient for the Court. A plaintiff challenging a districting plan therefore only needs to claim that the plan "rationally cannot be understood as anything other than an effort to separate voters into different districts on the basis of race, and that the separation lacks sufficient justification" (*Shaw v. Reno* 1993, 649).

The determination of whether a particular district is a *Shaw*-type gerrymander has focused on the shape and other features of that district. A single district can constitute a racial gerrymander, according to the Court in *Shaw,* if it was designed without regard to "traditional districting principles such as compactness, contiguity, and respect for political subdivisions" (*Shaw v. Reno,* 1993, 647). The burden of proof that plaintiffs face in these cases is simply to convince judges that race trumped "traditional districting principles" in determining the design of the districts—that race, in short, was the reason for departures from these other criteria. *Shaw*-type cases therefore focus not on the "special harms" alleged to result from the violations, which remain "purely theoretical" (Brischetto 1998, 62), but rather on whether these districting principles have been violated, and if so, the reasons for the violations.

The majority in *Shaw* acknowledged that there is no federal constitutional requirement that these districting criteria be followed in the design of election districts (*Shaw v. Reno* 1993, 647). It could have noted as well that there is no federal statutory requirement either; indeed, contiguity and compactness were dropped from the federal reapportionment statute in 1929 and have been excluded from the subsequent statutes, and respect for political subdivision boundaries has never been included in those statutes (see O'Rourke 1998, 197, 221 n. 5). (Nor were any such criteria required for congressional districts by the state constitution or statutes in North Carolina [see *Shaw v. Hunt* 1996,

934–35, Stevens, J., dissenting].) Yet the Court emphasized these principles "because they are objective factors that may serve to defeat a claim that a district has been gerrymandered on racial lines" (*Shaw v. Reno* 1993, 647).

If a district is found to be a racial gerrymander, even for a benign purpose, the Court held that federal judges must subject it to a standard of review called "strict scrutiny." This is the most rigorous level of scrutiny used to determine whether a state action or policy is consistent with the Equal Protection Clause. Under this standard, districts that are not *"narrowly tailored to further a compelling* governmental *interest"* are unconstitutional (*Shaw v. Reno* 1993, 658, emphasis added). What these expressions actually require is far from clear, but the application of this standard is popularly described as "strict in theory but fatal in fact." Indeed, it proved to be fatal to the Twelfth Congressional District in North Carolina when the Supreme Court, three years later in *Shaw v. Hunt* (1996), concluded that it did not satisfy this standard and therefore was unconstitutional.

The *Shaw* decision stimulated additional litigation in numerous settings in which majority-minority districts had been adopted following the 1990 census and also complicated subsequent cases involving more traditional claims of gerrymandering adverse to minority groups.

Clarifying Standing and Standards under Shaw

The *Shaw* decision held that the claim of district-specific racial gerrymandering was justiciable, but many questions concerning how such claims are to be adjudicated were left unanswered. The Court further reinforced the district-specific dimension to this type of gerrymandering allegation in a 1995 case in which it held that the special harms identified in *Shaw* only threaten those who reside in the gerrymandered district. In *United States v. Hays,* the Court vacated a lower court judgment that a majority–African American congressional district in Louisiana was an unconstitutional racial gerrymander. That judgment, based on *Shaw,* was discarded because none of the plaintiffs challenging the district lived in the district. According to the Court, "Voters in [racially gerrymandered] districts may suffer the special representational harms racial classifications can cause in the voting context," but a person residing in another district, even an adjacent district, "does not suffer these special harms" and therefore has no standing to challenge the district on this basis *(U.S. v. Hays* 1995, 745). Districting of course involves placing an entire population within a set of mutually exclusive districts, so how one district is drawn affects other districts, especially those that are adjacent to it. As one Louisiana congressman noted about the creation of a new majority–African American district in that state, "How you shape it shapes all the others" (quoted in Engstrom and Kirksey 1998, 243). The fact that the district challenged in *Hays* was adjacent to the district in which the plaintiffs lived and that the racial composition of one had a direct effect on the racial composition of the other simply did not matter to the Court. The spillover effects of an alleged gerrymander do not constitute, according to the Court, "a cognizable injury" under the Equal Protection Clause (*U.S. v. Hays* 1995, 746). The plaintiffs in *Hays* therefore did not have standing to complain about the majority–African American district. A plaintiff must live in a district, the Court held, to challenge that district.[11] (This requirement had no impact on the case, other than to prolong it, as residents of the district were simply added to the list of plaintiffs, and the district was again declared unconstitutional [*Hays v. State of Louisiana* 1996].)

The evidentiary standard articulated in *Shaw* was clarified in another 1995 case involving a majority–African American congressional district, *Miller v. Johnson.* At issue in *Miller* was the Eleventh District in Georgia. Justice Anthony Kennedy noted that the shape of the Eleventh, while irregular, "may not seem bizarre on its face," at least when compared to other districts (*Miller v. Johnson* 1995, 917). But that did not immunize the district from constitutional attack, he concluded, because *Shaw* had never held that a bizarre appearance was a necessary condition for a constitutional violation (*Miller v. Johnson* 1995, 912–13). The issue was whether the district was the result of race-based districting, which could be demonstrated through shapes and demographics or through other evidence. *Miller* provided plaintiffs alleging that a particular district, by itself, constitutes a racial gerrymander with a more clearly articulated statement of their burden of proof:

> The plaintiff's burden is to show, either through circumstantial evidence of a district's shape and demographics or more direct evidence going to legislative purpose, that race was the *predominant* factor motivating the legislature's decision to place a significant number of voters within or without a particular district. (*Miller v. Johnson* 1995, 916, emphasis added)

The Court returned to its focus on what it identified as traditional districting principles in *Shaw,* and explicitly added another, "communities of interest," to the list, when it continued:

> To make this showing, a plaintiff must prove that the legislature *subordinated* traditional race-neutral districting principles, including but not limited to compactness, contiguity, respect for political subdivisions or communities defined by actual shared interests, to racial considerations. (*Miller v. Johnson* 1995, 916, emphasis added)

Strict scrutiny was again fatal, as the Georgia district was also found to be in violation of the Equal Protection Clause.

Traditional Districting Criteria

Shaw and *Miller* have significantly elevated the importance of the four "traditional districting principles" identified in those decisions: contiguity, compactness, respect for political subdivisions, and recognition of "communities of interest." There is little doubt that these criteria will be more important referents in future districting decisions. Indeed, these criteria now serve, in the words of Justice O'Connor, as "a crucial frame of reference" in the evaluation of districts (*Miller v. Johnson* 1995, 928, O'Connor, J., concurring). Those who design and/or adopt districting plans will not want to subject their product to strict scrutiny and therefore will be less inclined to deviate from these criteria. This will certainly be the case in the design of many majority-minority districts. It can be expected to apply to districts more generally as well, if only to avoid allegations of racial double standards in the application of these criteria. (Allegations of a racial bias in their application have already resulted from *Shaw* and its progeny [see, e.g., Bybee 1998, 151; Kelly 1996, 230, 268; Whitby 1997, 141; Karlan 1998, 732, 747; Buery 1999; McKinney 1999, 36–37].)

Elevating the importance of these criteria in the design of districts might appear, on first impression, to reduce significantly the number of ways districts can be drawn and therefore make the districting task much easier. But this is not the case. To the contrary, the "political thicket" of districting is now even more entangled, as what exactly these criteria entail is a matter of considerable confusion. The absence of clear definitions for some of these criteria, as well as agreed-upon standards for identifying when they have been "respected" and when they have been "subordinated," leaves districting cartographers, and judges, in a conceptual thicket. This has been apparent in the post-*Shaw* decisions of the lower federal courts. This ambiguity is exacerbated by the fact that these traditional criteria are often in conflict rather than in harmony. Emphasizing one criterion can interfere with implementing another. Communities of interest, for example, may not be geographically distributed in a compact fashion and can be split by county and municipal boundaries (see, e.g., *Chen v. City of Houston* 2000, 515, 520 n. 13). No agreed-upon hierarchy of these criteria exists to help resolve such conflicts.

Even assuming that these criteria can be clearly defined and readily measured, and therefore are capable of providing an unambiguous frame of reference, what exactly the standard for comparison will be also remains unclear. Will the respect accorded these criteria be measured through deviations from some absolute standard, deviations from the extent to which they have been implemented in past plans, or deviations from the extent to which they are respected in the design of other districts within a plan? Given that the Supreme Court has acknowledged that none of these criteria is constitutionally required, it is not likely that some absolute standard will be judicially imposed.[12] Nor, presumably, will the tolerance for deviations from these criteria be less because a gerrymandering allegation concerns race. Justice O'Connor's statement, in her concurrence in *Miller,* that "certainly the standard does not treat efforts to create majority-minority districts *less* favorably than similar efforts on behalf of other groups" (*Miller v. Johnson* 1995, 928, emphasis in original) indicates that deviations tolerated in the past, for nonracial purposes, will continue to be acceptable in the racial context. If that is the law, then the frame of reference will have to allow substantial deviations in many states and local political jurisdictions, for the application of these criteria has not been particularly strict. Indeed, instances of their subordination to political considerations have been legion, even when they have been explicitly required by state constitutions or statutes or by city charters (see esp. *Gaffney v. Cummings* 1973).

The conceptual ambiguity surrounding these districting criteria and the new subordination standard is a cause for serious concern. Adherence to these traditional principles does not extricate those responsible for districting from the political thicket but confronts them with capricious definitions and contrasting measurements, as is evident in the litigation spawned by *Shaw.* Elevating the legal importance of these criteria without more precise guidelines for their application will not bring us closer to the goal of "fair and effective representation" through geographical districting (*Reynolds v. Sims* 1964, 565–66). While these criteria may be neutral on their face, districting is unfortunately an activity in which "the potential for mischief in the name of neutrality is substantial" (Butler and Cain 1992, 150).

The districting criteria identified in *Shaw* and *Miller* are reviewed below. Special attention is given to their treatment by the federal district courts in the gerrymandering litigation spawned by the *Shaw* decision and to their new role as a frame of reference in the post-*Miller* districting process. Unfortunately, the increased attention given to these criteria has contributed to the conceptual confusion rather than providing clarification.

Contiguity

Contiguity and compactness are criteria widely invoked in the evaluation of districts. They are conceptually distinct criteria that concern different aspects of the geographical form of districts. Many state constitutions, statutes, and local charters require representational districts to be contiguous; far fewer require that they be compact (see Grofman 1985, 177–83; Pildes and Niemi 1993, 528–31; Lyons and Jewell 1986, 76).

Contiguity is, or at least was, the most straightforward of the criteria identified by the Court. It is a simple dichotomous concept. A district is either contiguous or it is not. The test for determining this is not complicated: "A contiguous district is one in which a person can go from any point within the district to any other point [within the district] without leaving the district" (Note 1966, 1284). In short, contiguity requires that districts not be divided into discrete geographical parts.

Prior to *Shaw* there was little confusion about what contiguity entails. Neither the concept nor its application was often a matter of dispute. The major issue concerning contiguity has been whether the ability to travel throughout a district is a theoretical or a literal requirement. This usually arises when bodies of water connect what are otherwise separate parts of a district. It has been common for water to be treated the same as land for contiguity purposes. The Florida Supreme Court, for example, has held that the test for contiguity identified above "does not impose a requirement of a paved, dry road connecting all parts of a district," nor does it require "convenience and ease of travel, or travel by terrestrial rather than marine forms of transportation" (*In re: Constitutionality of SJR 2G* 1992, 279). The Florida constitutional mandate that state legislative districts be contiguous therefore was not violated, that court held, by "the presence in a district of a body of water without a connecting bridge, even if it necessitates land travel outside the district in order to reach other parts of the district" (*In re: Constitutionality of SJR 2G* 1992, 280; this holding was noted, without any trace of disagreement, by the U.S. Supreme Court in *Lawyer v. Department of Justice* 1997, 581 n. 9). The New York City charter, on the other hand, contains a contiguity requirement that specifies that there be an actual transportation linkage across any water separating parts of a district, stating that "there shall be a connection by a bridge, a tunnel, a tramway or by regular ferry service" (New York City Charter chap. 2, sec. 52[2]). Another issue that has arisen regarding contiguity is whether having parts of a district that connect only at a point satisfies the criterion (see Cirincione, Darling, and O'Rourke 2000, 196).

Until *Shaw*, it could be said that "Contiguity is a relatively trivial requirement and usually a noncontroversial one" (Grofman 1985, 84). Lower-court decisions following *Shaw*, however, have created confusion about what contiguity now requires. Some judges have not been convinced that districts that meet the traditional definition of contiguity satisfy this principle. In a case involving Louisiana's congressional districts, for example, a federal court held that a majority–African American district that was only eighty feet wide in places complied with this criterion, "but only hypertechnically and thus cynically," and that "Such tokenism mocks the traditional criterion of contiguity" (*Hays v. State of Louisiana* 1993, 1200). A district court in North Carolina went even further and held that contiguity had been "disregarded" in that state's reconstruction of its Twelfth Congressional District in 1997, finding that the new district contained "narrow corridors" that left it "barely contiguous" (*Cromartie v. Hunt* 1998, 8, 12, 13, 28; see also *Cromartie v. Hunt* 2000, sl. op. at 12). The expression "technical contiguity" has been applied to other majority-minority districts in other post-*Shaw* decisions (see *Shaw v. Hunt*

1994, 468; *Johnson v. Miller* 1994, 1368).[13] Some courts have even begun to treat contiguity as a continuous concept, as if some districts can be viewed as "more" or "less" contiguous than others (*Shaw v. Hunt* 1994, 452; see also *Vera v. Richards* 1994, 1338, 1342).

This approach to contiguity has been an unfortunate development. It commingles the notion of contiguity with that of compactness, treating the two as if they are synonymous. A district that is never less than eighty miles wide may well be "more compact" than one that is eighty feet wide at points, but it should not be considered "more contiguous" for that reason as well. These are distinct criteria that concern different aspects of the geographical form that districts can assume. A district should not be found to violate the contiguity criterion simply because its shape violates the compactness criterion.[14]

Compactness

In contrast to contiguity, the compactness criterion has always been a matter of considerable ambiguity (Webster 2000, 144). It concerns the shape of districts, not whether they contain geographically discrete parts. Compactness is a continuous concept. Districts can be considered more or less compact, and therefore this criterion, unlike contiguity, has been the object of a great variety of quantitative measurements (see, e.g., Niemi et al. 1990). There is "no generally-accepted definition" of what exactly compactness entails, however, and therefore no generally accepted measure of it (*Shaw v. Hunt* 1994, 452; see also *Johnson v. Miller* 1994, 1388).

Compactness is legally required less often than contiguity (Lyons and Jewell 1986, 76), and there is far less consensus about its importance in the design of districts. The linkage between the shapes districts assume and the quality of representation district residents receive has long been questioned. As candidly expressed by one set of commentators:

> It is, in truth, hard to develop a powerful case for the intrinsic value of having compact districts: If the representative lived at the center of a compact district, he or she wouldn't have to travel any more than absolutely necessary to campaign door-to-door or meet with constituents, but other than that, uncompactness does not seem to affect representation in any way. (Backstrom, Robins, and Eller 1990, 152)

A compactness requirement is widely touted, however, as an impediment to gerrymandering. It will rarely preclude gerrymandering, at least the dilutive kind, because that type of gerrymandering is not limited to funny-shaped districts. Indeed, a compactness rule in some circumstances could even serve as an excuse for this type of gerrymander (see Butler and Cain 1992, 149–50). But it is at least a constraint on the way in which district lines can be drawn and therefore an impediment to the manipulation of those lines for political advantage. And of course odd-shaped districts do stimulate suspicions of deliberate manipulation.

Since *Shaw* elevated the concern for compactness, lower courts have been confronted with a wide array of quantitative indicators that supposedly reveal the relative compactness of districts (see *Johnson v. Miller* 1994, 1388–90; *Vera v. Richards* 1994, 1329–30; *Diaz v. Silver* 1997, 114–15; *Cromartie v. Hunt* 1998, 5–9; *Cromartie v. Hunt* 2000, sl. op. at 13–14, 16, 21–22). These measures emphasize different aspects of shapes, however, and therefore can and do result in conflicting conclusions. Even bizarrely shaped districts can satisfy some of the tests (see Young 1988; Scher, Mills, and Hotaling 1997, 95). The measures also vary greatly in complexity. The simplest is based on the length of district boundaries. The shorter the boundary, the more compact a district is considered to be. Other measures examine the extent to which district shapes deviate from some standard, such as a circle or a square, or the extent to which a district fills the area of a polygon encasing it.

The ambiguous connection between district shapes and representation is the reason, no doubt, that attempts have been made to separate the concept of compactness from any notion of geographical shape whatsoever. New quantitative measures of compactness have been proposed that depart from the notion of geographical appearances, focusing instead on the physical distances between the homes of the people residing within a district (see Niemi et al. 1990, 1162, 1165–66). A federal court in California recently departed even further from the traditional concern for shape and adopted the notion of "functional compactness," holding that "Compactness does not refer to geometric shapes but to the ability of citizens to relate to each other and their representatives and to the ability of representatives to relate effectively to their constituency" (*DeWitt v. Wilson* 1994, 1414; see also *Johnson v. Mortham* 1996, 1512–13, Hatchett, J., dissenting; *Cromartie v. Hunt* 1998, 15, Ervin, J., dissenting). "Functional compactness" has evolved into a concept, much like communities of interest (discussed below), in which virtually anything can be treated as an indicator. One commentator has considered topography, transportation linkages, communication systems, economic bases, and local government boundaries as indicia of whether districts are functionally compact or noncompact (McKaskle 1995, 61–63). Rather than treat these other factors as valid reasons to deviate from a geographical-compactness constraint, which they may be, given the tenuous linkage between compactness and representation, the concept itself is being redefined even more ambiguously, permitting these other factors, in effect, to be part of the definition itself. A panel of the Fifth Circuit Court of Appeals has appropriately noted that "functional compactness" is "an inherently nebulous term" that is "open to abuse" (*Chen v. City of Houston* 2000, 507 n. 2).

The variation in approaches does not end here, either. Just as the federal court in Louisiana commingled compactness with contiguity in *Hays,* the federal court in Georgia handling the *Miller* case commingled communities of interest with compactness. After reviewing several approaches to measuring geographical compactness, that court chose to rely on a population-based approach that would "require an assessment of population densities, shared history, and common interests; essentially whether the populations roped into a particular district are close enough geographically, economically, and culturally to justify them being held in a single district" (*Johnson v. Miller* 1994, 1389; see also *Vera v. Richards* 1994, 1341; *Johnson v. Mortham* 1996, 1512–13, Hatchett, J., dissenting). A federal court in Illinois, in turn, has commingled respect for political subdivisions with compactness, concluding that a finding that the state's Fourth Congressional District "did not excessively split political subdivisions" supported the view that the district was "reasonably compact" (*King v. State Board of Elections* 1997, 626 n. 5). The Supreme Court has affirmed the California, Georgia, and Illinois decisions without commenting on what compactness actually entails (see *DeWitt v. Wilson* 1995; *Miller v. Johnson* 1995; *King v. Illinois Board of Elections* 1998).

With this type of confusion over the concept of compactness, requiring that districts not be subordinated to a compactness standard will not simplify the districting task. Districting decisions are likely to be more, not less, difficult in this context. Without some clarity concerning this constraint, those designing and/or adopting districts cannot be expected to know the limitations under which they must work. They can also be expected to choose an approach to this concept that provides the least constraint to implementing other goals through the design of districts.

Political Subdivisions

The third traditional criterion identified by the Court in *Shaw* is respect for political subdivisions. Local units of government, especially counties, have often served as building blocks for state legislative and congressional districts. Prior to the Supreme Court's adoption of the one person, one vote principle, counties were even the units to which legislative seats were apportioned in many states (see Jewell 1955). Not dividing counties among districts unless necessary to equalize populations has been a common districting constraint (Grofman 1985, 177–83). Following established political boundaries such as these is said to keep districts more cognizable to voters.

Political subdivisions are recognized by law, and there should be no problem in identifying them and in determining whether or not they have been divided by representational district lines. This is a simple matter of counting. There may be arguments, however, over which political subdivisions to include in the count. Counties, as noted, had been the major focus prior to *Shaw* and *Miller,* but the treatment of other subdivisions could be examined as well. The district court in Louisiana, for example, referenced the number of times the state's congressional districts divided "major municipalities" as well as counties (*Hays v. State of Louisiana* 1993, 1201; *Hays v. State of Louisiana* 1994, 121).[15] The list could also include other units, such as school districts, other types of special districts, or townships. Where the list ends is an issue in need of resolution.[16]

Simply counting the number of units divided by a district or districts may not be the appropriate basis for evaluation, either. Whereas the court in Louisiana found the splitting of municipalities to be objectionable per se, the federal court in the Texas congressional districting case responded very differently. The fact that cities in Texas had been divided between districts was not viewed as a negative, even though the divisions were along racial lines. The court noted instead that these divisions "gave the Congressmen a toe-hold in such cities and effectively doubled the cities' representation in Congress" (*Vera v. Richards* 1994, 1345; compare, however, the same court's comments at 1334–35 n. 43).[17] Indeed, the Supreme Court, in a case involving a state senate district in Florida, noted without any disapproval that dividing counties "increases the number of legislators who can speak for each county, a districting goal traditionally pursued in the State" (*Lawyer v. Department of Justice* 1997, 14 n. 9). Other issues include such things as "How many splits are too many?" and "Is a little split from a single unit as bad as a big split?" (Backstrom, Robins, and Eller 1990, 153).

Another related issue is the respect to be accorded precinct lines. Precincts are not governmental jurisdictions but merely administrative units for elections. It is often argued that precincts should not be divided by districts, but this is simply a matter of administrative convenience and therefore "precincts do not merit the same emphasis on boundary preservation as do political subdivisions" (*La Comb v. Growe* 1982, 165). Requiring districts to follow pre-existing precinct boundaries can impede the achievement of other, more important districting goals, such as creating majority-minority districts, and courts should not allow this constraint to be a pretext for discriminatory districting. Precincts can be changed relatively easily to accommodate more important districting criteria.

Communities of Interest

Districts are preferably more than arbitrary aggregations of individuals. The use of geographically based districts is premised on the notion that people who reside close to one another share interests. When "communities of interest" exist, it is often suggested that they be maintained intact within representational districts. Serious problems arise, however, in identifying such communities, as well as in deciding which deserve to be recognized, and thereby favored, in the design of districts. The Supreme Court added "communities defined by actual shared interests" to its list of traditional districting principles in *Miller* (1995, 916) but unfortunately provided little guidance as to how this concept is to be applied.

Despite being identified as a "traditional" principle by the Court, recognition of communities of interest is legally required in only a few states (Malone 1997, 466–67), and exactly what this criterion entails is even less clear than what the principles discussed above entail. Indeed, it is "probably the least well defined" criterion for drawing districts (Morrill 1990, 215; see also Leib 1998, 688–89; O'Rourke 1995, 764–66). The application of this concept has certainly been far from systematic. When employed as a referent for districts, or as an after-the-fact rationalization for districts, these so-called communities have been "identified on an ad hoc basis" (Malone 1997, 483) with virtually no limitation as to what may qualify for inclusion under the concept.

Judicial decisions prior to *Miller* contained "widely divergent concepts of communities of interest" (Malone 1997, 467). This is another area in which judicial efforts at definition have added to the conceptual confusion rather than provide clarity. A federal district court in South Carolina, for example, when faced with adopting congressional and state legislative districts for that state after the 1990 census, announced that "a community of interest . . . is an amalgamation of sometimes amorphous qualities best understood when considered on a backdrop of time" (*Burton v. Sheheen*, 1992, 1360–61 n. 60). Rather than attempt to deal with such "amorphous amalgamations," a federal district court in Illinois took what may be a much more rational approach. When faced with adopting a congressional districting plan in 1991, it stated that the concept of communities of interest was "both subjective and elusive of principled application" and simply declined to consider it (*Hastert v. State Board of Elections* 1991, 660).

Since "community of interest" has been elevated in importance as a districting criterion by the Supreme Court in *Miller,* its application has remained just as subjective, and limitless, as before. A federal district court in Florida, for example, while reviewing a state senate district, gave the concept careful consideration in light of *Miller* and concluded:

> Describing the notion of community is a stubborn problem. Viewed optimistically, a community is definable as individuals who sense among themselves a cohesiveness that they regard as prevailing over their cohesiveness with others. This cohesiveness may arise for numerous sources, both manifest and obscure, that include geography, . . . history, tradition, religion, race, ethnicity, economics, and *every conceivable combination of chance, circumstance, time and place.* (*Scott v. United States Department of Justice* 1996, 1254, emphasis added)

Nothing in *Miller* or in subsequent decisions by the Supreme Court has provided any guidance that will reduce the subjectivity in the application of this concept.[18]

An important question stimulated by the *Miller* decision is whether the "shared interests" must be among people living in geographical proximity to each other or whether this concerns the degree to which districts themselves combine people with similar interests. In *Miller,* Justice Anthony Kennedy stated that "A State is free to recognize communities that have a particular racial makeup, provided its action is directed toward some common thread of relevant interests" (*Miller v. Johnson* 1995, 920). The fact that this comment was immediately followed by a quote from *Shaw* indicating that it would be legitimate to concentrate minority group members in a single district—when they "live together in one community"—suggests that the concept may require geographic proximity (*Miller v. Johnson* 1995, 920). But when Justice Kennedy concluded that the Eleventh Congressional District in Georgia "tells a tale of disparity, not community," he was explicitly referencing "the social, political and economic makeup" of the district as a whole. African Americans in the Savannah area had been joined with African Americans in metropolitan Atlanta, thereby linking, according to Kennedy, African Americans who were "worlds apart in culture" (*Miller v. Johnson* 1995, 908). Presumably, if these African Americans were not so culturally disparate, at least in Justice Kennedy's opinion, then combining them within a district would at least be a legitimate recognition of their shared interests.

Many would no doubt argue with Justice Kennedy's unsupported assertion that African Americans living in the metropolitan area of Atlanta are "worlds apart" from those who happen to reside in Savannah, especially when it comes to politically "relevant interests." Evidence presented at the trial in the *Miller* case clearly shows that in statewide elections across Georgia and in the state's congressional elections, African Americans overwhelmingly shared the same candidate preferences and that these preferences, at least when they were for an African American candidate, were not shared by the state's white voters. Geographical proximity certainly was not a variable explaining voting behavior in these Georgia elections (see Lichtman 1994a, 7–18, app. 1; 1994b, 11–12; Weber 1994, 22–31, attachment E; Katz 1994, 18–21). This simply reflects the fact that race constitutes a major political division in Georgia. As one commentator has noted, "Perhaps African Americans in suburban Atlanta have distinct interests from poor rural African Americans 100 miles to the east, but poor rural African Americans may have even less in common with white merchants and farmers who live in the very same county" (McKaskle 1995, 47).[19] Many of the most relevant political interests that people share transcend geography (Webster 2000, 144–46). This is no doubt the case among African Americans. As expressed by Kelly:

> the importance of race also transcends place, creating a community that has little to do with geography but everything to do with the larger political and cultural community of color. This larger community generally recognizes the reality of

racism, the pleasure of a common culture, and the need to act together to effectuate common interests and to remedy common problems that repeat themselves
across geographical divides. (Kelly 1996, 234–35; see also Leib 1998, Malone
1997, 486–90; *Theriot v. Parish of Jefferson* 1999, 486–87)

Concern for shared interests that transcend geography was central to the
North Carolina congressional districting case. In North Carolina the district
court, after *Shaw v. Reno* was remanded, identified the state's two majority–
African American congressional districts as distinctive in character, one being
rural and the other urban, and concluded that this was a result of the legislature's concern that districts reflect "significant communities of interest" (*Shaw
v. Hunt* 1994, 471). Unlike the typical ad hoc application of more place-
specific notions of community, the application of this criterion to these districts was systematic. A guideline was adopted that at least 80 percent of the
population in one district reside outside cities with populations exceeding
twenty thousand and at least 80 percent of the population of the other reside
within cities exceeding twenty thousand. This resulted in districts that were far
from compact but that, according to the district court, have "substantial, relatively high degrees of homogeneity of shared socioeconomic—hence political—interests and needs among its citizens" (*Shaw v. Hunt,* 1994, 470). The
Supreme Court in its second *Shaw* decision did not dismiss this application of
the concept but simply held that it "came into play only after the race-based
decision had been made" (*Shaw v. Hunt* 1996, 907). Despite maintaining a
pronounced urban character in its next version of the Twelfth Congressional
District, two federal district court judges still concluded that North Carolina
had "disregarded" the community of interest criterion (*Cromartie v. Hunt*
1998, 9), prompting the following response from a dissenting judge:

> District 12 also was designed to join a clearly defined "community of interest"
> that has sprung up among the inner-cities and along the more urban areas abut-
> ting the interstate highways that are the backbone of the district. I do not see how
> anyone can argue that the citizens of, for example, the inner-city of Charlotte do
> not have more in common with citizens of the inner-cities of Statesville and
> Winston-Salem than with their fellow Mecklenburg County citizens who happen
> to reside in suburban or rural areas. (*Cromartie v. Hunt* 1998, 15)

Justice Kennedy stated in *Miller* that the "mere recitation of purported communities of interest" will not successfully invoke this criterion (*Miller v. Johnson* 1995, 919). Simply referencing well-known geographical place names presumably will not suffice. Identifying an area as containing people with
particular traits, such as ethnic or religious identifications or lifestyle preferences, may be sufficient, if the particular interests shared are documented. But
the application of this concept by federal courts following *Miller* continues to

be no more than a "mere recitation of purported communities of interest." It remains as ad hoc as before, and there is no attempt to specify the "common thread of relevant interests" reflected by these considerations. This is well documented by what happened in *Miller* itself, when the federal district court in Georgia adopted its own districting plan for the state in 1995. The court referenced "community of interest" considerations liberally in its description of its plan, but the specific "shared interests" involved must be assumed, because they were never identified, let alone documented (*Johnson v. Miller* 1995). The new Eleventh District in the court's plan, for example, was described by the court as "a relatively compact grouping of counties which follow a suburban to rural progression and have Interstate Eighty-Five as a very real connecting cable. The road net, the area's commerce, its recreational aspect, and other features produce a palpable community of interests" (*Johnson v. Miller* 1995, 1564). What shared interests are denoted by these generalized references to commerce and recreation, or to a road net, or to "other features," is anyone's guess.[20]

Even more revealing of the unsystematic application of the communities of interest concept by the court in Georgia is its failure to cite any such justification for the design of some of the other districts in its plan. The new Eighth District in the court's plan, for example, appears to be no less a "tale of disparity, not community" than was the unconstitutional version of the Eleventh. A geographer's examination of the district produced the following commentary:

[M]uch as the Court questioned the wide variety of interests in the old 11th district, one can question where the communities of interest are that tie together the Court's 8th district. The wedge-shaped district runs some 360 kilometers (225 miles), starting on the border of the Atlanta MSA before heading southeast through Macon, central Georgia farm country and forestry areas of south Georgia, before ending up in the Okefenokee Swamp and at the Florida border. (Leib 1998, 695)

Needless to say, the concept of community of interest remains just as "subjective and elusive of principled application" (*Hastert v. State Board of Elections* 1991, 660) after *Miller* as before. Which shared interests deserve recognition in districting and how such interests are to be identified continue to be determined in a very capricious, ad hoc manner. This is a districting criterion that has never been, and is likely never to be, well specified. It has been described, appropriately, as "a 'sponge' concept that may absorb any number of meanings, depending on the parameters defining the community group" (Brischetto 1998, 63). An Australian Electoral Commission workshop concerning the use of this concept as a criterion for districts resulted, not surprisingly, in the following admission:

At the end of the day there was no consensus on exactly what community of interest "meant" or how it might be operationalized. . . . If anything, there was a healthy skepticism that as the phrase would be taken up by those who wished to argue an essentially political case and used for their own purposes, there was limited scope for developing it into an analytic tool. (Australian Electoral Commission 1985, 1)

This should be no less of a concern in the American context.

Frame of Reference

Traditional race-neutral districting criteria are now supposed to provide "a crucial frame of reference" for evaluating *Shaw-* and *Miller*-type gerrymandering allegations (*Miller v. Johnson* 1995, 928, O'Connor, J., concurring). The four districting criteria discussed above are those that the Supreme Court has explicitly recognized as falling within that category. The increased attention that these criteria have received as a result of those decisions has illuminated, and in many cases even added to, the ambiguity inherent in this frame of reference. As students of the districting process have appropriately warned, "when [these criteria] are viewed closely and analytically, they invariably fail to provide useful guidelines" (Scher, Mills, and Hotaling 1997, 95). The inconsistent application of these criteria will no doubt continue. Neither legislative nor judicial discretion is greatly constrained by this framework, as "nebulous concepts like 'compactness' or 'communities of interest' . . . can easily be manipulated to rationalize any plan" (Kousser 1998, 187–88).

The Court also stated in *Miller* that it did not consider these four criteria to constitute an exhaustive list of the traditional criteria (*Miller v. Johnson* 1995, 916). What other criteria the Court may include is not known. The list of candidates, however, is virtually endless. An illustrative set of possible criteria, some of which may have clear referents but little, if anything, to do with the political interests that people share, has been provided by Kubin:

> Other examples of potential redistricting criteria are respect for media markets, newspaper circulation areas, historic district boundaries, telephone exchanges, high school athletic districts, river basins, employment characteristics, rainfall patterns, and neighborhood subdivisions. (Kubin 1997, 851 n. 78)

The majority on the federal district court panel in the *Cromartie* case in North Carolina found that the state, in designing a new congressional district, had "disregarded" another impressive sounding criterion, "geographical integrity" (*Cromartie v. Hunt* 1998, 28). No referent whatsoever was provided for this expression, however, prompting the dissenting judge to confess, understandably, that he was "not clear exactly what they mean by that" (*Cromartie v. Hunt* 1998, 44, Ervin, J., dissenting).[21]

Another question regarding the use of these criteria as a frame of reference concerns the standard for comparison. Even assuming that these criteria can be clearly defined and readily measured, and therefore are capable of providing an unambiguous frame of reference, what exactly the standard for comparison will be remains unclear. Will courts compare the extent to which the challenged districts conform to these criteria to some absolute standard? Or will the comparison be to the extent to which districts in that particular state or locality conformed to these principles in the past? Or will it be the extent to which the other districts in the plan at issue conform to them?

Given that the Supreme Court has acknowledged that none of these criteria is constitutionally required, it is not likely that some absolute standard will be judicially imposed. A particularly sensitive issue, however, is whether the Court will impose a double standard. Is it necessary to conform to these criteria more closely when they conflict with racial rather than other considerations? Districts frequently deviate from compactness, for example, for reasons having nothing to do with race. If the deviation from some compactness ideal in one district is due to race, but that deviation is no greater than, or even less than, that in another district due to concerns about incumbent protection or an effort to gain partisan advantage, does the first deviation constitute "subordination" of that criterion sufficient to trigger strict scrutiny?

Justice O'Connor has indicated that the tolerance for deviations from these criteria does not vary, at least for her, with the group allegedly benefiting from the deviation. As noted above, in her concurrence in *Miller* she stated that "certainly the standard does not treat efforts to create majority-minority districts *less* favorably than similar efforts on behalf of other groups" (*Miller v. Johnson* 1995, 928, emphasis in original). Deviations considered acceptable in the past for nonracial purposes should continue, in her view, to be acceptable in the racial context. Justice Kennedy, however, seems to take a much different view. In a concurring opinion in *Bush v. Vera,* involving congressional districts in Texas, he held that districts that were not drawn for racial reasons "may take any shape, even a bizarre one" (*Bush v. Vera* 1996, 999). But his tolerance for noncompact districts would not apply if the same deviation was due to race. According to Kennedy, if "the bizarre shape of the district is attributable to race-based districting," then the district must be strictly scrutinized (*Bush v. Vera* 1996, 999).

More recently a five-person majority of the Court, through Justice David Souter, examined the actual implementation statewide of districting criteria in a Florida plan to determine whether they had been "subordinated" to race in the construction of a particular state senate district. The Court concluded, on the basis of the way these criteria had been applied in the other districts, that the departures from these criteria in the district at issue did not constitute a subordination to race. The departures simply were not exceptional in the context of Florida's plan. The Court stated that, given the other districts, the district at issue was "no different from what Florida's traditional districting principles could be expected to produce" (*Lawyer v. Department of Justice* 1997, 582; the four dissenting justices, including O'Connor, did not address this issue, see Scalia, J., dissenting). This standard was also adopted by the federal district court in a more traditional vote-dilution case involving city council districts in Chicago. The city had argued that the illustrative remedial districts presented by the plaintiffs would constitute racial gerrymanders under *Shaw* because those districts deviated from the criteria of compactness, communities of interest, and "continuity" (minimizing the number of people placed in a district with an identifying number different from that of their previous district). The court rejected this argument because the illustrative districts did not deviate from these criteria any more than majority-white districts in the plan adopted by the city itself (*Barnett v. City of Chicago* 1998, 755–58).

If the frame of reference is to be the actual application of these principles, either in the past or within the plan at issue, rather than some elevated standard applicable only to departures for racial reasons, then substantial deviations from these principles will not constitute subordination in many states and localities. As noted above, the application of these criteria, prior to *Shaw*, had not been particularly strict. Their subordination to political considerations was common, even when the criteria were explicitly required by state constitutions or statutes or by city charters (see, e.g., Wells 1979, 8–10; Engstrom 1977, 301–4). Indeed, departures from traditional criteria have been applauded by the Supreme Court when the purported reason was to implement a goal of proportional representation for two political parties. This occurred in *Gaffney v. Cummings* (1973), involving state legislative districts adopted by Connecticut following the 1970 census. The districts had been designed, the state claimed, to produce nearly proportional representation for the state's Democratic and Republican voters. This goal, which was not required by state law, took priority over state constitutional mandates that districts be compact and follow the boundaries of towns. When these constitutional criteria conflicted with the pursuit of proportionality, they were, the state admitted, simply ignored. Numerous towns were split in the plan, which contained districts that had, according to the trial court, "highly irregular and bizarre outlines" (*Cummings v. Meskill* 1972, 147; see also Engstrom 1977, 301–4). These departures from the constitutionally mandated criteria were not viewed as a problem by the Supreme Court, however. In *Gaffney* it stated, through Justice Byron White, that "judicial interest should be at its lowest ebb when a State purports fairly to allocate political power to the parties in accordance with their voting strength and, within quite tolerable limits, succeeds in doing so" (*Gaffney v. Cummings* 1973, 754).[22]

Two districting criteria that certainly qualify as traditional, at least in a de facto sense, have been protecting the reelection prospects of incumbents and manipulating district lines for partisan advantage. Designing districts in response to these concerns has been widely tolerated by the judiciary. They have been acknowledged referents for district lines, for example, in the *Shaw*-type challenges to congressional districting in North Carolina and Texas. While the Court has not included these criteria among those not to be subordinated to race, it has been very tolerant of the use of political data in redistricting, as long as the data do not deal, directly at least, with race (see *Bush v. Vera* 1996, 959, 963–68, 975; *Shaw v. Hunt* 1996, 907; *Hunt v. Cromartie* 1999, 15–19; *Hunt v. Cromartie* 2000, sl. op., 9–10, 16, 25, 29).

The conceptual ambiguity surrounding the districting criteria identified as traditional by the Court, and the new subordination standard, is a cause for serious concern. Adherence to these traditional criteria does not extricate those responsible for districting from the political thicket but rather confronts them with capricious definitions and contrasting measurements, as evident in the litigation spawned by *Shaw*. Elevating the legal importance of these criteria without more precise guidelines for their application will not bring us closer to the goal of "fair and effective representation" through geographical districting (*Reynolds v. Sims* 1964, 565–66). Indeed, even if the criteria are applied in a more rigorous manner, the representational benefits of adherence to them are at best ambiguous. The notion that these criteria will somehow result in districts that are politically fair is widely regarded as naïve. As noted above, while the criteria themselves may be neutral on their face, districting is, unfortunately, an activity in which "the potential for mischief in the name of neutrality is substantial" (Butler and Cain 1992, 150).

Time to Reconsider Our "Winner-Take-All" Election Arrangements

Conflicts over geographical districts are primarily a function of the "winner-take-all" nature of the elections within them. Only one person can be elected in a single-member district, the candidate favored by a plurality of the voters.[23] How the district is shaped can determine which collection of voters constitutes that plurality. When multimember districts are employed, a cohesive plurality can determine all of the winners in the district. The tendency for candidates of one party, or one racial group, to sweep all of the seats within multimember districts has been particularly pronounced (see, e.g., Niemi, Jackman, and Winsky 1991, 102–3; McDonald and Engstrom 1992, 138–39). Again, the geographical design of such districts can determine which group receives this electoral bonus. The real issues in legislative battles over districts and in the subsequent litigation over the lines, therefore, are about who is grouped with whom. One participant in the redistricting process has described it as "a power grab" (Texas state senator Eddie Bernice Johnson, quoted in Richie and Hill 1999a, 17). As expressed by one commentator, "Every district boundary, whether drawn by the interested legislator or randomly assigned by computer, shapes the opportunities for political mobilization and power" (Bybee 1998, 169). Another has stated that the expression "fair districts," in the winner-take-all context, is an oxymoron (Katz 1997, 190). The stakes are high, and the choice of districts has become, consequently, a "contentious," "conflictual," "acrimonious," and "nasty" part of American politics (Silverberg 1996, 913; Gelman and King 1996, 207; Holmes 1998, 221; Scher, Mills, and Hotaling 1997, 237).[24] The manner in which we structure electoral competition, in short, has itself become a subject of controversy. A central aspect of democracy in America, its implementation, is widely viewed, unfortunately, as tainted with bias.

While judicial review of the resulting districts has become commonplace, it has not eliminated the widespread allegations of bias. Judges themselves have been accused of being partisan and result oriented in their evaluations of districts (see, e.g., Kousser 1999, 370, 435–37; Williams 1994, 582–83, 591–93). The Supreme Court's recent requirement that districts be subject to strict scrutiny when racial considerations predominate in their design, imposed through 5-4 votes on the Court, will not eliminate the conflicts over districts but rather exacerbate them. Elevating the importance of these principles has already produced capricious definitions and inconsistent applications of these districting criteria. Even straightforward principles like contiguity, when the subject of adversarial judicial proceedings, become clouded with ambiguity. And more nebulous concepts like respect for communities of interests are ripe for self-serving identifications and measurement. The districting thicket is now filled with conceptual as well as political thorns, and the conceptual confusion will be manipulated for political ends. The districting thicket is, in short, more tangled than ever and is expected to stimulate a "litigation explosion" following the 2000 census (Hasen 1999, 1102; see also Karlan 1998, 733). Districting conflicts in the future will not, in reality, be over these traditional principles any more than those of the past have been over small deviations from population equality. The issue will still be who is grouped with whom, and the new conceptual thicket will be a medium for rationalizing what some perceive to be politically favorable groupings (Webster 2000, 155).

The persistent conflicts over district lines during the 1990s highlight the need to reconsider our attachment to winner-take-all electoral arrangements. Electing representatives in this manner is not a requirement of democracy. As Supreme Court Justice Clarence Thomas has noted, the use of such systems is "merely a political choice," not a constitutional mandate (*Holder v. Hall* 1994, 909). The recurring conflicts over the arrangement of geographical districts have grown increasingly intense and should cause us to question our continued use of arrangements in which election outcomes are so sensitive to district boundary choices. As expressed by James Campbell (1996, 224):

[A] system that is out of kilter, that systematically overrewards one party and underrewards another, that consistently and arbitrarily weighs the voices of some voters more heavily than those of others, that raises questions about the fundamental fairness of elections and the legitimacy of the representative process, is a system in which change should be seriously considered.

Other electoral systems that are at least as democratic as, if not more democratic than, those currently in place could be adopted that would reduce dramatically the importance of where district lines are placed and therefore reduce the controversies surrounding these choices. The allegations of manipulation, bias, and gerrymandering, whether to benefit a racial or language group, political party, or a particular incumbent or incumbents, that now so frequently accompany our implementation of democracy could easily be reduced, if not eliminated, in many states and localities by the adoption of these other systems.

The key to reducing the current emphasis on, and controversies over, district lines is to eliminate the winner-take-all nature of the elections within them. Democracy does not require that electoral competition be structured so that only the candidate or candidates favored by a plurality of voters are elected. Indeed, a distinct minority of the world's democratic countries employ this decision rule to elect the members of their national legislature (see Lijphart 1999b, 144–50; Rule and Zimmerman 1994). Systems in which pluralities of voters determine who wins some of the seats, but not necessarily all of them, can be employed instead. Eliminating the need to be a plurality allows other groups of voters the chance to elect candidates they favor. When electoral opportunities are not dependent on being a plurality within a district, the location of district lines is usually less critical to electoral success. Interest in these alternative systems has been especially keen among, but not limited to, those concerned with the representation of minority groups protected by the Voting Rights Act (see, e.g., Zimmerman 1978; Still 1984; Engstrom, Taebel, and Cole 1989; Karlan 1989; Engstrom 1992a; Mulroy 1998, 1999). The adoption of these systems has been recognized as a way to provide politically cohesive but residentially dispersed groups with electoral opportunities. The residential dispersion of Latinos, for example, has often resulted in their voting strength being divided across a number of districts, a situation that has contributed to their underrepresentation in many districted contexts (see, e.g., McDonald and Engstrom 1992; Welch 1990; Hardy-Fanta 1993, 112–14; and more generally Cain and Miller 1998, 153).

Interest in these systems has intensified in the wake of the Supreme Court decisions placing new constraints on the creation of majority-minority districts (see Engstrom 1998; Canon 1999a, 365). Acceptance of the limitations on minority electoral opportunities imposed by these recent decisions is no less "a political choice" than the use of the winner-take-all format itself. In fact, a different choice has been made by about a hundred local government units that have adopted an alternative system in response to complaints about minority-vote dilution. The subsequent experience with these systems has added to the interest in them among minority voting rights advocates, as minority candidates have usually been successful in the elections held under these alternative arrangements.

Modified Multiseat Electoral Systems

The alternative electoral systems receiving the most attention are the modified multiseat systems of limited, cumulative, and preference voting (Engstrom 1992a). These systems can be used in any multiseat-election context, whether "at-large," across an entire political jurisdiction like a city or a county, or within a multimember geographical district. They vary from the typical multiseat elections held in this country, however, in that the rules concerning how votes may be cast are different. The voting rules usually employed in multiseat elections are that (1) every voter is allowed to cast as many votes as there are seats to be filled but (2) only one of those votes may be cast for any particular candidate. The winners of the seats are then determined by a plurality-vote rule; the N candidates receiving votes from the most voters win the N available seats.

As a result of these voting rules, multiseat elections have been widely viewed as unfriendly to minorities. As noted above, a cohesive group of voters constituting a plurality of the applicable electorate can determine who wins all, or almost all, of the positions contested. The votes of a minority group, when it does not share the same candidate preferences as the plurality, are submerged within those of the plurality and rendered ineffective. Many at-large election systems and multimember district arrangements have been invalidated by courts for having this effect (see, e.g., *Thornburg v. Gingles* 1986). The use of multiseat elections under these rules has even been referred to as "institutional gerrymandering," in recognition of the fact that structuring electoral competition in this fashion can dilute minority voting strength just as effectively as a discriminatory delineation of district boundaries (Dixon 1971b, 54).[25] Single-member districts therefore have been considered as more "minority friendly" than multimember arrangements.

It is the voting rules employed with the multiseat format, however, not the format itself, that are responsible for these dilutive tendencies. Other voting rules consistent with the basic one person, one vote rule can be used with that format that can provide groups that constitute less than a plurality within a district, including the racial and language groups protected by the Voting Rights Act, with a realistic opportunity to elect candidates of their choice. Given the new constraints on the design of districts, alternative systems like limited, cumulative, and preference voting can provide minority voters in many settings with more electoral opportunities than will single-member districts (see McKaskle 1998, 1182–83).[26]

Limited Voting

Limited voting makes the simplest change in the voting rules. In this system each voter in a multiseat election is given a number of votes that is less than the number of seats to be filled. For example, if five people are to be elected at-large or from a geographical district, each voter in that electoral unit may be limited to casting only a single vote. The limitation could also be set at two, or three, or even four. The defining characteristic of limited voting is simply that the number of votes be less than the number of seats. Voters are still restricted to casting only one vote for any particular candidate. Winning candidates are determined by a simple plurality rule; the top N vote recipients are elected to the N seats at issue.

Limited voting provides minority voters with an opportunity to elect candidates in the multiseat context by reducing the ability of a cohesive plurality to win every seat. The restriction on the number of votes reduces the larger group's ability to submerge the votes of a smaller group. The smaller the number of votes allocated to each voter, the fewer votes the larger group has to distribute across the candidates of its choice, and the less dominant it is likely to be. The more limited the vote compared to the number of seats, therefore, the greater minority voters' opportunity to place a candidate or candidates of their choice among the winners. A group does not need to constitute a plurality of the voters for its preferred candidate or candidates to receive enough votes to finish among the top N candidates in a limited-voting election.

Cumulative Voting

Under cumulative voting rules, each voter may have as many votes as there are seats to be filled, but the restriction that only a single vote may be cast for any particular candidate is removed. Voters may still, if they wish, provide several candidates with one vote apiece. But they also have the option to cumulate their votes behind fewer candidates than there are seats being filled. Generally, the only restriction in distributing votes among the candidates is that the votes be cast in whole units. In a five-seat, five-vote election, for example, voters retain the option of voting for five different candidates, giving each a single vote. But if a voter prefers some candidates more intensely than the others, he or she may cast the five votes for fewer than five candidates. A voter with a strong preference for two candidates, for instance, could cast two votes for each of them and another vote for a third candidate, while a voter who strongly prefers the election of one particular candidate could cast all five of his or her votes for that candidate (a practice known as "plumping").[27] As with limited voting, winning candidates are determined by a simple plurality rule.

Despite the absence of any limitation on the overall voting strength of the plurality, minority voters can have opportunities to elect candidates of their choice under cumulative voting rules. The removal of the one vote per candidate limitation permits minority voters to cast, in effect, a more efficacious type of "single-shot" vote than they can in other multiseat elections. The single-shot voting strategy entails group members voting for only one particular candidate (or perhaps a few candidates, depending on the relative size of the group). Under the more traditional voting rules, when a group employs the single-shot strategy, it does not fully exercise its franchise. The group's voters cast a vote for the candidate that they want elected and withhold the rest of their votes from all of the other candidates so as not to add to the vote totals of those other candidates. The idea behind single-shot voting is that by voting for one candidate and not contributing votes to the others, the candidate preferred by the group might finish among the top N vote recipients and win one of the seats.[28]

When cumulative voting rules are used, a group will not need to withhold its remaining votes, as the group's voters may cast all their votes for the group's preferred candidate or candidates. Cumulative voting allows voters to concentrate their votes much more powerfully and thereby increases the opportunity that minority group voters have to elect the candidates they prefer. As with limited voting, a group does not have to constitute a plurality of the voters for its preferred candidate or candidates to receive enough votes to finish among the top N candidates.

Preference Voting

The third modified multiseat system receiving attention is preference voting, also known as choice voting (Richie and Hill 1999a, 15) and as the single transferable vote (STV). It is like the one-vote limited system in that every voter is allocated a single vote. Under preference voting, however, voters are allowed to indicate more than just their first choice among the candidates. Voters may also, if they wish, rank order candidates to reflect their relative preferences among them, ranking the first choice as 1, second choice as 2, third choice as 3, until they no longer care to distinguish among the remaining candidates.

Candidates are rank ordered in a preference-voting election because votes that would be "wasted" on one candidate can be transferred to another candidate. A vote is wasted in either of two ways. It could be cast in support of a losing candidate, or it could be a "surplus" vote cast in support of a candidate who would win without it. Rather than have the vote wasted in these situations, preference voting allows that vote to be transferred to another candidate, provided the voter has specified a subsequent preference. Preference voting is a system designed to increase the proportion of voters in an election whose vote will ultimately contribute to the election of a candidate.

The winning candidates in a preference-voting election are those whose votes equal or exceed a specified number. This number is usually based on the *Droop quota,* which is the lowest number of votes that can be required for election and yet limit the number of individuals elected to the number of seats to be filled. This quota is 1 more than the quotient obtained when the total number of votes cast in an election is divided by 1 plus the number of seats to be filled. If 3 seats are to be filled and 1,000 votes are cast, for example, the quota will be 251, the value that results from dividing 1,000 by (3+1), and then adding 1.

The first step in counting the votes in a preference-voting election is to allocate to each candidate the ballots on which he or she is listed as the first preference. If none of the candidates has a number of first preferences equal to or exceeding the quota, then the candidate with the fewest first-preference votes is considered defeated and the votes received by that candidate transferred to the candidates listed as the second preference on those ballots. Each candidate's votes are then recounted. If a candidate exceeds the quota, however, then that candidate is declared elected and any surplus votes (above the quota) received by the candidate are redistributed to the candidates listed as the next preference. Whereas transferring the votes of a defeated candidate is straightforward (all of that candidate's votes are transferred to the next most preferred candidates among the remaining candidates), transferring surplus votes is more complicated. Several methods are available for transferring surplus votes. The simplest is to declare a candidate elected once his or her vote matches the quota and then transfer all of the subsequent ballots that go to that candidate. Another method, used in Ireland where preference voting is employed to elect the Dail, the lower (and most significant) house of Parliament, is to select randomly a number of ballots equal to a candidate's surplus and transfer those ballots to the next available preference. A third method, probably the most preferable now that computers can be used to count votes, is to redistribute the surplus proportionally. Each remaining candidate (not already elected or eliminated) would be given a share of the surplus votes equal to the proportion of the ballots on which he or she was the next choice of the voters.[29]

A count of the ballots in a hypothetical preference voting election involving five candidates competing for three seats is contained in table 1.1. It assumes that 2,000 votes are cast, so the Droop quota is 501. The first preferences of the voters are distributed as reflected in the column labeled First Count. Candidate C1 receives 480 first preference votes, candidate C2 receives 470, C3 450, C4 350, and C5 250. Given that none of the candidates has met the quota, the lowest vote recipient, C5, is eliminated and his votes redistributed. Most of C5's

Table 1.1 A Hypothetical Single Transferable Vote Election for Three Seats

Candidate	First Count	Transfer	Second Count	Transfer	Third Count
C1	480	+15	495	+25	520 *elected*
C2	470	+25	495	+20	515 *elected*
C3	450	+10	460	+4	464
C4	350	+200	550 *elected*		
C5	250 *eliminated*				

Note: 2000 votes cast; Droop quota 501.

voters, 200, identified C4 as their second preference, and therefore C4 receives 200 votes via transfer from C5. The other candidates receive only a few of C5's votes, 15, 25, and 10, respectively, for C1, C2, and C3. When the second preferences are added to the first preferences, reflected in the column labeled Second Count, C4's new vote total is 550, which exceeds the quota. C4 is therefore declared elected and his 49 surplus votes redistributed. If these surplus votes are transferred proportionally, and C1 is the next preference among the remaining candidates on 281 of C4's ballots, C2 the next preference on 224 ballots, and C3 the next preference on 45, then C1 would receive 25 of the surplus votes; C2, 20; and C3 only 4. When these votes are added to the candidates' totals, the results, reported in the column labeled Third Count, put C1 and C2 over the quota. C1 and C2 are therefore declared elected to the two remaining seats and the counting of the votes concluded.

Preference voting, as noted above, is like limited voting when the number of votes is limited to one. This reduces the ability of a cohesive plurality to win all of the seats. In addition, the transfer feature allows a group to transfer what would otherwise be wasted ballots among multiple candidates preferred by its voters, a feature that makes intragroup competition less likely to cause the defeat of candidates preferred by the group.

Electoral Opportunities under Alternative Systems

All three of these modified multiseat systems satisfy the basic one person, one vote rule, or individual voter equality requirement, because every voter has the same number of votes and the same options for casting them. All voters, in short, are treated equally.[30] The alterations in the voting rules under these systems, however, can cleanse the multiseat format of its tendency to dilute the vote of a minority. These alterations in the voting rules can counter the submergence effect that so often accompanies the traditional rules and thereby can provide minority voters with opportunities to elect candidates of their choice, even when voting occurs along group lines.

The opportunities that these systems provide minority voters to elect candidates can be demonstrated theoretically through a coefficient known as the *threshold of exclusion* (see Rae, Hanby, and Loosemore 1971). This coefficient identifies the percentage or proportion of the electorate that a group must exceed in order to elect a candidate of its choice *regardless of how the rest of the voters vote*. This coefficient is based on a set of worst-case assumptions, from the minority group's perspective, about the behavior of the other voters. These assumptions are:

1. The other voters cast all of the votes available to them.
2. None of their votes are cast for the candidate preferred by the minority voters.
3. Their votes are concentrated entirely on a number of other candidates equal to the number of seats to be filled.
4. Their votes are divided evenly among those other candidates.

The other voters, in short, are assumed to cast their votes as efficiently as possible in a multiseat election.

The value of the threshold of exclusion for limited voting systems depends both on the number of seats to be filled and on how limited the vote is. The formula for calculating this threshold for limited voting, expressed as a percentage, is:

$$\frac{\text{(Number of Votes)}}{\text{(Number of Votes)} + \text{(Number of Seats)}} \times 100$$

If the vote is limited to 1, for example, the threshold value for a three-seat election is $[1/(1 + 3)] \cdot 100$, or 25.0 percent. In other words, if 251 voters out of 1,000 (25 percent + 1) all voted for candidate A, then candidate A must be elected to one of the three seats. Even if the other 749 voted according to the worst-case assumptions, casting all of their votes for only three candidates, B, C, and D, with B receiving 250, C also receiving 250, and D 249, candidate A would be the recipient of the most votes and would therefore win a seat. If the other voters did not vote according to the worst-case assumptions but instead cast their votes unevenly so that B receives 260 and C 255, for example, then the most D can receive is 234, and the minority preferred candidate, A, still wins one of the three seats.

Illustrative values of the threshold for limited voting, for various seat and vote combinations, are reported in table 1.2. For any number of seats, the more limited the vote is, the lower will be the value of the threshold. Likewise, for any number of votes, the larger the number of seats, the lower the threshold

Table 1.2 Threshold of Exclusion Values

Number of Seats	Cumulative & Preference Voting	Limited Voting		
		1 Vote	2 Votes	3 Votes
2	33.3	33.3	—	—
3	25.0	25.0	40.0	—
4	20.0	20.0	33.3	42.9
5	16.7	16.7	28.6	37.5
6	14.3	14.3	25.0	33.3
7	12.5	12.5	22.2	30.0
8	11.1	11.1	20.0	27.3
9	10.0	10.0	18.2	25.0

value. The threshold for a 2-vote, three-seat election, for example, is 40.0 percent , while that for a 1-vote, five-seat election is 16.7 percent.

The formula for calculating the threshold of exclusions value for cumulative voting systems, expressed as a percentage, is:

$$\frac{1}{1 + (\text{Number of Seats})} \times 100$$

This is the same as that for limited voting when the number of votes is 1. In the three-seat cumulative context, for example, the threshold is again 25.0 percent. In other words, if those 251 voters out of 1,000 (25 percent +1) each "plumped" all three of their votes for candidate A, giving him 753 votes, then A again must win one of the seats. The other 749 voters could distribute their 2,247 votes evenly across only three candidates, so that B, C, and D each receive 749, and A would still be a winner. Again, if the other voters deviated from the worst-case assumptions, giving more votes to two of their choices, their third choice would have even fewer votes and A would still win a seat. As in the 1-vote limited context, the more seats at issue the lower will be the value of the threshold for cumulative voting. Illustrative values of the threshold for the cumulative context for different numbers of seats are also reported in table 1.2.

If the Droop quota used with preference voting systems, which identifies the number of votes a candidate must receive in order to be elected, is expressed as a percentage of votes, it is also the same as the threshold of exclusion (plus 1 vote) for a 1-vote limited system or a cumulative system. As noted above, the Droop quota for a three-seat election with 1,000 voters is 251. This is the result of dividing 1,000 by (3 + 1) and adding 1. Any group, in short, that can provide a candidate with at least 25 percent plus one of the votes is elected to one of the three seats in a preference voting election, just as in a 1-vote limited or cumulative voting election. The threshold values for preference voting therefore also vary inversely with the number of seats, just as in the other systems.

The threshold of exclusion, it must be remembered, identifies the percentage of the voters in a particular election that a group sharing the same candidate preference must exceed in order to elect that candidate with no assistance whatsoever from the other voters. If the behavior of other voters deviates in any way from the worst-case assumptions, then a minority group may be smaller or less cohesive in its preferences and still have a realistic opportunity to elect a candidate or candidates of its choice through one of these voting systems.

Deviations from perfect cohesion among minority voters can of course negate their opportunity to elect a candidate, even when their presence in the electorate exceeds the threshold. In the previous illustration involving a three-seat, 1-vote election, for example, if just 10 percent of the minority voters (25 of the 251) had as their first preference another candidate, say E rather than A, then A would have received only 226 votes and would have failed to win a seat. In the 3-vote cumulative election, if a second candidate, E, received just 10 percent of the votes cast by minority voters (75 votes), candidate A would be left with 678 and again fail to win a seat. Electoral opportunities provided by limited and cumulative voting can thus be negated by intragroup competition.

Preference voting is more conducive to intragroup competition than is either limited or cumulative voting. As long as minority voters share a preference for a set of candidates, there can be competition among those candidates for the support of minority voters without that competition precluding the election of one or more of them, because votes can transfer among them. Preference voting in effect offers minority voters, and others, the equivalent of a primary election (or a series of primary elections) and a general election through a single ballot on the same day. In the previous illustration, for example, if those voting for candidate E preferred A to all of the other candidates, then in a preference voting election, A would have been elected when E's votes transferred to him following E's elimination for being the last-place candidate. Likewise, in the illustrative preference voting election in table 1.1, if C4 and C5 were candidates whose 600 votes came from minority voters, the fact that minority voters had initially divided their votes between them would not have precluded either from being elected. Rather, the minority voter cohesion, reflected by most of C5's voters listing C4 as their second preference, would allow C4 to win one of the seats. This feature of preference voting is particularly advantageous when the minority might have enough electoral strength to elect more than one candidate in a multiseat election. An uneven distribution of support across candidates is much less problematic, given the transfer feature, in a preference voting election than in a limited or cumulative voting contest. This is a reason that some commentators have expressed a preference for preference voting over the other options (e.g., Inman 1993, 2001, 2012, 2014–15; Briffault 1995, 435–41; Pildes and Donoghue 1995, 298–99; McKaskle 1998, 1127, 1152, 1161, 1163 n. 177, 1202; Mulroy 1999, 1906–23).

Electoral Experience with Alternative Systems

The different features of electoral systems are alleged to have numerous consequences, some good, some bad, and some about whose value commentators disagree. Many of these alleged consequences are exaggerated, however.[31] This is certainly the case with limited, cumulative, and preference voting arrangements. While opponents of these systems have alleged that numerous negative consequences result from these alternative voting rules, these consequences have not been, or cannot yet be, documented. There is one claim, however, that neither the proponents nor opponents of these voting rules can rationally dispute, and that is that these modified multiseat systems provide minority voters with opportunities to elect candidates of their choice.

Minority electoral opportunities within these systems are not just theoretical (see, e.g., Gerber, Morton, and Rietz 1998). Both cumulative voting and limited voting systems have been adopted in response to lawsuits, or the threat of lawsuits, alleging minority vote dilution. Courts have approved the adoption of these systems when they provided the basis for the settlement of such suits, and the Department of Justice has almost invariably granted preclearance to them (see Mulroy 1995; Hodgkiss 1999). Cumulative voting has been adopted by almost sixty counties, municipalities, and school boards in five states, while limited voting has been adopted by almost forty such units, also in five states.[32] Elections have now been held under these voting rules in almost all of these settings. These elections have demonstrated that when the minority's percentage of the electorate has exceeded, or even approached, the value of the threshold of exclusion for one of these systems, minority candidates have almost always been elected (Engstrom 1992a; Engstrom, Kirksey, and Still 1997a; Brischetto and Engstrom 1997; Arrington and Ingalls 1998; see also Brockington et. al. 1998, 1115). Exit polls conducted at a number of these elections have further confirmed that these minority candidates, many of whom were the first minority person ever to be elected to the particular governing body, have been the choices of minority voters. These results have been found regardless of whether the relevant minority has been African Americans (Engstrom, Kirksey, and Still 1997b), Latinos (Engstrom, Taebel, and Cole

1989; Cole, Engstrom, and Taebel 1990; Cole and Taebel 1992; Brischetto and Engstrom 1997), or Native Americans (Engstrom and Barrilleaux 1991).[33]

The critical factor in providing minority voters with electoral opportunities through these arrangements has been how closely the minority presence in the electorate matches the value of the threshold of exclusion for a particular system. Brischetto and Engstrom, for example, conducted exit polls at fifteen cumulative voting elections in Texas in 1995 in which at least one Latino was a candidate. These elections were for either a municipal council or a local school board. In all seven of the elections in which the ratio between the percentage of those signing in to vote that was Latino and the threshold of exclusion value exceeded .9, Latino candidates favored by Latino voters were elected. In the one setting where the percentage of Latino voters was almost twice the threshold of exclusion (1.93), two Latino candidates favored by Latino voters were elected. A Latino candidate favored by Latino voters was also elected in a setting where the Latino percentage of those signing in constituted almost two-thirds (.66) of the threshold.[34] In the other settings, in which the ratio ranged from .64 to .06, no Latino was elected, even though Latino candidates were favored by Latino voters in all but one of them (Brischetto and Engstrom 1997, 984–85).

Recent experience with preference voting in the United States has been much more limited. While twenty-two cities have used preference voting for councilmanic elections at some time during the 1900s, Cambridge, Massachusetts, is the only city continuing to use the arrangement today (Weaver 1986). In many of the cities that used preference voting in the past, African Americans were elected for the first time, and continued to be elected, under that arrangement (see Barber 1995). The success of minority candidates has been cited as a major reason for the abandonment of these systems, as opponents of the system often used the "race card" in their campaigns for repeal (Amy 1996/1997, 18; see also Barber 1995; Burnham 1997). Cambridge continues to use the preference system to elect both its city council and its school committee, bodies on which African Americans have been consistently represented (Amy 1993, 166). The system has also been used since 1970 in New York City to elect thirty-two community school boards, on which African Americans and Latinos have generally won close to a proportional number of seats (Amy 1993, 138; Brischetto 1998, 69, 103).[35]

While most commentators would consider the electoral opportunities provided by these modified multiseat arrangements to be a positive feature of the systems, there has not been complete agreement on this. These opportunities have been converted, in the rhetoric of some of the opponents of these systems, into unconstitutional electoral guarantees. Cumulative voting, for example, has been described as "a method of assuring proportional representation."[36] And limited voting has likewise been called "a race-based quota system."[37] Such characterizations, however, are simply not accurate. These systems, depending on how they are implemented, can provide minority voters with equal opportunities to elect representatives of their choice, but they guarantee no particular outcomes (see McKaskle 1998). They certainly do not assure the election of minority candidates, as was demonstrated by the Texas experience with cumulative voting. Even in the Texas jurisdictions where the Latino percentage of registered voters was well above the threshold of exclusion, Latino-preferred candidates lost because Latinos failed to mobilize on election day (Brischetto and Engstrom 1997, 985–87). Electoral outcomes are no doubt less predictable in these systems than in single-member district arrangements (see Arden, Grofman, and Handley 1997; Lublin 1997; Grofman and Davidson 1994, 311, 329; Grofman and Handley 1992), which is why many voting rights advocates continue to prefer single-member districts when majority-minority districts can be created.

There is nothing unconstitutional, of course, about providing minorities with an equal opportunity to elect representatives. This was recognized in a recent attack on a limited voting arrangement in Cleveland County, North Carolina. White voters in the county, citing the Supreme Court's decisions concerning majority-minority districts, attacked the settlement of a vote-dilution lawsuit that included the adoption of limited voting. Prior to the filing of that lawsuit, no African American had ever been elected to the county's five-member governing board, which was elected at-large, although African Americans constituted 20.9 percent of the county's population and 18.8 percent of its voting-age population. The settlement agreement explicitly stated that the change in system was "intended to improve the ability of black citizens to elect candidates."[38]

A federal district court dismissed the challenge to the settlement. It held that "the mere motivation to facilitate equal opportunity for representatives of all races" did not necessitate that the limited voting scheme be strictly scrutinized, let alone invalidated (*Cleveland County Association for Government by the People v. Cleveland County Board of Commissioners* 1997, 80). The court correctly observed that the arrangement, a four-vote, seven-seat system, "does not guarantee any seats on the Board of Commissioners to blacks, nor does it give black voters any more voting power than other voters" (*Cleveland County Association for Government by the People v. Cleveland County Board of Commissioners* 1997, 80). The system did not require strict scrutiny, the court held, because it did not classify individuals on the basis of race. Unlike the majority-minority districts that the Supreme Court had struck down, the limited voting arrangement "does not separate voters or distinguish among voters or candidates along racial lines. It treats all voters in the county—black or white—in precisely the same way" (*Cleveland County Association for Government by the People v. Cleveland County Board of Commissioners* 1997, 80).[39] Cumulative voting, likewise, has been found to "not compartmentalize voters according to their race" (*McCoy v. Chicago Heights* 1998, 983; *Harper v. City of Chicago Heights and the Chicago Heights Election Commission* 2000, 601–2).[40]

The provision of electoral opportunities for racial and language minorities, especially when they are not dependent on group-based classifications, are generally viewed as a positive feature of an election system. The opportunities provided by limited, cumulative, and preference voting do not entail such classifications (see Mulroy 1998, 350–52). Suggestions that these modifications in voting rules establish quotas and guarantees rather than opportunities can be dismissed as, at best, misguided hyperbole.

The Complexity Argument

There are other consequences that allegedly result from the use of these systems. One supposedly associated with cumulative voting is that it is too complex for voters to understand. This has rarely been a criticism of limited voting because that system retains the familiar restriction that each voter may cast only one vote for any candidate. Nor is the ranking of candidates in preference voting viewed as onerous to voters, provided that it does not require that distinctions be made among all candidates on a ballot (see McKaskle 1998, 1161; Mulroy 1999, 1913; Farrell and Gallagher 1999, 310–11).[41] Cumulative voting, however, increases the number of ways in which votes may be cast, and this is allegedly a source of considerable confusion for voters (see Canon 1999a, 367; 1999b, 260). The confusion caused by these additional permutations is expected to be most pronounced among less educated voters, and therefore among minority voters, as disproportionate numbers of them tend to be among the less educated, at least in a formal sense. This confusion, it is suggested, could negate the electoral opportunities that cumulative voting otherwise provides minority groups (see Note 1981, 1829; Note 1982, 155; Dunn 1972, 655–58; Everson et al. 1982, 23).

This notion that cumulative voting is so confusing to voters that they will not be able to cast their ballots effectively can be safely rejected. Exit polls conducted at cumulative voting elections reveal very little voter confusion. Only about 10 to 15 percent of the respondents in these polls reported that casting ballots in these elections, which were conducted with paper, machine, and computer ballots, was more difficult than voting in other local elections. And any possible increase in difficulty did not appear to impede seriously the use of the cumulative options, as 90 percent or more of the voters typically reported that they understood that they could cumulate votes. Minority voters were actually somewhat less likely than other voters to report that they found the system more difficult and much more likely to actually exercise the option to cumulate (Cole, Engstrom, and Taebel 1990; Engstrom and Barrilleaux 1991; Cole and Taebel 1992; Engstrom, Kirksey, and Still 1997b, 301–8).

Voters in the Texas exit polls were given a response option to the question about relative difficulty that voters in the other polls did not have. Whereas the question used in the other settings simply asked whether cumulative voting was "any more difficult to understand," in the Texas exit polls respondents were provided with a more complete range of responses. These included whether cumulative voting, compared to the voting methods used in other elections, was "any easier, about the same, or more difficult to understand." The results may be surprising to many, as over a fourth (28 percent) of the respondents indicated that cumulative voting was *easier* to understand. Indeed, more respondents reported that it was easier than reported it to be more difficult (16 percent). This was especially true of the Latino respondents, 53 percent of whom said it was easier compared to only 8 percent reporting it to be more difficult (Brischetto and Engstrom 1997; for similar responses among African Americans, see Engstrom and Brischetto 1998, 825, 833). In addition, the less educated voters, among both Latinos and Anglos, were not more likely to find the system more difficult. Voters who had not graduated from high school were in fact the most likely, within both groups, to indicate that the system was easier to understand (Engstrom and Brischetto 1998, 822–24, 830; also 825, 833 for similar results concerning African Americans).

That voting under cumulative rules is reported to be easier than voting in other local elections should not necessarily be surprising, however. In multiseat elections, the cumulative options could very well make voting easier for voters with intense preferences for particular candidates. In the more traditional multiseat context, in addition to voting for their preferred candidates, these voters also have to decide whether to cast their remaining votes for candidates competing with their more preferred choices. Votes cast for less preferred candidates can help to defeat their more preferred choices, and therefore not casting a complete ballot can be very rational. Indeed, the single-shot voting strategy, in which voters withhold votes, has been advocated as a way for minority voters to compete more effectively in multiseat elections (Engstrom and McDonald 1993). Voters with relative preferences among candidates may find that the option to cumulate votes simplifies their decision. This may help explain why so many of the Latino voters in Texas reported cumulative voting to be easier.

If cumulative voting makes it more difficult to cast ballots, then the degree of difficulty would presumably increase as the number of votes available to cumulate, and therefore the number of permutations in which votes may be cast, increases. The exit polls in Texas were conducted at elections in which voters had either two, three, or five votes to cast. When the relationship between the number of votes and the relative difficulty of cumulative voting was examined, this expected relationship was present among the Anglo voters but not among the Latino voters. Among the Anglo respondents participating in two-vote elections, 29 percent said cumulative voting was easier. This percentage dropped to 20 in the three-vote context and to 12 in the five-vote situation. The percentage of Anglos voting in the two-vote context who found cumulative voting to be more difficult was 12. This percentage increased to 23 in the three-vote and to 28 in the five-vote settings. For Latinos, the relationship was reversed. The percentage reporting cumulative voting to be easier increased from 48 in the two-vote situation, to 55 in the three, and to 59 in the five. The percentage reporting it to be more difficult changed only minimally, from 7 in the two-vote context to 9 in the three-vote and 10 in the five-vote context (Brischetto and Engstrom 1997, 979–81). These differences between the groups were not attributable to educational differences between them (Engstrom and Brischetto 1998, 823–24, 831).

An exit poll was also conducted at a seven-vote cumulative election in Chilton County, Alabama, in 1992. Among the white respondents to that poll, 28 percent reported cumulative voting to be more difficult, but 88 percent also indicated that they understood they could cumulate their votes and 78 percent reported doing so. Among the African American respondents, only 12 percent reported the system to be more difficult, while 96 percent indicated that they knew votes could be cumulated and 91 percent reported cumulating them. Educational differences among the voters again had minimal if any impact on their understanding of the system (Engstrom, Kirksey, and Still 1997b, 301–8).

Cumulative voting does not appear to be so confusing that it impedes the ability of voters to use their ballots effectively. In fact, some voters may find the ability to cumulate votes simplifies rather than complicates their voting decisions in multiseat elections. There certainly is no evidence that the additional complexity introduced by cumulative options will negate the electoral opportunities the system provides minority groups. Minority voters have not only understood cumulative voting but have also used it to elect their preferred candidates.

Alleged Systemic Consequences

The simple revisions in the voting rules that these alternative systems entail are alleged to have much broader systemic consequences as well. These consequences are also matters of dispute, however. Empirical evidence comparable to that documenting minority electoral success through these systems, or the lack of serious voter confusion in cumulative voting elections, is not available to assess these other alleged consequences. Many of these supposed consequences, however, especially the often "apocalyptic forecasts" asserted by opponents of these systems (Persily 1999, 10), are clearly exaggerated, and the associated predictions can be dismissed as hyperbole.

The center of the debate concerns the perceived advantages or disadvantages of the greater diversity in representation that these systems facilitate, including, but certainly not limited to, that for racial and language minorities. There is no doubt that these alternative voting systems structure electoral competition in a way that more widely diffuses electoral opportunities. Proponents of these systems tout this expansion in opportunities as a positive feature. They argue that these systems allow more of the salient interests within government jurisdictions to be represented in their legislative bodies than do the traditional multiseat systems or single-member districts, and thereby enhance the decisions and legitimacy of these institutions. Alternative voting rules, it is said, allow like-minded voters to form "voluntary constituencies" based on their interests. Many of these interest groupings would not be able to elect their favored representatives under the other arrangements. Voters with these interests would either be submerged in multiseat elections using the more traditional voting rules or they would be dispersed among districts in a single-member district arrangement (see Weaver 1984, 194; Karlan 1989, 213–36; Still 1991, 358–60; Guinier 1994b, 94–101, 109–14, 149–56; Still and Karlan 1995).

Geographic proximity is certainly not a necessary condition for shared interests. Many of the most salient interests of people are not place related. Ideological beliefs, religious values, and ethnic identities are just some sources of shared political interests that are rarely distributed in a geographically compact fashion. Voters concerned with particular clusters of issues, such as gender discrimination, gay rights, or environmental protection, do not all share neighborhoods (see, e.g., Rosenblum 1996; Bloch 1998). Alternative voting systems allow voters to determine which interests are most important to them and to vote accordingly. Voters concerned with place-related interests can vote on the basis of those interests. But those who find other interests of greater importance can vote on the basis of those concerns. The effectiveness of a person's vote, therefore, will not be so dependent on where she happens to live (Inman 1993, 2004). As expressed by Guinier, writing about cumulative voting, "*all* voters have the potential to form voluntary constituencies based on their own assessment of their interests" (Guinier 1994b, 149).

Opponents of these systems view the potential increase in representational diversity differently. The more decision-making bodies resemble the voters, they argue, the more problematic they become. They maintain that these systems will "balkanize" politics by stressing group or issue differences among voters. Candidates, they claim, will make divisive campaign appeals, attempting to win election on a narrow base of support. In partisan settings, these systems will allegedly encourage small political parties to contest elections, which opponents claim will endanger the two-party system. Fringe or extremist candidates, it is also argued, are more likely to be elected under these voting rules. And the more diverse governing bodies elected through these systems, opponents claim, will experience greater internal conflict and even be susceptible to gridlock. Politics, in short, will become more polarized (see, e.g., Thernstrom 1999; Busch 1999; Clegg 1999; and more generally Weaver, 1984, 194–95).

The Party System

One of the most frequent themes of critics of alternative systems is that they constitute a threat to the American two-party system. This criticism relies largely on the association between proportional representation (PR) election systems and the presence of representatives of multiple political parties in parliaments around the world. These multiparty systems in turn are associated with coalition governments, and coalition governments are said to be unstable or otherwise weak governments. Winner-take-all elections, such as those in the United States, are more likely to force electoral competition to be between two parties, resulting in single-party control and more stable and effective government. These linkages between election systems and the stability or strength of governments, however, are not as strong or clear as often portrayed by the opponents of the alternative systems (see esp. the exchange between Pinto-Duschinsky 1999a, 1999b and Powell 1999, Lijphart 1999a, Vowles 1999, Shugart 1999; and more generally Lijphart 1999b). Nor are other democracies' experiences with electoral systems necessarily exportable to the United States (see Taagepera 1998, 87–88).

An example of how these arguments are exaggerated occurred recently in the congressional hearings on the States' Choice of Voting Systems Act. This bill, sponsored by Rep. Melvin Watt of North Carolina, would allow states to elect members of the U.S. House of Representatives through multimember districts, provided those districts do not violate the Voting Rights Act. This condition would virtually preclude the use of traditional multimember elections in areas with large numbers of minority voters. Elections within multimember districts in these areas would need to be conducted under alternative voting rules in order to avoid the dilution prohibitions of the Voting Rights Act, unless it could be demonstrated that the candidate preferences of voters did not differ along group lines (see *Thornburg v. Gingles* 1986, 46–51). The hearings therefore focused, not surprisingly, on the alternative voting rules.[42]

Opponents of the bill generally equated alternative voting arrangements with PR systems and warned of a resulting fragmentation of politics through multiple parties. One witness raised the specter of excessive fragmentation by referring to atypical examples of proportional representation systems. This witness stated that

> countries using some form of proportional representation or other multi-member district methods are more prone, *like Italy or Israel,* to political instability and/or a situation in which groups having the support of only a small proportion of the population nevertheless hold the decisive political balance. (Busch 1999, 2, emphasis added)[43]

Another witness stated that if cumulative voting were used in the new multimember districts, Congress would consist of "a variety of warring parties" (Thernstrom 1999, 3).

In response to these critiques, proponents of alternative election systems can note that not everyone is enamored of a two-party system. Winner-take-all electoral systems impose "stability" through two parties by distorting the translation of popular votes into legislative seats, typically providing the plurality party in the electorate with an exaggerated majority of seats in a legislature (see, e.g., Campbell 1996, 34–36), and sometimes even manufacturing a legislative majority for a party that did not receive a plurality of the votes (see Lijphart 1999b, 165–68).[44] The American two-party system has been said to inhibit the major parties from taking clear positions on issues, thereby impeding debate over policy, leaving voters uncertain about what the parties stand for, and making it difficult to hold parties politically accountable. As expressed by one political scientist who would like more electoral options, "The Republican and Democratic parties are immobilized by having to promise too many things to too many people" (Lowi 1999, 177). This sentiment appears to be shared by many of America's voters as well. A nationwide survey conducted by the National Opinion Research Center in 1996 found that 82 percent of Americans thought that "both parties are pretty much out of touch with the American people" (Shea 1999, 38), and other surveys during the 1990s consistently showed that a majority of the public would like to have at least a "third major political party" option (Collett and Hansen 1996, 239, 252 n. 1).[45]

Regardless of whether one prefers the two-party arrangement, however, the apocalyptic scenarios of these opponents can be dismissed as hyperbole. One cannot simply export political conditions in Italy or Israel to the United States by changing an election system. First, the linkages between election systems and party systems, while empirically well documented, are far from uniform. Political conditions in Italy and Israel are certainly not typical of countries with proportional representation arrangements. In a comment that could be written to apply to Israel as well as Italy, Shugart has noted:

> Anti-PR polemicists . . . take as a given that all PR systems can be damned by stating one simple word: Italy. While there are indeed PR systems that have been characterized by frequent inter-election changes in government and an inability of elections to be framed as choices among competing governments—as in Italy—such characterizations do not apply to PR systems *as a class*. (Shugart 1999, 143, emphasis in original; see also MacIvor 1999, 25, 29; and, more generally, Reilly and Reynolds 1999)[46]

Electoral systems, it is well understood, are "by no means the sole determinant" of party systems (Lijphart 1999b, 144, 168–70). It has even been suggested, given recent election outcomes around the world, that "the conventional wisdom of a causal relationship between an electoral system and a party system is increasingly looking out of date" (Reilly and Reynolds 1999, 17).

Second, the election systems used in Italy and Israel are very different from the alternative system under consideration in the United States. Both use a list system of proportional representation in which the focus is on voting for parties rather than candidates. And the number of seats per district (called "district magnitudes") in each country is among the highest in the world (Cox 1997, 50–55). District magnitude is a crucial variable affecting the electoral opportunities of small parties. The higher the magnitudes, the more likely small parties are to win seats (Taagepera and Shugart 1989, 112–25).

For many years district magnitudes in Italy ranged from 1 to 53, with a median magnitude of 17.[47] All 120 seats of the Israeli Knesset are elected through one nationwide vote. Systems like these, classified as "extreme" cases of PR (Lijphart 1991, 73), are not being seriously contemplated in the United States (Benoit and Shepsle 1995, 61).

If other countries are to be cited as examples of the effects that alternative systems are likely to have on the American party system, then it would be much more appropriate to reference Malta, which uses a preference voting system rather than a proportional list system, with all districts electing only five members of parliament. This is much closer to the number to be elected, through alternative voting rules, in the multimember arrangements usually suggested by the proponents of these systems in the United States.[48] Malta, unlike Italy or Israel, has had a two-party system and one-party governments for many years (Lijphart 1999b, 75–77, 111, 168–70, 312).[49] An even better reference, however, would no doubt be the state of Illinois, which used cumulative voting in three-member districts to elect the lower house of its legislature from 1870 to 1980 and had a thriving two-party system the entire time (see Wiggins and Petty 1979; Kuklinski 1973; Dunn 1972; Blair 1960; and more generally Guinier 1998, 266–68).[50]

It must also be understood that the adoption of alternative voting rules in elections for legislative bodies would not eliminate other structural features of American politics that might have a greater impact on the number of viable parties. A crucial regime-level feature of American politics is the presence of a presidential rather than a parliamentary system of government. Although not originally designed as such, this system has evolved further into what is functionally a presidential-centered arrangement. In a presidential system, separate votes are cast for presidential and legislative candidates. While votes in the American presidential election are filtered through the electoral college, rather than aggregated into one official, nationwide count, this is still essentially a single-person, winner-take-all election. As Lijphart has stated, "[P]residentialism tends to foster a two-party system, as the presidency is the biggest prize to be won, and only the largest parties have a chance to win it." The advantage that larger parties have over smaller parties in presidential elections, he further notes, "often carries over into legislative elections as well." This spillover effect has been the case even when countries with the presidential system use proportional representation rules for their legislative elections (Lijphart 1991, 73; see also Lijphart 1999b, 155–56, 164, 168; Reichley 1999, 14).

The presidential structure is of course also replicated in the governments of all fifty states, and in many local governments as well. Governors and many mayors are directly elected by the people, rather than through a vote of state or local legislators. In addition, at the federal level, Congress is a bicameral institution, and although every state is apportioned two members to the upper chamber, the Senate, Article 1, section 3 of the Constitution specifies that senatorial terms be staggered, making senatorial elections also winner-take-all, single-person elections (see McKaskle 1998, 1199 n. 327). The use of alternative election systems in these elections therefore would require a constitutional amendment, and this is rarely, if ever, advocated by proponents of these systems.

Other structural features are considerable obstacles to the development of a multiparty system within the United States as well. The requirements for having party candidates listed on election ballots, for example, vary from state to state but are typically much more restrictive than those in other democracies (Katz 1997, 260–61). Primary elections, widely used to select party nominees in this country, are said to "give strong incentives for dissidents to try their luck in one of the major party primaries instead of establishing separate small parties" (Lijphart 1999b, 164). Campaign finance laws are also among a variety of election laws and regulations that are considered to be "heavily biased against the formation and maintenance of anything other than the two-party system" (Lowi 1991, 172). These laws and regulations appear to be legally secure as the Supreme Court has taken a protective attitude toward the two-party system, holding recently that states may "enact reasonable election regulations that may, in practice, favor the traditional two-party system" (*Timmons v. Twin Cities Area New Party* 1997, 367).

Racial Polarization

Racial polarization is often predicted to increase if alternative voting rules are adopted. Racial polarization, it is even suggested, will become manifest in partisan polarization, in the form of racially specific parties. The witness testifying against Rep. Watt's bill who stated that Congress would degenerate into "a variety of warring parties" testified as well that if cumulative voting were used in the new multimember districts, "There will be a David Duke party and a black nationalist party" (Thernstrom 1999, 3).[51] Another witness asserted that cumulative voting "discourages coalition building and facilitates identity politics and, especially, racial politicking" (Clegg 1999, 4–5). Defendants objecting to a cumulative voting remedy for a dilutive at-large system in a Maryland county argued that the system would "increase and entrench racial polarization" in the county.[52] A political scientist testifying on behalf of the county, Donald Horowitz, claimed that because the African American percentage of the voting age population in the county (20) was close to the threshold of exclusion for the five-vote system (16.67), minority candidates were likely to exploit "divisive racial issues" in their campaigns. White candidates, he said, were also "likely to engage in racial appeals" if that system were used (Horowitz 1994, 9). "In the name of remedying racial polarization," Horowitz concluded, "cumulative voting would be likely to entrench it" (Horowitz 1994, 10).

No empirical evidence has been marshaled to support these suggestions that alternative systems will result in increased racial polarization. The only study that has addressed the broader racial consequences of the use of one of these systems is that of cumulative voting in Chilton County, Alabama, by Pildes and Donoghue (1995). African Americans constituted, as of 1990, 9.9 percent of the voting age population in Chilton County. The threshold of exclusion for the county's seven-vote system is 12.5. The close correspondence between these two figures suggests that this is a setting, according to Horowitz's theory, in which racial polarization is likely to become more intense. Pildes and Donoghue, however, found just the opposite effect.

No African American had ever been elected to the Chilton County commission until cumulative voting was implemented in 1988. The victorious African American in that contest, Robert Agee, finished first despite receiving very little of the white vote (Still 1992, 189, 193–94). He was reelected in 1992, finishing second despite again receiving relatively little of the white vote (Engstrom, Kirksey, and Still 1997b, 306; Pildes and Donoghue 1995, 289, 303, 306). Agee's victories clearly depended on the ability of the county's African American voters to cumulate votes on his behalf. According to Pildes and Donoghue, even in 1992, when Agee was an incumbent, he "would not have stood a chance" of being elected under the previous at-large election system (Pildes and Donoghue 1995, 288).

In both 1988 and 1992, African Americans preferred Agee over another African American candidate, Robert Binion. According to Pildes and Donoghue, Agee was considered a moderate candidate, whereas Binion, endorsed by the state's major African American political organization, the Alabama Democratic Conference, was viewed as more radical (Pildes and Donoghue 1995, 293). Agee is credited with bringing about more equity in county services and appointments (Pildes and Donoghue 1995, 278–79) without being a polarizing presence on the commission. He reportedly received more contacts and requests for assistance from white than African American residents of the county (Pildes and Donoghue 1995, 297). His colleagues even chose him to serve as the chairperson of the commission. Interviews with other commissioners revealed that Agee was elevated to that position because of his "judgment, temperament, and ability" (Pildes and Donoghue 1995, 281).

Cumulative voting has not caused the racial divisions in candidate preferences in Chilton County. The African American voters' preference for an African American candidate and the white voters' preference for white candidates (Still 1992, 189, 193–94; Engstrom, Kirksey, and Still 1997b, 306; Pildes and Donoghue 1995, 289, 303–7) did not result from the option to

cumulate votes. That option, however, has permitted the African American residents of the county to elect an African American to serve on the commission,
which not surprisingly has had the beneficial effect of making the African
American minority feel "more connected to local government" (Pildes and
Donoghue 1995, 279). And contrary to the predictions of some opponents of
alternative election systems, the election of an African American has not exacerbated racial polarization in the county. Pildes and Donoghue discovered, to
the contrary, that it has "begun to decrease racial polarization in politics"
(Pildes and Donoghue 1995, 297; see also Webster 2000, 158).

Balkanization

Increases in political parties and racial polarization are only two dimen-
sions of the "balkanization" of politics alleged to result from the use of alternative systems. As noted above, one witness testifying on Rep. Watts bill stated that cumulative voting would "discourage coalition building and facilitate
identity politics" (Clegg 1999, 4–5). Another witness warned of "increased
ethnic divisions," "the deliberate cultivation of ethnic identity or separatism,"
and "increased leverage held by political groups outside the mainstream"
(Busch 1999, 5, 6). The election of "extremists" supported by a small proportion of the electorate (such as neo-Nazi members of a future "David Duke
party") is frequently forecast by opponents of these systems.[53]

As is the case with the claims of increased racial polarization, there is no
evidence supporting these predictions. Alternative systems, as already noted,
do diffuse electoral opportunities, and therefore legislatures elected through
these systems are likely to reflect better the diversity of views in the electorate, but this does not equate with the election of extremists. Indeed, as
Mulroy has pointed out, "There is no evidence that where alternative systems
have been tried in the United States, there has been any marked increase in
[even] the number of candidates considered 'radical' or 'extremist,'" let alone
the number elected (Mulroy 1998, 354 n. 110; see also Pildes and Donoghue
1995, 292).

A study comparing votes cast in the Illinois House of Representatives, during and after the period in which that chamber was elected by cumulative voting in three-member districts, with those cast in the Illinois Senate, elected
through single-member districts, found that there was more diversity in the
voting behavior of the members of the house while cumulative voting was in
effect. The study examined the percentage of times each legislator voted in
agreement with the "pro-business" position of the Illinois Political Action
Committee (IPAC), an organization with ties to the Illinois Chamber of Commerce, on a set of "key votes" identified by that group. The results revealed
that there was more variation in support for IPAC's positions in the house
while cumulative voting was used than in the senate, or than in the house when

that body was elected in single-member districts (Adams 1996, 140). Although one commentator has interpreted this as demonstrating that "the cumulative system in Illinois produced more *ideologically extreme* members of the state assembly than did the single member district system" (Canon 1999a, 366; 1999b, 290), nothing in the study indicates that the behavior of any of the legislators elected under cumulative voting, on the basis of this measure, could be considered "ideologically extreme" (see Engstrom 1999, 470).

Many advocates of alternative voting rules argue that rather than discouraging the creation of electoral coalitions across group lines, these systems will encourage them. As expressed by Guinier, "Voters are not coerced into voting based on race or any other affiliation simply because of where they live or what they look like" (Guinier 1999, xii; see also Viteritti 1994, 254, 270). The ability to form "voluntary constituencies," rather than being trapped within winner-take-all geographical districts drawn to favor particular groups of voters, provides an incentive for candidates to appeal to voters across groups. Efforts to build coalitions based on interests and issues rather than identity, it is argued, are more, rather than less, likely if alternative rules are used (see, e.g., Lewyn 1995, 212; Bloch 1998, 29; Mulroy 1998, 353–55; and Webster 2000, 158).[54] In addition, elections under these systems are expected to offer voters more candidates from which to choose, to be more competitive, and therefore to stimulate more voter interest and participation than found in the frequently "safe" districts currently in place (see, e.g., Mulroy 1998, 350; Lewyn 1995, 212–13; Richie and Hill 1999a, 13; Webster 2000, 158).

The multiple-vote feature of these systems is also alleged to decrease the polarization so often engendered by electoral campaigns in single-member districts. When voters have only a single vote to cast, candidates often attempt to distinguish themselves from the others through negative attacks on their opponents. Candidates who think they are behind, as indicated by polls, for example, are thought to be especially prone to "go negative" (see Guinier 1998, 92, 254–55). Attack advertising has become "the dominant message of modern political campaigns" (Ansolabehere and Iyengar 1995, 101; see also Magleby 2000; Thurber, Nelson, and Dulio 2000). When voters have more than one vote, however, as may be the case in limited voting and is the case in cumulative voting, or when their vote may transfer among candidates, as in preference voting, candidates will be less likely to engage in negative campaigning, it is argued, because they will not want to alienate voters favorably disposed to other candidates. They will be more likely to distinguish themselves from the other candidates in this context through positive messages about themselves rather than negative messages about the others (Inman 1995, 2013–14; McKaskle 1998, 1198 n. 324). Campaigns under these systems, therefore, are less likely to become, as a recent state legislative contest in a single-member district in Louisiana has been described, "a political knife fight" (Donze 1999, B1).

Proponents and opponents of particular election systems often make exaggerated claims about the advantages and disadvantages of those systems. This is no doubt true of both the proponents and opponents of alternative voting systems. Everson has correctly noted that:

> Political reform usually fails to achieve either the heaven on earth described by its proponents or the hell feared by its opponents. One reason for this is that the conditions reformers wish to alter are usually the product of multiple causes and reform usually focuses on a single factor. (Everson 1992, 190)

To date, little has been documented about the consequences of alternative election systems other than that they can, depending on where the threshold of exclusion is set, provide minority voters with electoral opportunities. The opponents of these systems claim, with considerable rhetorical flair, that while this goal may be admirable, the numerous negative consequences that will result from their use far outweigh this benefit. These other alleged consequences, however, have yet to be documented, and what little empirical evidence exists points to their absence rather than their presence. It will not be surprising if empirical research ultimately reveals that these other consequences do not occur, at least not to the degree that the opponents predict. This was the conclusion, for example, of a study of the use of preference voting in five Ohio cities early in the twentieth century. Members of minority groups that had been unrepresented, or severely underrepresented, on councils prior to the adoption of preference voting had their representation increased after its adoption. When it came to the parade of horribles predicted by the system's opponents, however, it was found that the system was never "as damaging to the polity as its opponents claimed" (Barber 1995, 308).

Conclusion

The implementation of democracy in the United States, unfortunately, has not been a neutral, nonpartisan process. The way in which electoral competition is structured has become a subject of recurring controversy in many states and localities. Allegations of bias in the arrangements used to elect our legislative bodies are common. Bruising legislative battles over the design of geographical districts have been followed by contentious and costly litigation, which may resolve such disputes, at least in terms of declaring winners and losers, but does little to instill confidence that either the process or the outcome is impartial.

The design of election districts has often been an "acrimonious," even "nasty," issue because it can be a crucial factor affecting election outcomes. Elections in single-member districts are winner-take-all elections—a plurality of votes wins the seat, and all of the other votes, no matter how close the election may have been, may as well be discarded. When multimember district elections are held under the traditional voting rules, a plurality group often wins all of the seats, or at least a vastly disproportionate number of them. Who is grouped with whom, therefore, becomes a major referent in evaluating the lines, and a major cause of conflict.

The redistricting stimulated by the 1990 census was especially contentious. The application of new computer technology made it possible to manipulate district boundaries and to assess their likely consequences more effectively than ever before. Demands for population equality among the districts became excuses to fine-tune the maps to satisfy the personal interests of incumbents and/or the collective interests of various groups, particularly political parties. Instead of the people choosing their representatives, many critics said, election outcomes were predetermined by the representatives choosing the people they would represent. The basic structure through which elections are conducted is infected, many claim, with undemocratic gerrymandering, a problem that is endemic to the system and often immune to judicial review.

During the 1990s many of the gerrymandering allegations focused on racial and language minorities protected by the Voting Rights Act, primarily African Americans and Latinos. Unlike previous decades, however, the 1990s witnessed not only the traditional allegations of gerrymandering against these groups, which the Voting Rights Act is supposed to prevent, but also allegations of gerrymandering in their favor to avoid violations of that act. The perceived racial consequences of different plans were tied directly to different expected electoral outcomes for various incumbents and political parties, a fusion that made the districting thicket even more entangled politically than it had been in the past.

The Supreme Court has responded to the allegations of gerrymandering in favor of protected minorities by elevating the importance of what it has identified as "traditional districting principles." The increased emphasis on these principles certainly does not eliminate efforts to bias districting arrangements to favor some groups of voters at the expense of others. Although the principles are labeled as "traditional," the constraints they place on those drawing and adopting districts are far from clear. Some of the principles, like compactness and respect for communities of interest, lack agreed-upon definitions and therefore are subject to considerable manipulation. Others, like contiguity, once had unambiguous referents but are now, as a result of judicial scrutiny, conceptually muddled. Even assuming that agreement is reached on the definitions and measures of these criteria or that they are simply imposed by the Court, the standards for assessing when they have been "respected" and when they have been "subordinated" remain uncertain at best. The post-2000 round of redistricting will be not only politically entangled but also more conceptually ensnarled than ever before.

While the so-called traditional principles are race neutral on their face, they may not be neutral in application (see Webster 2000, 158–59; Lennertz 2000, 183). In the context of our system of winner-take-all geographical districts, they will no doubt tend to favor plurality groups that are relatively evenly dispersed geographically, as these groups are the most likely to benefit from a strict compactness requirement (see Wildgen and Engstrom 1980). This means that they will work, in application, to advantage Anglos more often than African Americans or Latinos, given their respective numbers and residential distributions. The medium for providing racial and language minorities in this country with opportunities to elect representatives of their choice has typically been the majority-minority single-member district. The fact that the Court's new concern for these districting principles has resulted, at least to date, in the dismantling of only these types of districts is no accident.

The ability to create majority-minority districts has been diminished by the new constraints on the design of districts. Fewer such districts are expected to be created after the 2000 census than were created after the 1990 census. This situation is, as noted above, a political choice, not a requirement of democracy. Not surprisingly, this has stimulated interest in other possible choices, especially in election systems in which minority electoral opportunities are not dependent on, or at least less dependent on, district lines. Two such systems, limited voting and cumulative voting, have now been adopted to provide these opportunities by about a hundred local governmental units, and a third, preference voting, has been frequently proposed for this purpose. These opportunities, as noted above, are neither electoral guarantees nor recipes for racial polarization.

The ability of minority voters to elect candidates favored by them but not by other voters when these types of voting rules are used has been documented in numerous elections. This has often resulted in a minority candidate being elected to the respective governing body for the first time. The minority electoral opportunities provided by these systems, in short, are not just theoretical, provided the threshold of exclusion is not set too high relative to minority electoral strength.

These electoral opportunities are provided without treating members of racial or language minorities any differently from other voters. Minority voters need not constitute majorities within districts, or other electoral units, to have opportunities to elect representatives of their choice, so there is less need for district boundaries to selectively include and exclude group members. Electoral opportunities provided in these multimember districts are therefore much less dependent on districts that bear the "resemblance to political apartheid" that the Supreme Court found in some single-member district arrangements in the 1990s (*Shaw v. Reno* 1993, 647). Indeed, what the Court has identified as "traditional race-neutral districting principles" should be easier to apply when creating the larger multimember districts used with these

alternative systems. Concerns for contiguity, compactness, and other governmental boundaries are less likely to conflict with the provision of minority
electoral opportunities within these larger multimember districts, and geographically based "communities of interest" are less likely to be dissected by
their boundaries (see Engstrom 1995b; Morrill 1996a, 1996b; Webster 1997).

A variety of other consequences, some good and some bad, are alleged to
result from the use of these voting systems. No evidence has been gathered,
however, documenting these effects in any of the jurisdictions using the systems. Indeed, the only consequence that is well documented is the ability of
minority voters to elect their preferred representatives, who are themselves
members of the minority group, when the group's electoral strength is close to
the threshold of exclusion. Some critics of the systems have suggested that the
election of such candidates will result in increased racial antagonism and
polarization. This is another allegation for which evidence has yet to be presented. There is certainly no evidence that racial hostilities will be higher when
these systems are used than when minorities remain systematically underrepresented as a result of dilutive electoral arrangements. What little evidence
exists suggests just the opposite, that racial polarization is likely to decline
when minority-preferred representatives serve on governmental bodies (Pildes
and Donoghue 1995).

While invalidating a majority-minority single-member district for being an
impermissible "racial gerrymander," one federal court stated, "The time has
come to contemplate more innovative means of ensuring minority representation in democratic institutions" (*Johnson v. Miller* 1994, 1393). The American
experience with electoral systems has been severely truncated. There are
numerous ways to conduct democratic elections, many of which, like limited,
cumulative, and preference voting, can provide minorities with electoral
opportunities without gerrymandering district lines (see, e.g., Lijphart 1994,
10–56; Rule and Zimmerman 1994; Farrell 1997). Recognition of this fact is
an important development in American politics. The new legal restrictions on
majority-minority districts need not, and should not, become an excuse to limit
minority electoral opportunities in this country. Tolerance of such a limitation,
it must be recognized, would be "another political choice" made by Americans
(*Holder v. Hall* 1994, 911, Thomas, J., concurring), not a constitutional, and
certainly not a democratic, necessity.

Notes

1. See *Fouts v. Harris,* C.A. No. 98-10031 (S.D. Fla.); *Cromartie v. Hunt,* C.A.
No. 4:96-CV-104-H2 (E.D. N.C.); *Thompson v. Smith,* C.A. No. 97-A-715-E (M.D.
Ala.); *Maxwell v. Foster,* No. CV98-1378 M (W.D. La.); *Daly v. Leake,* C.A. No. 5:96-
CV-88-V (E.D. N.C.); *U.S. v. City of Lawrence, Mass.,* C.A. No. 98-12256-WGY (D.

Mass.); *Sanders v. Dooly County, Ga.,* C.A. No. 5:98-CV-412-2 (M.D. Ga.); and *Wilson v. Jones,* C.A. No. 96-1952-M (S.D. Ala.).

2. See Silverberg 1996, 229; Clymer 1991, 13A; *Hays v. State of Louisiana* 1993, 1199.

3. See *Wesberry v. Sanders* 1964 ; *Reynolds v. Sims* 1964; *Avery v. Midland County* 1968; and *Hadley v. Junior College District of Metropolitan Kansas City* 1970.

4. All members of the U.S. House of Representatives from the forty-three states with more than one member are elected from single-member districts, as are almost all state legislators. (The 7,424 state legislators in the United States [Stanley and Niemi 2000, 60] are elected from 6,743 geographical districts [Lilley, DeFranco, and Diefender 1994, xi], an average of 1.1 per district.) In addition, the 1992 census of governments indicates that 74.9 percent of the members of county governing boards, 36.3 percent of the members of elected school boards, and 21.3 percent of the members of municipal governing boards are elected from geographical districts (Bureau of Census 1995, 9, 12, 16).

5. On the work of these commissions, see Lyons 1970; Butler and Cain 1992, 117–39; Butler and McLean 1996; Johnston, Rossiter, and Pattie 1996; Maley, Morling, and Bell 1996; Bowden and Falck 1996; and Rossiter, Johnston, and Pattie 1999.

6. Litigation concerning city council districts in Chicago following the 1990 census lasted about seven years and may cost that city roughly $20 million. This includes about $12 million paid to three law firms representing the city (Simpson 1999) and almost $7.3 million the city has been ordered to pay the lawyers representing the successful African American plaintiffs (*Barnett v. City of Chicago* 2000). The litigation focused primarily on the racial composition of one of the fifty council districts in the city.

7. See Handley, Grofman, and Arden 1998; Brischetto 1998, 49–50, 96; Lublin 1997; Arden, Grofman, and Handley 1997; Grofman and Davidson 1994; and Handley and Grofman 1994.

8. For a review of the many issues, legal and factual, involved in implementing sections 2 and 5, see Hebert et al. 1998, 116–38. The Supreme Court has determined that only changes with a retrogressive purpose or effect (i.e., plans that are intended to leave, or do in fact leave, a protected minority in a worse situation) may be denied preclearance under section 5 (see *Reno v. Bossier Parish School Board* 1997 regarding retrogressive effect and *Reno v. Bossier Parish School Board* 2000 regarding retrogressive intent).

9. The number of members of the U.S. House of Representatives, currently 435, as well as their election through single-member districts, is specified by federal statute. Following each decennial census, seats in the House are apportioned to the various states through the method of "equal proportions." The number of seats apportioned to a state, and consequently the number of districts to be adopted by that state, may therefore vary from census to census (2 USCS secs. 2a, 2c). Changes in the size of state and local legislative bodies occur only rarely.

10. In 1996 the Supreme Court held North Carolina's Twelfth District unconstitutional in *Shaw v. Hunt,* necessitating a revision in the districts before the 1998 congressional elections. A third districting arrangement was used for the 2000 election (see *Cromartie v. Hunt* 2000, stayed *Hunt v. Cromartie* 2000).

11. See also *Shaw v. Hunt* 1996, 904 (dismissing the complaint against North Carolina's First District because no plaintiff lived in that district); and *Bush v. Vera* 1996, at 957–58.

12. A panel of the Fifth Circuit Court of Appeals stated recently, "It would seem obvious to us that there is more than one way to draw a district so that it can reasonably be described as meaningfully adhering to traditional principles, even if not to the same extent or degree as some other hypothetical district" (*Chen v. City of Houston* 2000, 519).

13. An argument that a judicial election subdistrict in Louisiana was defective because it was only "technically contiguous" because areas of the district were "separated by uninhabited swamp" was not accepted in *Oren v. Foster* (1999, sl. op., 9–10).

14. Adding even further to the confusion has been the suggestion by one court that "'contiguity' is not an abstract or geometric technical phrase. It assumes meaning when seen in combination with concepts of 'regional integrity' and 'community of interest'" (*DeWitt v. Wilson* 1994, 1414).

15. One commentator has suggested that, because of racially selective annexation practices, following municipal boundaries in designing districts may often result in districts that disadvantage minority voters (McKaskle 1995, 85; see also Fleischmann 2000, 111).

16. The Ohio Constitution specifies that if a division must be made, the unit to be divided shall be, in order of preference, "a township, a city ward, a city, and a village" (Art. 11, sec. 7(C)).

17. See also *Theriot v. Parish of Jefferson* 1999, 483 n.14, 485 n. 17, noting that the city council of a city within a parish (county) preferred that the city continue to be split among three county council districts in order to have access to, and influence over, three county council members.

18. A panel of the Fifth Circuit has recently commented: "Because of the inherently subjective nature of the concept, it would seem that reasonable people might disagree as to what constitutes a community. We thus caution against general over-reliance on the communities of interest factor" (*Chen v. City of Houston* 2000, 517 n. 9).

19. Essentially the same argument was made concerning African Americans in East Baton Rouge Parish and Caddo Parish (Shreveport) by witnesses in the *Hays* case in Louisiana (Engstrom and Kirksey 1998, 251; see also Kelly 1996, 268–69).

20. A federal district court in North Carolina concluded that the legislature in that state had "eschewed" the "community of interest" criterion when it revised the Twelfth Congressional District in 1997. The court provided no reference whatsoever, however, indicating how that criterion had been violated (see *Cromartie v. Hunt* 2000, sl. op., 24). A dissenting judge, in contrast, found that the Twelfth reflected "a clear community of interest" consisting of three urban areas known as "the Piedmont Crescent," which "share common characteristics and face similar problems" (*Cromartie v. Hunt* 2000, sl. op., 14, Thornburg, J., dissenting). A panel of the Fifth Circuit rejected an allegation that the City of Houston violated the "communities of interest" principle in a 1997 revision of councilmanic districts because the plaintiffs' evidence lacked specificity. Evidence of socioeconomic variation within districts that approached 200,000 in population did not impress the court, which expressed greater interest in anecdotal and

statistical evidence concerning specific districting choices made by the city (*Chen v. City of Houston* 2000, 512–17).

21. In the *Cromartie v. Hunt* decision of 2000, "geographical integrity" was again identified as a "traditional districting criterion" that had been "eschewed" by the North Carolina legislature in its 1997 revision of the Twelfth Congressional District (*Cromartie v. Hunt* 2000, sl. op., 24). The court failed to provide any indication of the meaning of this criterion in the later opinion as well. The expression "geographic integrity" has been used by geographers when writing about districting, but unfortunately it remains undefined in their work as well (see Morrill 1994, 117, 133; Webster 2000, 156).

22. The results of the 1972 election held under the plan were hardly proportional, however. They were more consistent with the plaintiffs' allegation that the plan was "nothing less than a gigantic political gerrymander" (*Gaffney v. Cummings* 1973, 752) in favor of the Republican Party. While the plan was alleged to have contained about seventy districts that were "safe" for the Democratic Party, that party won only fifty-eight districts in 1992. This no doubt disappointing outcome for the Democrats was not due to an unexpected landslide vote for the Republicans, whose candidates won only 52.9 percent of the votes (and 61.1 percent of the districts) (Engstrom 1977, 301, 304).

23. A simple plurality is the usual requirement for election in this country, although a majority of the votes is sometimes specified as a minimum criterion for certain offices, primarily at the local level.

24. The high stakes involved in districting are illustrated by the $1 million in contributions, by or through the National Republican Congressional Committee and its chairman, Rep. Thomas Davis III of Virginia, to Republican state legislative candidates in Virginia in 1999. The election produced a gain of three seats for the Republicans, which provided the party with control of the legislature. Davis is quoted as stating, "A million dollars for three seats is pretty expensive. But it's worth it because we now control the redistricting process" (Hosler 1999).

25. There are variations in how multiseat elections can be structured, such as the attachment of designated places or posts and "full-slate" requirements, that can enhance even further this dilutive potential (see Engstrom and McDonald 1987, 1993).

26. Other Supreme Court decisions have also made it more difficult for minority voters to force local governments through litigation to change from at-large electoral arrangements to single-member districts, which has also stimulated interest in alternative ways to structure electoral competition within the at-large format (on these decisions, see Engstrom 2000, 24–31).

27. It is not necessary that voters cast votes in whole units. In Peoria, Illinois, for example, a five-vote cumulative system has been adopted whereby voters simply identify up to five candidates they wish to vote for, and then their five votes are allocated evenly among those candidates. If a voter votes for only one candidate, five votes are allocated to that candidate. If a voter votes for two candidates, then two and one-half votes are allocated to each, and so on.

28. The successful application of the single-shot strategy depends not only on a group's voters complying with it but also on the other voters dispersing their votes across more candidates than there are seats to be filled (see Engstrom and McDonald, 1993, 386–87).

29. Voters are not necessarily required to rank all of the candidates on a preference voting ballot. When they do not, some ballots may become nontransferable, resulting in the quota not being obtained by the required number of candidates. When this happens, the remaining seat(s) may be filled by applying a simple plurality rule after the final set of transfers.

30. As one court stated recently about cumulative voting, "By allowing each voter the same number of votes, cumulative voting subscribes to the one-person, one-vote requirement with numeric exactness" (*McCoy v. Chicago Heights* 1998, 984; see also *Kaelin v. Warden* 1971; *LoFrisco v. Schaffer* 1972; *Orloski v. Davis* 1983).

31. See, e.g., the findings of Welch and Bledsoe concerning the nonracial consequences of electing city councils through districts or at-large elections, which indicate far more modest effects on the types of people elected and their behavior in office than are typically asserted by the advocates of either of these systems (Welch and Bledsoe 1988, 104).

32. Cumulative voting has been adopted by local governments in Texas, Alabama, New Mexico, South Dakota, and Illinois. Limited voting has been adopted by local jurisdictions in Alabama, North Carolina, Texas, Georgia, and Arizona.

33. A study that matched the actual ballots cast in the 1991 cumulative voting election for the city council in Peoria, Illinois, with the racial composition of the city's precincts, however, found that while an African American was elected, he was not the preferred candidate of African American voters. The African American voters divided most of their votes between three other African American candidates, resulting in none of the three being elected (Aspin and Hall 1996).

34. Only two of the nine Latino candidates elected were also among the candidates preferred by the Anglo voters. One was an incumbent who three years earlier, in the city's first cumulative voting election, had become the first Latino ever to be elected to the city council. He was the second choice of the Anglo voters among three candidates (one a write-in candidate) in a two-seat election. The other was elected in a three-seat election in which only two Anglos and one other Latino were candidates.

35. Unlike limited and cumulative voting, preference voting has not been adopted in response to vote dilution allegations. Minority group leaders, touting the electoral opportunities it provides minority voters, have been instrumental in getting it placed on the ballot for voter consideration in Cincinnati in 1988 and 1991 and in San Francisco in 1996, however. The system was rejected in both cities as the result of racially divided votes in which African Americans were supportive of the system but whites were not (Engstrom 1993, 801, 804; DeLeon, Blash, and Hill 1997, 21–26, 48–55; DeLeon, Hill, and Blash 1998, 271–72; see also Engstrom 1990). In all three instances preference voting received around 45 percent of the total vote, an encouraging response to many of its supporters (see, e.g., Electoral Reform Society 1996; DeLeon, Hill, and Blash 1998, 270, 272–73).

36. Reply Brief of Appellants, *Worcester County, Md., et al. v. Cane, et al.*, Fourth Circuit Court of Appeals, No. 94-1579, July 2, 1994, 8. See also Thernstrom and Thernstrom, who assert that the alternative systems discussed herein "are designed to guarantee true proportionality" (1997, 651 n. 20).

37. Second Amended Complaint, *Cleveland County Association for Government by the People, et al. v. Cleveland County Board of Commissioners, et al.*, United States

District Court, District of Columbia, Civil Action No. 96-1447-SSS, February 30, 1997, 10.

38. *M. L. Campbell, et al. v. Cleveland County Board of Commissioners, et al.,* No. 94-0845-SSS, (D.C. D.C. 1994) (consent decree), 5.

39. This decision was reversed on appeal because the changes specified in the consent decree had to be implemented, according to state law, through a county referendum or a state statute. The appellate court did not express any disagreement with the constitutional interpretation of the district court, however, and specifically held that limited voting was otherwise permissible, stating: "We do not hold that the limited voting scheme provided for in the consent decree is itself contrary to 'public policy' or even the law of North Carolina—indeed . . . it has been successfully implemented in several other jurisdictions in the state" (*Cleveland County Association for Government by the People v. Cleveland County Board of Commissioners* 1998, 478).

40. In the Chicago Heights case, the district court adopted cumulative voting as a remedy for a dilutive municipal election system (*McCoy v. Chicago Heights* 1998). While acknowledging the "virtues" of cumulative voting, the appellate court reversed the district court's choice of this system, which was not part of a settlement, on procedural grounds similar to those cited in the Cleveland County case. See *Harper v. City of Chicago Heights and the Chicago Heights Election Commission* 2000, 601–2.

41. The complexity of preference voting occurs after the votes are cast. Voters may not fully understand how votes are transferred, especially those identified as "surplus" votes for a winning candidate, and many voters may not know which of the candidates they ranked ultimately received their vote (see McKaskle 1998, 1162; Rosenblum 1996, 142 n. 124).

42. A similar bill, called the Voters' Choice Act (H.R. 2545), was introduced in 1995 by Rep. Cynthia McKinney of Georgia. This bill would have permitted multimember districts for U.S. House elections provided they were combined with limited, cumulative, or preference voting specifically. McKinney's bill never received a hearing.

43. Italy and Israel have been exceptional among PR systems in terms of the number of parties holding seats in parliament (see MacIvor 1999, 29; Katz 1999, 105). Italy has had an extremely fragmented multiparty system in which coalition governments have been the norm. From June 1945 to June 1992, Italy had fifty different "governments," close to a government every nine months, on average, with as many as six different parties in the governing coalition (Partridge 1998, 190–91). Israel elects the 120 members of the Knesset through a party list system of proportional representation based on a nationwide vote. Any party with more than 1.5 percent of the vote is entitled to a seat (prior to 1992 the minimum was only 1.0 percent). The number of parties holding seats in the Knesset under this system has ranged from ten to fifteen, and small religious parties are said to often have disproportionate influence on the governing coalitions that result (Peretz and Doron 1997, 119).

44. These "manufactured majorities" have been called the "gravest democratic defect" of single-member district systems by Lijphart (1999a, 134) and its "worst pathology" by Shugart (1999, 144).

45. The two-party system is viewed negatively by many African Americans, who feel that, given the unresponsiveness of the Republican Party to their needs, the Democratic Party can be, and often is, complacent about those needs. Rather than having a

two-party option, African Americans are said to be a "captured constituency" for one of the parties (see Frymer 1999).

46. Another commentator has stated more bluntly, "It's time to dispense with the notorious Italian red herring on this matter" (Milner 1999, 44 n. 7).

47. Italy adopted a mixed-member PR system in 1993. Under this arrangement 475 members of the Chamber of Deputies are elected in single-member districts while the other 155 are elected, through a list PR system, in 26 multimember districts. Parties must obtain at least 4 percent of the votes in the list elections to be awarded a seat (see Partridge 1998, 41).

48. Richie and Hill 1999a, 26; 1999b, 186–87; and McKaskle 1998, 1181, recommend three-seat districts, while Arrington 1999, 5; and Webster 2000, 156–57, suggest three-, four-, or five-seat arrangements.

49. In 1981 the party that received a majority of the first preference votes in the Maltese election did not win a majority of the seats in Malta's House of Representatives. This prompted a constitutional amendment in 1987 that guarantees that a party receiving a majority of first-preference votes wins a majority of seats. If the majority party does not win a majority of the district seats, that party will receive as many additional seats as necessary to give it a one-seat majority in the legislative chamber. Another amendment in 1996 makes the same provision for any party winning a plurality of the first-preference votes, provided only two parties have won district seats (for details of Malta's election system, see Hirczy de Mino 1996).

50. In one of the few places in the United States where an alternative system—cumulative voting—has been applied to a partisan ballot, Chilton County, Alabama, Republicans were elected for the first time to both the county commission and the school board (Still 1992, 187–90). This happened in the first and subsequent seven-vote cumulative voting elections there (Engstrom, Kirksey, and Still 1997b, 187–90; Pildes and Donoghue 1995, 275), and of course was a boost rather than a threat to any two-party system in that county. No independent candidates or candidates affiliated with parties other than the Democrats or Republicans have been elected in any of the county's cumulative voting contests.

51. David Duke is a former leader of both the Louisiana Knights of the Ku Klux Klan and the National Association for the Advancement of White People. He also has had ties to the American Nazi Party. He became "America's most famous state legislator" (Boeckelman, Arp, and Terradot 1995, 33) while serving in the Louisiana House of Representatives from 1989 to 1992 (on Duke's political positions, see Ellison 1991).

52. Brief of Appellants, *Worcester County, Md. v. Cane, et al.,* Fourth Circuit Court of Appeals, No. 94-1579, June 10, 1994.

53. Ironically for these arguments, the most publicized case of an extremist being elected in the United States in recent years was David Duke's election to the Louisiana legislature in 1989 (see note 50, above). Duke was elected after winning a majority of the votes in a runoff election in a single-member district (on this election, see Powell 1992).

54. Alternative systems can, in particular, avoid interminority conflict over the boundaries of geographic districts (see Ramirez 1995, 975–77). Conflicts over districts are not uncommon, for example, between African Americans and Latinos (see Reed 1992, 769–79; Macchiarola and Diaz 1993, 1225–31; Marable 1994, 36–37; Jennings and Lusane 1994, 57; McClain 1996, 60).

2

The Hidden Costs of Electoral Reform

Mark E. Rush

Electoral Reform on the Congressional Agenda

On September 23, 1999, the House Judiciary Committee's Subcommittee on the Constitution held a hearing on H.R. 1173, the States' Choice of Voting Systems Act. The bill, which was sponsored by Mel Watt (D-N.C.), would eliminate the requirement that states elect their representatives from single-member districts. It would permit them to use single-member districts or alternative arrangements such as multimember districts or a combination of single- and multimember districts to choose their representatives.

Charles Canady, chair of the subcommittee, pointed out that the bill's proponents asserted that it would assist state legislatures with the difficult task of congressional redistricting. Summarizing the impetus for the bill, Canady nicely stated the tensions and constraints that hamper state efforts to redraw congressional and legislative district lines. The redistricting process, he noted,

> requires States to balance a number of competing considerations, including avoiding contests between incumbents, placing candidates in the same districts as their supporters, party affiliation, the "one person, one vote" standard, and the like. States must also ensure that its [*sic*] districts do not dilute or lead to retrogression of minority voting strength. Moreover, this process must conform to the Supreme Court's decisions striking down redistricting plans in which race was the predominate factor in drawing districts. (Canady 1999)

The hearing produced a variety of arguments in favor of and against the use of alternative voting schemes.

Those in favor of the act argued that it would "further the process of representative government" and "make the election system more effective in translating votes into seats on governmental bodies" (Arrington 1998). Critics of the bill urged that the existing system of single-member districts operates well and therefore does not cry out for repair (Thernstrom 1999). Insofar as introducing a new electoral system would also introduce an element of uncertainty into the electoral process, others argued that H.R. 1173 would probably "do more harm than good" (Everett 1999).

More guarded observers played down the potential impact of the bill. Nathaniel Persily (1999) noted that the impact of a shift to multimember districts would be conditioned by the changes (or nonchanges) in other electoral rules that might accompany the enactment of H.R. 1173. Citing the fallout from previous reforms, others warned of the unintended consequences that would certainly arise in the wake of any change in electoral laws (Busch 1999; Rush 1999).

Anyone familiar with the decennial reapportionment process and the endless litigation that now accompanies it can certainly understand why Congress would entertain *any* alternative that would diminish the controversy that surrounds the redistricting process. It is, as Dick Engstrom notes in his chapter, a highly partisan, contentious, and expensive ordeal that, in the end, does little to resolve the issues of gerrymandering and political fairness that inflame debates about the electoral process.

At the root of any debate about electoral reform is a deeper debate about the rules by which politics is conducted. To what are the various groups that comprise a polity entitled? What constitutes *legitimate* majority rule, and when must corresponding minorities acknowledge the legitimacy of the governing coalition or majority? At any given time specific groups may feel that the electoral system treats them unfairly. However, the performance of any political system must be judged over time—not by discrete electoral results.

If we are to discuss the rules of the political game, we first must decide what rights we have when we engage in the political process. When I say I have the *right* to vote, what exactly does it imply? Does it mean simply that I have the right to express my opinion at the ballot box on election day, or does the franchise entail more than simply the right to cast a vote? Conservative critics of the Supreme Court's voting rights jurisprudence argue that the scope of the franchise should entail no more than free access to the polls. In contrast, advocates of minority voting and representation rights argue in favor of the more expansive vision.

More broadly, the debate about electoral reform and voting rights also addresses questions about the democratic process and the environment in which elections are conducted. Scholars and political activists find much to analyze and criticize about the American electoral process. Currently, even an unsophisticated search on the Web will produce hundreds if not thousands of sites dealing with political reform proposals ranging from calls for proportional representation (PR) to campaign spending restrictions to term limits to revised ballot access provisions to increased use of the initiative and referenda. All of these reform agendas have one thing in common: a desire to improve the performance of the American political process by repairing specific aspects of the electoral structure that fail to work as well as critics would like.

The problem with all these proposals is that they are too narrow and too broad at the same time. On the one hand, they focus on perceived defects in specific aspects of an immense, complex constitutional system and political process. On the other, they hope to deliver a new and improved democratic process essentially by tinkering with what amounts to a lone widget in that broad constitutional and political system.

Proponents of reform tout the benefits of their proposals, but they are seldom as eager to discuss the costs that such reforms would necessarily entail. Political reform always comes at a price, usually in the form of unanticipated or unintended consequences (see, e.g., Ceaser 1982; Polsby 1983). Steven P. Erie, in *Rainbow's End* (1988), describes a classic example of such unintended consequences as he chronicles the impact of progressive reforms on Irish American urban political machines. Erie notes that there have been no records of African American political success to rival those of Tammany Hall or the Cook County Democratic machine. In their efforts to destroy political machines, reformers—and African American leaders in particular—dismantled the one practice (patronage) that had assured political ascendancy to the groups that had managed to gain control over urban governments (Erie 1988, 6). Thus, the improved functioning of the political system did not translate into tangible benefits for all political groups.

This same tension between group-specific benefits and systemwide political reform haunts contemporary American debates about electoral reform and minority voting rights. In the American context, proportional and alternative electoral systems are hailed by minority rights advocates and electoral system reformers who contend that the single-member plurality (SMP) electoral system is an unfair and inaccurate method of translating votes into legislative seats.[1] But, despite the common calls for alternative electoral arrangements, the desires of minority rights advocates are fundamentally at odds with the goals of electoral system reformers. The former interpret the Voting Rights Act (VRA) as requiring adjustments to the electoral system that would ensure representational opportunities for specific, discrete minorities. This vision is fundamentally at odds with the goals of systemic reformers whose desire to ensure that the fairness of the function of an electoral system is not driven by the fates of any particular political group.

Electoral system reformers contend simply that something is wrong when an electoral system such as SMP can deliver 100 percent of the political power to a group that makes up as little as 50 percent + 1 (or less) of the electorate, merely because the geographic distribution of voters allows this result. If by simply reorganizing the voters you can get a radically different electoral result, the means of counting votes is suspect.

If we put a premium on the proportional translation of votes into legislative seats, there is little that anyone can muster in defense of SMP. It has been criticized for delivering such skewed electoral results for the better part of two centuries. On the other hand, if we consider that the function and value of voting entail more than simply allocating legislative seats in a manner that reflects social divisions, then the issue of proportionality becomes less compelling. Advocates of a strong two-party system contend that SMP is better because voters know who will make up the government when the polls close. In a PR system with more than two parties, there is always the possibility that none of the parties will gain a legislative majority. As a result, postelection bargaining will ensue until a majority coalition can be formed. While PR advocates state that this arrangement is bound to be representative of a broader cross-section of the polity's social divisions, critics of PR respond that it is in fact a less democratic arrangement because it lets legislators, not the voters, decide ultimately who the government shall be (Pinto-Duschinsky 1999a, 1999b).

Across the world, more and more countries are converting to PR (Farrell 1997; Reynolds and Reilly 1997). In the United States, a small number of municipalities have changed to alternative electoral methods such as cumulative voting. PR advocates contend that this worldwide trend is due to the benefits to be gained from PR: less gerrymandering, better representation of minorities and women, higher voter turnout, and more issue-oriented campaigns (Amy 1993; Lewyn 1995). Accordingly, they argue that a conversion to a different electoral system would most certainly improve the performance of American democracy. While such statements are certainly not *inaccurate,* it remains to be seen whether a conversion to PR would actually remedy the problems of American elections that either minority rights advocates or systemic reformers identify.

Different electoral systems work differently in different countries. The better (or, depending on how you measure it, worse) performance of countries with different electoral systems cannot be attributed simply to the way they count votes. Their histories, party systems, constitutional organization, and political cultures all have an impact on the conduct of politics. Accordingly, when we encounter a call for electoral reform, we must assess both the nature of the reform itself and the conditions—and constraints—under which its proponents have observed its operation.

A very important constraint on electoral reform in the United States is the Voting Rights Act. Insofar as it protects the representational opportunities of specific minorities, it may actually stand in the way of some electoral reforms despite the good intentions of their proponents. In fact, at the hearings on H.R. 1173, Deputy Assistant Attorney General Anita Hodgkiss asserted that the Department of Justice's support for the bill "absolutely depends on the bill containing the explicit requirement that any multi-member congressional districts must comply with the Voting Rights Act" (Hodgkiss 1999).[2]

In this chapter, I address arguments made in favor of minority voting and representation rights and electoral reform and the extent to which the two complement and work against each other. I shall demonstrate that no electoral system can possibly maximize all aspects of democratic fairness. As a result, there will always be critics of any electoral system. The electoral system debate in the United States, however, remains hampered by the constraints imposed by the Voting Rights Act's commitment to the representational opportunities of specific minorities. So long as the group-specific goals of the VRA remain in tension with the systemic concerns of electoral reformers, the American voting rights dialogue will remain unresolved. I turn first to discuss the criticisms of the American electoral system made by advocates of proportional representation. I will then discuss the tension that has developed between the study of electoral systems and the American movement to ensure minority representation rights.

The Case for PR and against the Current Electoral System

In one of the strongest, most systematic contemporary criticisms of the American electoral process, Douglas Amy begins *Real Choices, New Voices* with the following assertion:

> The American election system is unfair, outmoded and undemocratic. Worse, few Americans are even aware of these problems. To be sure, the American public frequently expresses a great deal of anger and frustration about some aspects of our elections, such as poor quality candidates, the constant reelection of incumbents, and the role of special interest money in campaigns. But when it comes to the most basic mechanics of our electoral system—the method of casting votes and electing winners—we rarely give our system a second thought. It would hardly occur to us that this voting system is deeply flawed or that it routinely violates the principles of fairness and equal representation that we believe are the hallmarks of our political system. (Amy 1993, 1)

He identifies numerous problems that are symptomatic of the electoral system's malfunction: low turnout, "tweedle dee and tweedle dum candidates," two-party monopoly, wasted votes, issueless campaigns, lack of representation for women and minorities, and gerrymandering (Amy 1993, 5–7).

There is no doubt that each element of Amy's list accurately identifies a symptom, if not a shortcoming, of contemporary American politics. But these elements beg a fair response: Will switching to PR resolve them? I suggest that the answer is at best a qualified maybe. Many other democracies (most of which use some form of PR) do seem to perform better than the United States in that their turnout is higher, parties are stronger and more ideologically coherent, and so forth (see, e.g., Jackman 1987; Powell 1986). Still, the fact that turnout is higher in a country that uses proportional representation does not prove that PR is the source of higher turnouts.

Thus, in order to make the case for PR in the United States, we need to assess the problems that advocates of PR identify and then consider whether a switch to PR would enhance the likelihood of their resolution. Changing the electoral system will have an impact on the conduct of politics. But whether that impact will be positive or even desirable remains to be seen.

What's Wrong with American Politics:
The PR Advocates' Assessment

The major problem with the single-member plurality electoral system is that "large numbers of voters come away from elections without any representation" (Amy 1993, 21–22). The only voters who are represented in our electoral system are those who, in any given electoral district, are lucky enough to have cast a ballot for the winning candidate. As a result, Amy concludes that "voters on the losing side in an SMP election have no more political influence than if they were officially denied the right to vote" (22).

This criticism echoes that posed by John Stuart Mill (1994, 277–80), who pointed out that in an SMP system, a winning candidate needs to garner only 50 percent + 1 of the votes in an election. Accordingly, as many as 50 percent + 1 of the voters in his constituency could have no voice in the legislature. Furthermore, said Mill, a government formed on the basis of majority votes in electoral districts would not only minimize the number of opinions that could be represented but would also militate against groups who were not geographically compact enough to elect districtwide majorities. In fact, SMP could actually produce *minority* rule. For all intents and purposes, Mill explained, 50 percent + 1 of the legislature was free to govern the rest of the country. However, legislators could be elected by the narrowest margins (50 percent + 1) in each of their districts. The result would be that legislators who represented slightly more than 25 percent (50 percent + 1 of 50 percent + 1) of the population would be governing the entire country (1994, 279).

There is a response to this criticism, which PR advocates dismiss. Insofar as voters for the losing candidate in district A may not be represented by their legislator, the district system compensates by permitting the election of candidates from other districts who may share those losing voters' views. PR advocates contend, however, that this offers losers in district A little in the way of effective representation. First, no two candidates of the same party are identical. The fact that two candidates bear the same party label does not, at least in the United States, indicate that they have similar views or that they will vote the same way in the legislature. Log Cabin Republicans do not see eye-to-eye with members of the Christian right (see, e.g., *Johnson v. Knowles* 1997; *Republican Party of Texas v. Dietz* 1997), liberal Democrats won't have much in common with Reagan Democrats, and extremist elements of a party may not get along with the rank and file (*Duke v. Massey* 1996).

Gerrymandering

In general, then, SMP distorts the will of the people, at least as it is expressed at the polls. No matter how one draws the districts, the translation of popular votes into legislative seats is likely to be inaccurate because it is theoretically possible for half of the voters to have no voice in the legislature. Thus, a principal target of PR advocates is the SMP system's propensity to foster gerrymandering—the manipulation of electoral districts in order to achieve electoral results or partisan ends that do not necessarily reflect the will of the voters. Depending on how the district lines are drawn, partisan votes can be wasted in any number of ways. As a result, the districts themselves distort the popular will. In table 2.1, Douglas Amy shows that the manipulation of district lines can turn a 58 percent electoral majority into 100 percent control of the legislature or condemn it to 20 percent of the legislative seats.

Gerrymandering has a long and sordid history in the United States. While the event that resulted in the coining of the term "gerrymander" occurred in Massachusetts in 1812, perhaps the starkest recent example of the use of gerrymandering to disenfranchise a group of voters occurred in Tuskegee, Alabama, and led to the Supreme Court decision in *Gomillion v. Lightfoot* (1960). What had been an aesthetically pleasing Tuskegee with a square border was transformed into a twenty-eight-sided figure—all in an effort to disenfranchise African American voters by placing them outside the city limits.

Yet, even if district lines are not intentionally gerrymandered, Amy's example shows that the location of a district line can have a determinative impact on electoral outcomes. PR seems to offer a way out of the gerrymandering dilemma because it limits the ability of mapmakers to draw district lines in a strategic manner. By definition, PR requires fewer districts than an SMP system. Fewer district lines will result in fewer disputes over their location and correspondingly fewer cries of "gerrymander."

Or so it would seem. Thus far, the argument against the SMP system boils down to the assertion that a more accurate translation of votes into seats results in a fairer and more representative electoral system. Certainly, PR will make the process of drawing district lines less contentious, if not unnecessary. Nonetheless, there is more to the analysis of votes and seats than the translation of the former into the latter. Before addressing this, let us first set forth the rest of the indictment of the SMP system.

Table 2.1 Hypothetical Votes and Seat Allocations under Different Systems of Representation

District	Example 1		Example 2		Example 3		Example 4		Example 5	
	Party A	Party B	Party A	Party B	Party A	Party B	Party A	Party B	Party A	Party B
1	58,000	42,000	65,000	35,000	71,000	29,000	77,500	22,500	94,000	6,000
2	58,000	42,000	65,000	35,000	71,000	29,000	77,500	22,500	94,000	6,000
3	58,000	42,000	65,000	35,000	71,000	29,000	77,500	22,500	49,000	51,000
4	58,000	42,000	65,000	35,000	71,000	29,000	77,500	22,500	49,000	51,000
5	58,000	42,000	65,000	35,000	71,000	29,000	45,000	55,000	49,000	51,000
6	58,000	42,000	65,000	35,000	45,000	55,000	45,000	55,000	49,000	51,000
7	58,000	42,000	47,500	52,500	45,000	55,000	45,000	55,000	49,000	51,000
8	58,000	42,000	47,500	52,500	45,000	55,000	45,000	55,000	49,000	51,000
9	58,000	42,000	47,500	52,500	45,000	55,000	45,000	55,000	49,000	51,000
10	58,000	42,000	47,500	52,500	45,000	55,000	45,000	55,000	49,000	51,000
Total Vote	580,000	420,000	580,000	420,000	580,000	420,000	580,000	420,000	580,000	420,000
Seats	10	0	6	4	5	5	4	6	2	8

Source: Amy 1993

Issue-Oriented Campaigns

PR advocates note that candidates in SMP systems avoid taking strong stands on issues to decrease their chances of offending any discrete groups of voters (Amy 1993, 64). In fact, in *Considerations on Representative Government*, John Stuart Mill identified this as a principal reason that American parties invariably produced inferior nominees.

> The necessity of not dividing the party, for fear of letting in its opponents, induces all to vote either for the first person who presents himself wearing their colours, or for the one brought forward by their local leaders; and these . . . are compelled . . . to bring forward a candidate whom none of the party will strongly object to. . . . [Thus] the strongest party never dares put forth any of its strongest men, because every one of these, from the mere fact that he had been long in the public eye, has made himself objectionable to some portion or other of the party, and is therefore not so sure a card for rallying all their votes as a person who has never been heard of by the public at all until he is produced as the candidate. (1994, 280–81)

Whether or not this behavior is an evil is a matter for debate[3] and certainly has as much to do with the nature of political parties and party discipline as it does with the method of vote counting. Political parties in Great Britain and Canada are much more ideologically coherent than their American counterparts. Yet, all three countries use the SMP electoral system. The difference in candidate behavior arises (as I discuss later) from competing philosophies of the role of political parties.

Nonetheless, PR advocates contend that the need to obtain a districtwide majority of the vote in the SMP system entices candidates to water down their ideological stands so that they will essentially be less unattractive to voters who are not already supporting them. Because PR does not require the attainment of a majority of the vote in order to win an election, advocates argue that candidates and parties can and do focus on real issues in PR elections instead of avoiding them at all costs for fear of alienating some constituency.

As Amy notes, elections in PR systems are more issue oriented because they are perceived more as contests among parties than among individual candidates. In fact, American elections are so focused on personality and candidate idiosyncrasies that the party programs are almost irrelevant. As Katz and Kolodny point out:

> Ambivalence about party is reflected in American attitudes toward representation. Members of Congress see themselves, and are seen by their constituents, primarily as agents of their districts or states, rather than as members of national organizations taking collective responsibility for government. Even presidential candidates, whose constituency is national, and who are expected to attend to the national interest, are seen more as individuals than as partisans. In most

democracies to say "I vote for the candidate not the party" would be regarded as evidence of political immaturity; in the United States it is exactly the reverse. (1994, 26)

Commenting further on the weaknesses of the Democratic and Republican Parties, Maurice Duverger (1984, 36) notes that "the two American parties are mere receptacles containing too haphazard a mixture of different elected members to properly represent the diverse tendencies of [American] public opinion."

In party-list PR systems, voters don't even vote for candidates. They vote for slates of party nominees. Candidates are essentially conduits for conveying the party program to voters. They receive their campaign funds from the parties (Amy 1993, 96) and are pledged to adhere to and support the party program. Instead of running against the legislature as American candidates do, they run on the basis of their parties' performance or promises (see Fenno 1978; Fiorina 1989). Furthermore, as Amy notes, there is very little individualistic behavior on the part of candidates after they are elected: "[L]egislators must vote with their parties on important parliamentary votes or be subject to disciplinary action, including expulsion from the party" (Amy 1993, 96–97). As a result, voters are able to hold the governing party or coalition accountable for its program.

Amy also suggests that such strong parties would minimize the impact of lobbyists and special interests. Insofar as members of Congress are left to raise their own funds for reelection, they must depend on wealthy constituents and interests. European candidates, on the other hand, remain much more beholden to their party organizations for support. They can't afford to pander to special interests because they cannot vote against their party's program.

Breaking the Two-Party Monopoly and Electing Women and Minorities

Advocates of PR point out that American politics is truly outstanding in many ways, especially when viewed in a global perspective. The United States has only 2 parties. The average worldwide is 2 parties in plurality systems, 2.8 parties for majority systems, and 3.6 parties for PR (Blais and Massicotte 1996, 26). For years, scholars have pointed out that the SMP electoral system tends to produce two parties while proportional representation (or, at least, systems that require majorities instead of pluralities) will foster more parties (Downs 1957; Duverger 1984, 1986; Rae 1971; Riker 1984, 1986). Nonetheless, there are some outstanding exceptions to this rule. Canada and India both use SMP. Canada currently has five major parties represented in the federal parliament (Liberal, Reform, Bloc Québecois, Progressive Conservative, and New Democratic Party) and India has numerous parties vying for office.

Proponents of PR point out that the American duopoly is reinforced by laws that the Democrats and Republicans have passed to enhance their positions of dominance. Such laws ensure that it will be quite difficult for third and minor parties to grow, get on the ballot, or, perhaps, play more than a symbolic role in American politics (Rosenstone, Behr, and Lazarus 1996). For example, in many states and at the federal level, ballot access laws place heavy burdens on new parties seeking to get their nominees' names placed on ballots. In some cases, petition laws require enormous numbers of signatures. In addition anti-fusion laws, which prevent minor parties from sharing the nominees of major parties, have been sustained by the Supreme Court (Rosenstone, Behr, and Lazarus 1996; *Timmons v. Twin Cities Area New Party* 1997).

Because of the restrictions created by laws such as these, PR advocates point out that the American electoral system not only preserves the Democrats' and Republicans' duopoly, but it also makes it harder for women and minorities to gain representation. Women, who actually form a majority of the American population, are grossly underrepresented at all levels of government. In PR systems throughout the world, they are represented in far greater numbers (Amy 1993, 102–3; Rule and Zimmerman 1992; 1994).

Turnout

A final assertion by PR advocates is that SMP actually depresses turnout and therefore undermines the legitimacy of the government to the extent that it represents that many fewer people. According to one study by Blais and Carty (1990), a conversion from SMP to PR would result in a turnout increase of approximately 7 percent. There is no gainsaying the fact that electoral turnout in the United States is low by world standards. Teixeira (1992, 6) notes, for example, that turnout in presidential elections dropped from about 60–65 percent in the 1950s and 1960s to roughly 50–55 percent in the 1990s. On average, American turnout in "on-year" elections (i.e., those in presidential election years) to the House of Representatives from 1960 to 1995 ran about 54 percent. Out of thirty-seven democracies surveyed, the United States ranked thirty-fifth in voter turnout (Franklin 1996, 218).

Still, such data must be viewed in the proper perspective. Turnout in the thirty-seven countries studied by Franklin ranged from a high of 95 percent (Australia) to as low as 51 percent (Poland). Switzerland, which uses PR, tied the United States with a 54 percent turnout rate. Thus, while American turnout rates are low, they fall within the range of turnout rates that characterize PR systems.

American turnout may rank low on a world scale, but it is also important to note that turnout is declining worldwide, despite the fact that democracy and PR are spreading (Lijphart 1997, 6). In fact, the turnout issue is so pressing that Arend Lijphart has gone so far as to recommend the establishment of compulsory voting in order to ensure voter participation (1997, 6).

The Verdict?

Even a short survey of American politics such as the preceding one presents a bleak picture of the health of the American political system. It would seem, in fact, that the case for electoral reform of any sort would be easy to make. So, why have we not converted to PR?

There are many plausible answers to this question. They range from the cynical ("The Democrats and Republicans don't want it") to the more pragmatic ("There is more to elections than the mere attainment of proportional representation"). It only stands to reason that those who benefit from the status quo (the Democrats and Republicans) would be least likely to support reforms. Nonetheless, if we can put cynicism aside, we will see that there may be very good reasons for not switching to PR despite its many undoubtedly attractive qualities.

There is no question that a change in electoral rules could bring about more diverse legislative bodies and thereby alter political power relationships. This was clearly manifested in places like Alamogordo, New Mexico (see Engstrom, Taebel, and Cole 1989), Sisseton, South Dakota (Engstrom and Barrilleaux 1991), and Chilton County, Alabama (*Dillard v. Chilton County Board of Education* 1988; Pildes and Donoghue 1995), to name a few. On the other hand, alternative systems have also been implemented and subsequently repealed in Ohio (Barber 1995), New York City (Zeller and Bone 1948), and, most recently, Alamogordo (Engstrom 1998, 228). So PR has been the subject of experimentation in the United States. While Cambridge, Massachusetts, still uses PR (the single transferable vote) in its city elections, it has not taken as strong a hold in other places.

Ironically, SMP was actually implemented to remedy problems that arose with the at-large method of voting. The at-large electoral system was originally established as a progressive reform to break the power of political machines and their "ward bosses" (see, e.g., Weaver 1986, 140–41; Barber 1995). Yet, it was also used in the south to counter the mobilization of African American voters that occurred in the wake of the civil rights movements of the 1950s and 1960s (see, e.g., Thernstrom 1987, 22–24, 73–75; Davidson and Korbel 1989; Davidson and Fraga 1989). In response, the Justice Department and minority rights advocates have supported the creation of single-member "majority-minority" districts in order to ensure that concentrations of minority voters can have the opportunity to function as a majority and elect their candidate of choice. The creation of such districts undoubtedly enhances the electoral prospects of minority representatives. However, as Amy (1993, 122)—as well as other critics such as Supreme Court justices Clarence Thomas and Antonin Scalia (see *Holder v. Hall* 1994) and Lani Guinier (1994a)—points out, it is still a ham-handed attempt to enhance minority representation because the targeted group is not always concentrated or dispersed enough to enable it to take advantage of single-member districts.

The key point to bear in mind is that there are many different elements and emphases of democratic theory, not all of which are compatible. While democratic theory is founded upon notions such as popular self-government, the common good, and so forth, theorists and critics can differ with regard to the means by which those ends can be achieved. In order to assess the merits of PR as well as the claims made by its supporters, we need to undertake several analyses. First, we need to address questions of representation theory that underpin debates about electoral reform. What constitutes a "wasted" or "gerrymandered" vote? Would PR really decrease the likelihood of such wasted votes? Would this, in turn, put an end to gerrymandering?

Second, we need to consider the role and rights of voters in a democracy as well as the function and value of elections. Advocates of PR emphasize the need to ensure that legislatures come as close as possible to forming a microcosm of the society that they govern. However, there is an equally compelling vision of the electoral process that does not base governmental legitimacy on proportionality. While PR advocates contend that interests are entitled to be heard in proportion to their numbers, other theorists, including James Madison and John Stuart Mill, suggest that one of the most important elements of democracy is to subjugate the demands of discrete interest groups in order to promote the common good.

Accordingly, before we seek to graft PR onto the American political system, we need to ponder what, besides PR, characterizes the electoral systems to which its advocates compare the United States. While such systems are characterized by higher turnout, less lobbying, more proportionate representation of women and minorities, stronger parties, and so forth, there is more to distinguish those other systems than mere differences in the way votes are counted and translated into legislative seats. The constitutional architecture and organization of politics in other countries is different from that of the United States. Simply injecting PR into the American constitutional structure is unlikely to bring about the effects desired and promised by PR advocates—unless we also implement other, fundamental changes to the structure of the government and the rules by which politics and elections are conducted.

The Mechanics of Different PR Systems

With the exception of a relatively small number of localities, the SMP electoral system is employed throughout the United States. It is also known as the "winner-take-all" or "first past the post" system of elections. Worldwide, while only a small number of countries still use SMP, a large proportion of the world's "free" population is governed by it. As of May 1997, sixty-eight countries (32 percent), making up 45 percent of the free world's population, employed the SMP electoral system (Reynolds and Reilly 1997, 20). Critics

Table 2.2 A Hypothetical Distribution of Votes and Seats

	District					Total	% of	Seats
	1	2	3	4	5	Votes	Votes	Won
Party A	300	260	255	255	10	1,080	43	4
Party B	200	240	245	245	490	1,420	57	1
Total Votes	500	500	500	500	500	2,500	100	

point out, however, that these numbers are somewhat misleading: two of the countries that still use SMP, India and the United States, account for an overwhelming share of the people who are currently governed under that system. Nonetheless, the proportion of countries using PR has remained fairly constant (hovering around 60 percent) since 1920 (Blais and Massicotte 1996, 52).

The principal appeal of PR is that it tends to produce a more heterogeneous legislature. Whereas SMP tends to foster a two-party system, PR fosters multiparty systems. In the following examples (see tables 2.2–2.5), we elaborate upon Amy's example in table 2.1 to show how different systems can produce radically different legislative outcomes. These examples organize the numbers of, and divisions among, voters in the manner most convenient for the purposes of illustrating the worst- and sometimes the best-case scenarios. While it is unlikely that any electoral arrangement will produce results as clean or extreme as those displayed in some of the examples, such doctored hypotheticals demonstrate the starkest contrasts between and among various electoral formulas.

Let us consider a hypothetical election under the single-member system in which two parties compete for five seats, each of which represents a constituency of 500 voters. It is possible for party A to win four of the five seats even though party B received a majority (57 percent) of the vote.

As we saw in table 2.1, these districts could theoretically be reorganized in a manner that could also deliver the exact opposite result, as shown in table 2.3. Under PR (in which the voters were not divided into districts), we would expect party B to win three of the five seats. But the actual distribution would differ depending on the formula used to divide the voters between the parties.

The Importance of Quotas and Division

There are numerous versions of PR and numerous formulas by which votes can be allocated among seats. Two factors distinguish among PR formulas: the quota and the method of seat allocation. In an early exegesis of proportional

Table 2.3 Distribution as in Table 2.2, but with Different Results

	District					Total	% of	Seats
	1	2	3	4	5	Votes	Votes	Won
Party A	200	200	200	200	280	1,080	43	4
Party B	300	300	300	300	220	1,420	57	1
Total Votes	500	500	500	500	500	2,500	100	

representation, *The Machinery of Representation* (1857), Thomas Hare suggested the establishment of a "quota" (essentially a "price" for a seat in terms of votes) based on the number of votes cast in an election divided by the number of seats at stake (v/s). Thus, in table 2.2, the quota would be 500 votes (2500/5).[4] Having established the quota, we would then divide both parties' vote totals by the quota. In this case, party A, with 1080 votes, has two quotas plus 180 extra votes. Party B has two quotas plus 420 extra votes. Who should get the fifth seat?

Intuitively, party B is entitled to it because it clearly has more of a quota (84 percent) left with its remaining votes, while party A has only 16 percent of a quota. If we use the *largest remainder* method of allocating seats, then our intuition would be served and party B would get the fifth seat. The resulting distribution of legislative seats (60 percent–40 percent) would be almost an exact reflection of the distribution of votes (57 percent–43 percent).

Factors Affecting Quotas and Electoral Formulas

The Hare quota is just one of several quotas used in different PR systems. Throughout the last three centuries, different quotas have been proposed by different practitioners because of their impact on parties of different size, simplicity of calculation, and so on (see Carstairs 1980, 20–23). The Droop quota divides the number of votes by the number of seats *plus 1;* the Imperiali quota uses a divisor of the number of seats *plus 2.* Had we used the Droop quota, the distribution of seats would have been the same, but the process by which they were allotted would have been simpler because all seats would have been accounted for by the new quota of 416.7 (2500/6):

Party A: 1080—2 quotas + 246 extra votes
Party B: 1420—3 quotas + 169 extra votes

So, clearly, the rules do matter. In both cases, the party that more efficiently used up its quota of votes benefited more from the proportional distribution of seats.

Table 2.4 Seat Allocation under SMP and PR with Largest Remainder

| | District | | | | | Total | % of | Seat Allocation | |
	1	2	3	4	5	Votes	Votes	with SMP	with PR
Party A	300	200	200	20	5	725	29	3	2
Party B	50	50	50	365	50	565	23	1	1
Party C	50	25	75	100	300	550	22	1	1
Party D	75	50	170	10	100	405	16	0	1
Party E	25	175	5	5	45	255	10	0	0
Total Votes	500	500	500	500	500	2,500	100		

This, of course, raises the issue of what would happen if the number of parties were to increase. It is commonly assumed that with a conversion from a plurality electoral system to a system of PR, the number of parties would increase because parties no longer would have to obtain as many votes to attain legislative representation. In table 2.4 we observe a situation in which five parties are now competing for the same five seats.

Under a plurality system, we see that it would be possible for party A again to obtain a disproportionate share of seats (60 percent) owing only to the fortuitous distribution of its voters. In a PR system using the Droop quota (417), the distribution would be much fairer:

> Party A: 725—1 quota + 308 extra votes
> Party B: 565—1 quota + 148 extra votes
> Party C: 550—1 quota + 133 extra votes
> Party D: 405—0 quota + 405 extra votes
> Party E: 255—0 quota + 255 extra votes

In this case, parties A, B, and C would each get one seat because they surpassed the quota. The question then arises: How should we distribute the remaining two seats?[5]

There are two widely accepted methods of dealing with the remaining seats. The first, which is used in the first two examples, is called the *largest-remainder* system. After determining which parties have attained the quota, the remaining seats are then allotted on the basis of the number of remaining votes. Thus, in table 2.4, party D would get the fourth seat because it has the largest remainder of votes. Seat 5 would go to party A because its remainder is next in line.

Still, a critic might contend that there is something inherently unfair about this method of distributing seats even though it is clearly fairer than

Table 2.5 D'Hondt Highest-Average Method of Seat Allocation

	Total Vote	Divisor			
		2	3	4	5
Party A	**725**	**362.5**	241.7	181.3	145
Party B	**565**	282.5	188.3	141.3	113
Party C	**550**	275	183.3	137.5	110
Party D	**405**	202.5	135	101.3	81
Party E	255	127.5	85	63.8	51

Note: Numbers in bold indicate seat awarded.

the plurality system. Should party A get 40 percent of the seats with 29 per-cent of the vote while party E gets no representation when it has 10 percent? Should party A get twice as many seats as party B when the difference in their proportion of the vote is a mere 6 percent? A second method of seat distribution, the d'Hondt *highest-average* method addresses such dispari-ties—to a point.

The highest-average method divides vote totals sequentially by the number of seats available. Using the d'Hondt highest-average method, seats are assigned on the basis of the cell entries in a table such as that in table 2.5. Thus, based on their total number of votes (divisor = 1), party A gets the first seat, party B gets the second, C gets the third, D gets the fourth, and party A gets the fifth seat. However, if there are many small parties in a polity, such a system might still leave a significant number of parties or portion of the pop-ulace without legislative representation. In this case, the d'Hondt highest-average method is subject to the same challenge as the largest-remainder method.

One solution to this problem is to augment the d'Hondt method by changing the nature of the division. In this case, a second method can be employed that uses different divisors, the *St. Lague* method. Instead of dividing and forming averages on the basis of the divisors 1, 2, 3..., the St. Lague method uses the sequence 1, 3, 5, 7. This produces the results shown in table 2.6: the fifth seat would be awarded to party E instead of party A.

The same result could have been achieved under the largest-remainder method if we chose to use the Hare quota (v/s) instead of the Droop quota (v/[s+1]). Using the Hare quota of 500, the distribution of seats would be based on the following allocation:

Party A: 725—1 quota + 225 extra votes
Party B: 565—1 quota + 65 extra votes

Table 2.6 St. Lague Highest-Average Method of Seat Allocation

		Divisor	
	Total Vote	3	5
Party A	**725**	241.7	145
Party B	**565**	188.3	113
Party C	**550**	183.3	110
Party D	**405**	135	81
Party E	**255**	85	51

Note: Numbers in bold indicate seat awarded.

Party C: 550—1 quota + 50 extra votes
Party D: 405—0 quota + 405 extra votes
Party E: 250—0 quota + 250 extra votes

Under these circumstances, party E would get the fifth seat because its remainder is larger than party A's. Of course, while such an allocation makes the legislature more diverse, it also clearly cheats party A, which, with almost a third of the vote, has only 20 percent of the representation.

Do the Mechanics Matter?

What is important to note from all this is that any electoral system can be manipulated—"gerrymandered," that is—to achieve a particular result. And any electoral arrangement can be presented in either the worst or best possible light if we make certain assumptions about the distribution of voters. While PR systems may remove the appearance of gerrymandering that so clearly haunts the process of redrawing the boundaries of single-member districts, any alteration of the formula by which votes are translated into seats can change an electoral outcome. Accordingly, PR supporters' advocacy of the flexibility of different systems actually affirms the fact that all systems, no matter how fair they may be in theory, can be manipulated in practice (see Katz 1998).

Insofar as this is the case, we can turn to look more closely at the actual impact of SMP and PR on electoral outcomes. Invariably, comparisons of this sort focus on two issues: the wasting of votes and the fates of specific groups that would be more successful under one electoral system than under another. But since all electoral systems can be augmented to help or harm some group's electoral fortunes, we must look at other criteria for assessing the benefits or drawbacks of specific systems.

Wasted and Diluted Votes

If we define a wasted vote as one that is cast for a candidate or party that is not elected, there is no question that PR decreases the number of votes that are wasted in any given election. Insofar as single-member districts (SMDs) ensure that some votes (barring unanimity in the district) will be cast for a losing candidate, critics of SMDs assert that those "losing" voters have wasted their efforts. By lowering the quota of votes necessary to elect a candidate and increasing the number of options for which a voter may vote, PR increases the likelihood that more votes will have an impact on the outcome of an election. But while specific votes may count more under PR, the *effectiveness of government* may not necessarily be increased.

Choosing between PR and SMP still leaves unresolved the separate issue of whether we wish to maximize voter choice among candidates or maximize party responsibility. In the United States, for example, the use of the direct-primary method of nominations provides voters with a tremendous amount of control over who the candidates will be. However, this has been accompanied by widespread criticism of the lack of accountability of parties and candidates (see Fiorina 1989; Polsby 1983). Since party leaders (or, at least, card-carrying, dues-paying party members) cannot control the choice of their party's nominee, they cannot be held responsible for who the nominee is. In the place of party leaders, we now have participants in direct primaries who cannot be held collectively accountable for the nominee.

Insofar as candidates seeking party nominations need to distinguish themselves from one another, campaigns become quite individualistic and focus more on personalities than on issues and partisan programs. Parties are therefore challenged to adopt coherent partisan platforms on which to appeal to voters because they cannot control who will be on their slate of candidates for a general election. In addition, candidates are also forced to spend (and therefore solicit) vast sums of money in order to campaign effectively. The result of this system in which candidates—not parties—make the principal appeal to the voters is an absence of party cohesion.

Were party organizations to strengthen and thereby exercise more control over nominations, voters would probably have more meaningful choices on election day because candidates would be presented for election because they conform to their party's ideology. However, the last time the parties exercised such control over their nomination process (at least at the presidential level) was 1968. Hubert Humphrey received the Democratic nomination that year, despite his failure to run any primary campaigns. Robert Kennedy and Eugene McCarthy did run primary campaigns and claimed to represent the party rank and file, not the insiders in the "smoke-filled rooms" who ultimately handed the nomination to Humphrey. The result was chaos. McCarthy's supporters walked out of the convention, protests erupted, and, ultimately, reforms were implemented that weakened the party's control over the nomination process (see Polsby 1983, 1–37).

Thus, any electoral system involves a trade-off between voter control of candidates and nominations and the quality of the choice with which voters are presented. Different PR systems have different emphases as well. For example, the single transferable vote (STV) provides voters with the most freedom to choose, allowing them to vote for candidates regardless of party affiliation.[6] While this system permits voters to vote for whomever they want, it does not lend itself to the maintenance of strong, issue-oriented parties. Since voters vote for *candidates,* STV increases the likelihood that candidates under the same party banner will compete against one another and, as a result, weaken the bonds of party cohesion (see Blais and Massicotte 1996, 78–79; Katz 1986). The result of an election under STV may then be that more voters are represented because a broader diversity of candidates was elected. But, insofar as those candidates may be less bound to one another by shared party loyalties, the process of forming governing majorities may be made more difficult.

Party-list systems, on the other hand, restrict voter choice. Under such systems, voters may choose among *parties* only. When the votes are counted, seats are allocated among parties in proportion to their percentage of the vote. The party then fills the legislative seats on the basis of the order in which the candidates appear on its list. While this system is more likely to produce more cohesive parties, voters have less control over which party members are elected.

While PR decreases the probability that votes will be wasted in any given election, the question remains whether voters are any better represented. Advocates of the SMP system point out that it creates clearly defined geographic constituencies and therefore ensures that voters have a discrete representative with whom they can identify and whom they can hold accountable on election day. Critics contend, however, that SMP has very little else going for it.

In fact, the geographic basis for single-member districts is also their principal drawback. They discriminate against interests that are geographically dispersed and therefore unable to comprise a majority of the population in any one district. If 51 percent of a state's voters are Republican and they and Democratic voters are evenly and homogeneously distributed across the state, the Republicans will win every electoral contest by a 51-49 margin and control 100 percent of the legislative delegation, even though they make up only 51 percent of the population.

On the other hand, while individual votes may be wasted on a district-by-district basis, voters who cast those wasted votes are not necessarily *unrepresented.* If we assume that votes are cast strictly for candidates, then every vote cast for a loser is indeed wasted. However, if votes are cast for *parties,* voters (qua partisans) may still have their interests represented if their party's candidates are elected in other districts, wasted votes notwithstanding.

So long as elections are held in which some candidates are not elected, votes will be wasted. Candidate-centered PR systems such as STV enhance the probability that every voter will have a chance to cast at least one vote that counts toward the election of a candidate. But such electoral systems won't necessarily provide the sense of constituency that comes with single-member districts or the sense of accountability that comes from party-list or SMP systems.

Vote Dilution and Gerrymandering

As table 2.1 shows, district lines can transform any electoral majority into a legislative minority, or vice versa. While such gerrymandering can theoretically result in the denial of representation to voters, it can do so only under the right circumstances. While the percentage of votes cast for a given party's candidates may not be reflected in the percentage of legislative seats the party wins, the difference may have as much to do with the fact that votes are cast for *candidates* regardless of or despite their party affiliation. Thus, using the data in table 2.1, 42,000 Republican votes in district 1 will not necessarily translate into 42,000 Republican votes in district 2. Perhaps the Republican votes in district 1 represent an affinity for the candidate who just happened to be running under the GOP banner. Had he been running as an independent, voters would have been no less willing to vote for him. This sort of fickle behavior manifests itself when we study the impact of redistricting on partisan behavior.

Redistricting and Partisanship

Cries of gerrymandering and wasted votes make sense only if votes represent bona fide partisan sentiments. In other words, if we knew that voters made up their minds on election day as a result of the toss of a coin or a die, we would not attribute much meaning to whether a particular voter voted Republican or Democrat. On the other hand, if we knew that voters chose candidates on the basis of partisan sentiments, we could interpret a vote for candidate A as a vote in support of his or her partisan beliefs and affiliations.

Voting behavior—at least in the United States—is somewhere in between these two polar examples. Insofar as American parties are weakly organized and candidates run individualistic campaigns, "partisan affiliation" in America has been described by some critics as almost an oxymoronic concept (see Katz and Kolodny 1994, 26). This lack of "partyness" in American political behavior is manifested in the reaction of voters to changes in their election day options.

Table 2.7 Democratic Percentage of the Vote in Selected Montana Counties, 1972–1996

	1972	1974	1976	1978	1980	1982	1984
Liberty	38.0	38.8	56.4	47.8	49.3	58.1	25.8
Meagher	33.2	38.7	54.8	41.3	45.7	51.2	27.1
Pondera	44.2	48.3	65.3	50.8	55.8	60.0	30.8
Toole	40.2	49.2	54.9	48.2	53.3	58.2	28.4

	1986	1988	1990	1992	1994	1996
Liberty	41.1	33.9	26.1	32.6	40.1	34.7
Meagher	36.1	33.2	29.2	32.4	28.5	31.0
Pondera	46.9	41.8	32.0	38.7	39.3	38.4
Toole	42.5	41.6	30.4	40.8	43.5	37.8

Studies of the impact of redistricting on partisan behavior (Rush 1993, 1994, 2000) demonstrate that the partisanship of voters can change radically when the incumbent in their district retires or when they are redistricted. What is truly astonishing is the extent to which partisan fluctuation occurs. Table 2.7 shows the impact of congressional redistricting in Montana. Liberty, Meagher, Pondera, and Toole Counties, which had become strongly Democratic, became equally Republican after being redistricted in 1982 from a Democratic incumbent's district to one held by a Republican (Rush 2000, 253).

At first glance we might think that this was a classic attempt to bury several Democratic strongholds in a GOP district. But, as the table indicates, the four "Democratic" counties started voting Republican after they were redistricted.

Districts and Voter Choice

It is not the creation of bizarrely shaped districts that makes gerrymandering matter. A gerrymander can be perpetrated by using the most common geometric figures if the cartographer has sufficiently detailed political data and sufficiently powerful technology, and if the voters are distributed in an ideal manner. What makes gerrymandering truly "evil" and the dilution of votes so lamentable is the presumption that they both can contribute to the devaluing of certain groups' political voices. But if those political groups are as fluid in their makeup as the partisans in Montana's counties, it is almost meaningless to aggregate groups of people on the basis of how they cast their votes.

Thus, we might lament the loss of voting power experienced by the redistricted Montana counties. But their behavior indicates that we should have no regrets whatsoever. A lot of Democrats started to vote Republican, and vice versa. Accordingly, no one could claim that voters in the redistricted counties had lost voting power or that their votes were wasted. They weren't necessarily Democratic or Republican voters in the first place. Instead, they were voters who, given the choice between two candidates, happened to prefer the one bearing the Democratic party label. When they were moved and their candidate options changed, they ended up voting for the candidate with the Republican affiliation.

Some votes may have been wasted because they were cast for losing candidates. But the partisan behavior of the Montana counties indicates that we can't conclude that the voting power of Democrats or Republicans was diluted. If a voter votes for a Democratic candidate in one district, it does not imply that he or she would vote for another candidate bearing the same party label in another district. For a vote to be diluted, it has to be a clear expression of *partisan* support—not just a plug for a particular candidate.

Switching to PR would put an end to this problem only to the extent that it minimized the number of district lines that had to be drawn. If we substituted multimember districts for single-member districts (or, perhaps, dispensed with districts altogether), no one could claim that their partisan preferences had been constrained by the drafting of district boundaries. For example, if STV were used statewide, voters could vote for any candidate they wished. By dispensing with the use of electoral districts, such a statewide system of preference voting would ensure that all voters had the same choices in any given election. Thus, despite the fluidity that may characterize partisan voting, a conversion to some forms of PR would remove at least the opportunity to try to gerrymander voters by diluting partisan strength. However, this would not altogether remove the possibility of gerrymandering.

Gerrymandering is more than creative cartography. Whether we employ bizarre outlines or unsophisticated geometric shapes, the underlying concern about gerrymandering is that it constrains the choices presented to voters and therefore conditions electoral outcomes in an unfair or biased manner. In this respect, the manipulation of electoral thresholds in a PR system can be just as devastating as the most meticulous malicious cartography. Gerrymandering thus entails organizing your opponent's supporters so that they are unable to form a bloc large enough to cross the threshold of representation. Stated in this manner, gerrymandering covers *anything* that can be employed to condition an electoral outcome. This includes manipulating district lines or the size of the quota necessary to obtain a seat in a PR system (see Katz 1998).

In this respect, while an electoral system may not be intentionally gerrymandered, no electoral system can be counted upon to deliver proportional results all of the time. As a result, some group will always be able to claim that an existing electoral arrangement prevented it from gaining representation. In response, advocates maintain that PR is, nonetheless, a fairer *system* of representation because it enhances the representational opportunities of all groups, regardless of their cohesiveness.

In the United States, however, voting rights jurisprudence and scholarship have evolved to a point at which such systemic considerations are outweighed by those concerning the electoral fates of minority groups—specifically, those mentioned in the Voting Rights Act. This jurisprudence and scholarship are based on a very broad reading of the scope of the right to vote and definition of "vote dilution." Ironically, the attempt to enhance minority representational opportunities by expanding the scope of the right to vote has resulted in an approach to voting rights analysis that undermines the appeal of PR systems.

Vote Dilution and the Scope of the Right to Vote: The Impact of the Voting Rights Act

In the United States, the right to vote has gone through "three generations" of development largely as a result of court decisions and scholarly criticism in the wake of the passage of the VRA (Karlan 1993; Guinier 1994a). In its early reapportionment decisions (see, e.g., *Baker v. Carr* 1962; *Reynolds v. Sims* 1964; *Wesberry v. Sanders* 1964; *Lucas v. The Forty-fourth General Assembly District of the State of Colorado* 1964), the Supreme Court emphasized that the right to vote embodied one key component: individual equality. Accordingly, it struck down reapportionment schemes composed of legislative districts with unequal populations.

In *Allen v. State Board of Elections* (1969), the Supreme Court began to address (and expand) the scope of the right to vote. Section 5 of the VRA applies to "any voting qualification or prerequisite to voting or standard, practice or procedure with respect to voting." Section 14 of the act says that voting shall include "all action necessary to make a vote effective." In *Allen*, a divided Court concluded that the right to vote, so stated, could be infringed by changes in the method of elections (e.g., from a district to an at-large system), changes in ballot access restrictions, and changes of particular offices from elective to appointive status.

In *White v. Regester* (1973) and *Thornburg v. Gingles* (1986), the Court added substance to the expanded notion of the right to vote. It set forth criteria that, in addition to requiring equal weighting of individual votes, also established measures for determining whether a districting scheme diluted the power of minority voters. In *Regester*, the Court argued that an electoral scheme was subject to challenge if it could

> produce evidence to support findings that the political processes leading to nom-
> ination and election were not equally open to participation by the group in ques-
> tion—that its members had less opportunity than did other residents in the dis-

trict to participate in the political processes and to elect legislators of their choice. (*White v. Regester* 1973, 766)

After *Regester,* however, the Court ruled in *City of Mobile v. Bolden* (1980) that to challenge an electoral scheme under the VRA, a plaintiff group must prove that the challenged electoral scheme had been drafted with the *intent* of diluting minority voting power.

As it was originally drafted, section 2 of the VRA prohibited voting practices that were imposed or applied "to deny or abridge the right of any citizen of the United States to vote on account of race or color." In response to the *Bolden* decision, Congress revised the text of the VRA to rule out such an interpretation. The amended section 2 of the VRA now read:

> (a) No voting qualification or prerequisite to voting or standard, practice, or procedure shall be imposed or applied by any State or political subdivision in a manner which *results in a denial or abridgement of the right of any citizen of the United States to vote on account of race or color,* or in contravention of the guarantees set forth in section 1973b(f)(2), as provided in subsection (b).
> (b) A violation of subsection (a) . . . is established if, based on the totality of circumstances, it is shown that the political processes leading to nomination or election in the State or political subdivision are not equally open to participation by members of a class of citizens protected by subsection (a) . . . in that its members have less opportunity than other members of the electorate to participate in the political processes and to elect representatives of their choice. The extent to which members of a protected class have been elected to office in the State or political subdivision is one circumstance which may be considered: Provided, That nothing in this section establishes a right to have members of a protected class elected in numbers equal to their proportion in the population. (42 USCS sec. 1973 (1997), emphasis added)

In *Thornburg v. Gingles* (1986), the Supreme Court elaborated upon the criteria set forth in the amended VRA. While the Court acknowledged that intent was no longer a necessary part of a vote dilution claim, it stated nonetheless that a valid vote dilution claim required a plaintiff group to meet three criteria:

> [F]irst, the minority group must be able to demonstrate that it is sufficiently large and geographically compact to constitute a majority in a single member district. . . . Second, the minority group must be able to show that it is politically cohesive. . . . Third, the minority must be able to demonstrate that the white majority votes sufficiently as a bloc to enable it—in the absence of special circumstances . . . usually to defeat the minority's preferred candidate. (*Thornburg v. Gingles* 1986, 50–51)

Minority voting rights advocates criticized these criteria because they sent out conflicting signals. On the one hand, the Court acknowledged that a vote dilution claim *did not* require proof that an electoral scheme had been created intentionally to discriminate against a minority group. Thus, the Court established that the franchise included the right *not* to have an electoral system dilute a minority group's political influence. But, the "first prong" of the *Gingles* test now limited the VRA's protections to geographically compact groups. Critics argued that this was silly. First, it essentially limited protection against vote dilution to groups that were residentially segregated. Second, it assumed that geography—not shared interests—was determinative of a group's political cohesion (see Karlan 1989).

Insofar as the compactness standard ignored the possibility that a dispersed group can be politically cohesive, it worked against the notion that the franchise included a right to an undiluted vote. In cases such as *Shaw v. Reno* (1993), *Holder v. Hall* (1994), and *Miller v. Johnson* (1995), the Supreme Court was forced to wrestle with the tension that arose as a result of the limitations placed on vote dilution claims by the *Gingles* compactness requirement. In *Shaw* and *Miller,* the Court ruled that a redistricting plan whose lines are drawn in a manner so "bizarre" that it can be understood only as an attempt to segregate voters constitutes a racial gerrymander and violates the Fourteenth Amendment's Equal Protection Clause. These decisions were based on the assertion that race-conscious districting used to advance minority political fortunes is no more tolerable than similar redistricting used to retard them. Nevertheless, they exacerbated the tension between the Court's tolerance for single-member districts and its acknowledgment that the VRA defined vote dilution *only* in terms of the impact of an electoral system. If a system of single-member districts worked against the political fortunes of a dispersed minority group, it seemed logical that such a system would run afoul of the VRA.

Holder v. Hall

The tensions and logical contradictions inherent in the Court's reasoning were manifested most clearly in *Holder v. Hall* (1994), where a divided Court struck down a challenge to the Bleckley County, Georgia, single-commissioner form of government. The plaintiffs argued that the substitution of a five-member commission for the existing single-commissioner system would make it possible for African American voters to elect a representative to the commission and thereby have a say in the administration of the county. Therefore, they argued that the single-commissioner system ought to be replaced by a multimember council.

The challenge to the Bleckley single-commissioner system was a logical extension of the reasoning that had underpinned the development (and criticism) of the Court's jurisprudence. A vote dilution claim required only a showing of a discriminatory *impact* of an electoral system. To make a viable vote dilution claim, a group had to meet the *Gingles* criteria. The Court stated, however, that no "benchmark" existed by which the impact of the single-commissioner form of government could be measured. Accordingly, it was not prepared to strike down the government simply because one group was unable to control the election of the commissioner.

The divisions in the Court represented the ongoing debate over the scope and definition of the voting right. The majority resisted the plaintiff's desire to expand the notion of vote dilution to include the impact that the size of a governing body had on the ability of a discrete group to elect a candidate to it. The dissenters argued that the claim was legitimate and that a multimember commission could easily be established to ensure minority representation in the government.

The *Holder* decision clearly exposed the tension between *Regester* and *Gingles*: the latter places restrictions on the criteria outlined in the former and enshrined in section 2 of the VRA. If a vote dilution claim requires only a discriminatory impact on a group—not discriminatory intent—then the circumstances in *Holder* would seem to be tailor made for a section 2 violation. But, since the "district" in question in *Holder* was large enough to prevent a minority from functioning as a majority in the first place, the first prong of the *Gingles* test was not met. As a result, by the Court's own reasoning, there could be no vote dilution claim in *Holder,* absence of a benchmark notwithstanding. Thus, in the absence of any showing of discriminatory intent, the plaintiffs had no case in *Holder,* and, for all intents and purposes, the decision placed another limit on the notion of vote dilution.

Critics such as Lani Guinier (1994a) condemned the *Holder* decision precisely because it placed a limit on the expanding scope of the right to vote that had evolved through the VRA decisions. Guinier argued that the decision—especially Justice Thomas's concurrence—rests on a political theory of "individualized democracy" that is insufficient for protecting the rights of political groups that cannot gain access to legislative bodies (Guinier 1994a, 122).

Justice Thomas argued that the VRA had been interpreted too broadly and that the scope of the voting right should be read to include nothing more than free access to the polls. Otherwise, he noted, courts will become embroiled in debates about which political theory is best and which electoral system is least dilutive of a particular group's votes.[7] He suggested that the Court retreat from the vote dilution issue and dispense with its reliance on single-member districts. Also, he said that states and the Justice Department should turn to alternative voting schemes if they wished to enhance minority representation opportunities.

Guinier agreed with Thomas's second point but disagreed with the first one. She supports a conversion to an alternative electoral system because single-member districts are too restrictive of minority representational opportunities.

Nonetheless, she argued that Thomas had defined the scope of voting too narrowly. Guinier maintains that voting entails more than mere access to the polls or equality of representational opportunity. Instead, she offers a much more expansive notion of the voting right: "a system that gives everyone an equal chance of having their political preferences *physically represented* is inadequate. A fair system of political representation would provide mechanisms to ensure that disadvantaged and stigmatized minority groups also have a fair chance to have their policy preferences *satisfied*" (Guinier 1991, 1137). Thus, for Guinier, the VRA guarantees to minority groups an "effective vote" that comprises three components: "the right to cast a ballot, the right to cast a ballot that 'counts,' and the right to cast a ballot that embodies a fair chance to influence legislative policymaking" (Guinier 1994a, 126).

The debate between Thomas and Guinier is resolvable to no one's satisfaction. Thomas's narrow definition of the voting right and rejection of the notion of vote dilution would certainly make judges' lives a lot less complicated because it would put an end to legal challenges to even the most egregious gerrymanders, since a gerrymander is nothing more than another form of vote dilution. On the other hand, if we accept Guinier's definition of vote dilution, then there is virtually no electoral arrangement that would be beyond challenge because every electoral arrangement will dilute the impact of some group's voting power.

Despite this, minority voting rights advocates frequently suggest alternative electoral systems as a remedy for vote dilution (Engstrom, Taebel, and Cole 1989; Guinier 1991; Still 1991). Steven Mulroy (1998) suggests that using PR would provide "a way out" of the political thicket surrounding voting rights controversies. The beauty of PR, he argues, is that it lowers the threshold of exclusion (the number of votes necessary to elect a representative). Furthermore, Mulroy says, it would provide the useful, constant benchmark that was missing in the Supreme Court's resolution of *Holder* (370–71). A vote dilution claim, he argues, could be established by determining, simply, whether the threshold of exclusion was greater than the minority voting-age population (373).

But if we accept that protection against vote dilution is part of the voting right, then some forms of PR may not survive a VRA challenge. Under the right circumstances, PR may actually result in *less* representational opportunity for specific minority groups despite the fact that it would make the electoral marketplace more open for all minority groups. Such an occurrence would run afoul of the "nonretrogression" principle enunciated in section 5 of the VRA (see *Beer v. U.S.* 1976; *Reno v. Bossier Parish* 2000).

In general, more geographically compact groups will do better in single-member districts, while more dispersed ones will do better in a PR system with multimember districts. For example, in a state with five congressional seats elected by the SMP method, a geographically compact group of African American voters that comprises 15 percent of the electorate could be virtually assured of representation because it would make up a 75 percent majority in one of the districts. Conversion to PR actually might render this group without representation. The Droop quota in this case would be 16.67 percent of the vote (vote/6). If the white majority were to disaggregate into its constituent parts, the ideal situation (for the minority) that might occur would be the following:

Party A: 23—1 quota + 6 extra votes
Party B: 22—1 quota + 5 extra votes
Party C: 20—1 quota + 3 extra votes
Party D: 20—1 quota + 3 extra votes
African Americans: 15—0 quota + 15 extra votes

Under these circumstances, the cohesive bloc of African American voters would be able to elect its candidate of choice even though it did not attain the quota.

However, it would also be possible for *five* other groups to form, each of which made up 17 percent of the electorate. Under such circumstances, the seats/votes distribution would be:

Party A: 17—1 quota
Party B: 17—1 quota
Party C: 17—1 quota
Party D: 17—1 quota
Party E: 17—1 quota
African Americans: 15—0 quota + 15 extra votes

In this case, African American voters would not be represented. The conversion to the "fairer" system of PR could actually be a setback for minority voters and be subject to challenge under the nonretrogression standard set forth in section 5 of the Voting Rights Act.

Thus, under some circumstances, the plurality system with majority-minority districts might actually serve minority interests better, even though it might lessen their chances of obtaining proportional representation. As Campbell (1996, 208) shows, the use of majority-minority districts actually amplifies African American representation because it enhances African American representational opportunities despite the fact that turnout among African American voters in these districts is quite low. Were PR to be implemented, low turnout rates among minority voters might decimate their representation because it would prevent them from attaining the quota necessary to secure a seat (*United ed Jewish Organizations of Williamsburgh v. Carey* 1973, 162–65; Lewyn 1995, 213). While majority-minority districts may make legislative seats safer for minority candidates, they do little to enhance turnout—essentially because election of the minority-preferred candidate is assured. A PR system would, technically, be much fairer to *all* minority groups, but it would do much less for specific minority groups than the creation of special majority-minority districts. Accordingly, under a PR system minority group leaders would need to ensure that their constituents turned out and voted as a bloc. Otherwise they would run the risk of *losing* representation—*because* of the fairness of PR.

As a result, in the current American context, the prospect of PR poses a difficult problem, at least with regard to the fate of those minority groups itemized in the VRA. The conversion to PR would certainly put an end to the gerrymandering controversies that arise from the need to redraw district lines every ten years. But since the process of redistricting is currently constrained by the VRA to draw majority-minority districts, it ensures that the political marketplace *does not* function in a completely free manner. A conversion to PR would, as its advocates contend, make the political and electoral marketplace that much more open and fair. Fairness to all, however, might result in diminished representation for some.

Even if an alternative electoral system could survive a VRA challenge, the expansive definition of the right to vote embodied in the notion of vote dilution would still ensure controversy. First, to monitor the electoral process in this manner would require the establishment of some criteria to decide which groups "count" for purposes of a vote dilution challenge. This is an inherently controversial process because, inevitably, some groups would wish to be recognized but would fail to persuade the powers that be that they did, indeed, "count." This actually occurred in *United Jewish Organizations of Williamsburgh v. Carey* (1973). Hasidic voters challenged a New York State redistricting plan because it divided their community in order to construct two African American–majority districts. While the United Jewish Organizations claimed that the Hasidic community was distinct and had its own unique interests, the Court was unsympathetic. In a compelling passage, Justice William Brennan dismissed the Hasidics' claim essentially because the Court perceived of the vote dilution issue in "white" and "nonwhite" terms. Since the Hasidics were "white," they had no grounds to protest their being divided.

> Petitioners have not been deprived of their right to vote, a consideration that minimizes the detrimental impact of the remedial racial policies governing the §5 reapportionment. True, petitioners are denied the opportunity to vote as a group in accordance with the earlier districting configuration. . . . Yet, to the extent that white and nonwhite interests and sentiments are polarized in Brooklyn, the petitioners still are indirectly "protected" by the remaining white assembly and senate districts within the county. (*United Jewish Organizations of Williamsburgh v. Carey* 1973, 178)

A second controversy raised by the vote dilution issue is that it would most certainly require more (not less) gerrymandering of the electoral process— precisely to ensure that specific groups do not find their political power diluted. Any group that counted that also could not clear the threshold of representation (in even the fairest of PR systems) would be in a position to file a vote dilution claim. As a result, courts—or some authoritative body—would need to police the function of the electoral arrangement to ensure that the threshold of representation did not work against a particular minority group.

Minority rights advocates state that while it is clearly unconstitutional for a majority to gerrymander a political group out of power (or, at least, to dilute its power), it is all right for a majority to organize the outcome of elections in order to share power with a minority. In *Shaw v. Reno* (1993), Justice John Paul Stevens suggested that if a majority were to condition the electorate in a manner that would enhance minority political power, the resulting gerrymander would be permissible.

> The duty to govern impartially is abused when a group with power over the electoral process defines electoral boundaries solely to enhance its own political strength at the expense of any weaker group. That duty, however, is not violated when the majority acts to facilitate the election of a member of a group that lacks such power because it remains underrepresented in the state legislature. (*Shaw v. Reno* 1993, 677–78)

In rejecting Stevens's argument, the majority responded that "equal protection analysis is not dependent on the race of those burdened or benefited by a particular classification" (*Shaw v. Reno* 1993, 652). The *Shaw* Court accordingly suggested (albeit in unclear terms) that a legislature may not exercise excessive control over the process by which it is constituted (see Aleinikoff and Issacharoff 1993, 654; Polsby and Popper 1993, 676). This principle casts all gerrymanders in the same light: The legislature (or a majority thereof) may not "rig" electoral outcomes in favor of any political group.

By trying to prevent the dilution of a particular group's vote, minority rights advocates seek to gerrymander the electoral system in the sense that they are also trying to condition outcomes. In this respect, the minority rights advocates part company with advocates of PR. Whereas the former are concerned with ensuring that, at a minimum, voices of specific minority groups are not diluted and, at a maximum, that their preferences are satisfied, the latter have traditionally been concerned with ensuring the legitimacy of majority rule, the fates of specific minority groups notwithstanding.

Perspective: Democratic Theory and Minority Representation Rights

Contemporary PR advocates have a much narrower vision of the voting right (as well as the notion of representation) than minority rights advocates. While seeking to ensure minority presence in the legislature, PR advocates have not traditionally challenged the principle of majority rule or the notion that voting is an individual right. Instead, they have sought to reinforce the legitimacy of the governing majority by ensuring that it really reflects the interests of a majority of the populace and that the populace actually had a broad and meaningful choice on election day.

In her writings on the merits of PR, Enid Lakeman (1984) emphasizes the latter. She maintains that the legitimacy of democracy depends on ensuring that elections are not fraudulent in the sense that the choices they present are meaningless. Conversely, Maurice Duverger emphasizes the need to make sure that elections form effective governments:

> [D]emocracy does not consist of assembling a parliament which is a small-sized model of the distribution of the nation's different spiritual families in all their diversity and nuances. Voters should not choose their doubles who must resemble them as closely as possible. They should choose governments with the capacity to make decisions. . . .
>
> By dispersing the voters among numerous independent parties, PR prevents the citizens from expressing a clear choice for a governmental team. It transfers this choice to the party leaders. . . . PR properly expresses the citizens' diverse preferences, but it does not allow them to choose a concrete set of policies and a team to execute them. (Duverger 1986, 32)

Nonetheless, despite the values they emphasize, many contemporary analysts of electoral systems have concluded that the debate over which system is the best is moot. As Duverger notes, theories of representation pull in two irreconcilable directions:

> [One] requires that many parties present themselves to the citizens in order that each citizen can choose a candidate who is very close to his preferences. It also implies that the seats won should be exactly proportional to the votes received. [The other] needs completely opposite mechanisms. In order to enable the voters to impose the government of their choice and to give this government the means to act during the entire life of the legislature, a small number of parties is needed. . . . The ethical arguments about the authenticity of representation and the fairness of the distribution of seats compared with that of the votes are largely, if not completely, specious. One cannot seriously present PR as a moral and fair system, and the plurality and majority systems as immoral techniques, because they are alleged to be unfair. On the contrary, one must clearly state that PR generally weakens democracy and that plurality and majority systems strengthen it. (Duverger 1984, 33, 35)

Despite this lukewarm assessment of PR, Duverger still acknowledges that the United States would benefit from PR precisely because of the terrible state of the Democratic and Republican Parties (36). Similarly, Lakeman, who is an unabashed advocate of PR, acknowledges that there is a lot to be said for ensuring that, once the votes are counted, the voters know who will be governing instead of having to wait for coalitions to form among party leaders (1984, 47–48). Thus, the PR debate is, indeed, a practical one that involves trade-offs among competing values. The question we must confront is whether Americans would be willing to make those trade-offs in order to obtain the benefits of a PR system.

Advocates of PR frequently cite John Stuart Mill, whose advocacy of proportional representation was based on the desire to ensure that democracy would not tend towards government by "collective mediocrity" (1994, 287). His criticism of the single-member district system of representation was not accompanied by a desire to democratize the political process in the sense of making it easier for minority groups to ensure that their interests were addressed or their agendas enacted. Instead, he sought to ensure that the "instructed minority" (that is, smart folks like Mill and his friends) would be able to wield legislative influence despite their minority status.[8]

A district-based system of elections, he argued, would represent only "artificial units" such as towns and counties, which were, he contended "the creation of geography and statistics," not people. While he denied any desire to "annihilate" towns and counties, he saw no reason to limit representation to geographically based aggregations.

I cannot see why the feelings and interests which arrange mankind according to localities should be the only ones thought worthy of being represented; or why people who have other feelings and interests, which they value more than they do their geographical ones, should be restricted to these as the sole principle of their political classification. (Mill 1994, 292)

Furthermore, Mill contended that the single-member district system actually militated against the improvement of the legislature because it discouraged the most qualified candidates from running for office. "The natural tendency of representative government," he said, was toward "collective mediocrity." Only those who were willing to compromise their principles were able to get elected, because they would make unscrupulous appeals to the voters.

It is an admitted fact that in the American democracy, which is constructed on this faulty model, the highly-cultivated members of the community, except such of them as are willing to sacrifice their own opinions and modes of judgment and become the servile mouthpieces of their inferiors in knowledge, seldom even offer themselves for Congress or State Legislatures, so little likelihood they have of being returned. (1994, 288)

Mill therefore advocated PR to ensure not only that the legislative majority would be a more accurate reflection of the popular majority but also that the "instructed minority" would have an impact on the representatives of the less qualified masses. By enhancing the diversity of voices in the legislature, a PR system would actually improve the quality of legislative deliberations and, by extension, the quality of legislation (289).

Similarities between Mill and Madison

Critics of the use of SMDs in America might be surprised to learn that Mill's motivations were quite similar to those of James Madison. Whereas Madison sought to control the effects of "factions" by multiplying their number in an extended republic, Mill said that proportional representation would achieve essentially the same end by multiplying their number in the legislature. Both Mill and Madison believed that their visions would ensure that factional or minority groups would not tyrannize the rest of the populace and that such discrete groups would be consumed by the national interest.

Madison's "republican solution" to the problem of factions was to make it as difficult as possible for any faction to attain an unfettered majority of the legislative power. Accordingly, he broke with the tradition that had celebrated small-scale democracies and instead advocated the notion of an extended republic:

> The smaller the society, the fewer probably will be the distinct parties and interests composing it; the fewer the distinct parties and interests, the more frequently will a majority be found of the same party; and the smaller the individuals composing a majority, and the smaller the compass within which they are placed, the more easily will they concert and execute their plans of oppression. (Hamilton et al. 1961, 83)

To this point, Madison actually echoes Mill's complaints about the injustices that are likely to occur in a district-based system of representation: Once a local majority is formed, it need not listen to the appeals of voters who are not of the same mind. For all intents and purposes, those voters are without a voice in the legislature. Madison therefore concluded that a large polity was better than a small one:

> Extend the sphere and you take in a greater variety of parties and interests; you make it less probable that a majority of the whole will have a common motive to invade the rights of other citizens; or, if such a common motive exists, it will be more difficult for all who feel it to discover their own strength and to act in unison with each other. (Hamilton et al. 1961, 83)

Thus, in an extended republic, all factions would need to moderate their views in order to form alliances if they wished to be part of a governing majority. This process of making alliances among competing factions would, Madison assumed, ensure that no one group would dominate and that all groups would have a chance to join a governing coalition.

Mill made the same argument in favor of PR (1994, 287–91). Insofar as proportional representation would not artificially amplify the power of the majority, all groups would obtain representation in rough proportion to their numbers. As a result, aspiring majorities would be subject to the ever present possibility of "antagonism" from other groups—especially the instructed minority—who would be able to challenge majoritarian initiatives. Accordingly, Mill saw PR as a substantial bulwark against majority tyranny in the same way that Madison perceived his extended republic.

Had Madison foreseen the widespread use and impact of gerrymandering, would he have advocated a system of representation based on something other than geographically defined districts? Since representation in England was based on such geographically defined districts, it is no surprise that the Americans adopted them. In colonial legislatures, districts were in widespread use (Griffith 1907). Madison also notes in *Federalist* 56 that there would be one "representative for every *thirty thousand inhabitants*" in the new Congress (Hamilton et al. 1961, 350). He notes in *Federalist* 57 that the districts to be drawn for the congressional representatives would be approximately the same size as those drawn for the upper houses of several of the state legislatures (Hamilton et al. 1961, 355). Thus, he at least acknowledged their widespread use and envisioned the use of single-member districts for electing congressmen.

The compatibility of PR with the Federalist constitutional vision depends on whether single-member districts can be said to minimize the proliferation of interests that Madison had sought to ensure by "extending the sphere" of his proposed republican government. Since the purpose of the large republic was to increase the number of views represented in the legislature, Madison would not have been averse to the use of a system of proportional representation. As Robert Dixon notes, if enhancing the number of voices in the legislature was the goal of Madison's system,

> the representation system should be devised to maximize the likelihood that a variety of interests rather than a few dominant interests will be represented formally in the processes of government: hence the original constitutional system, with its varied provisions for direct and indirect election of the different parts of the legislature and the executive based on overlapping but distinct electorates. (Dixon 1968, 41)

In fact, Dixon goes on to argue that a Madisonian theorist would view winner-take-all systems "with suspicion" (42).

Regarding the framers' vision of representation and their fear of tyrannical factions, we are left with competing diagnoses of the SMP system. On the one hand, PR advocates themselves acknowledge that single-member districts make it difficult for discrete interest groups to organize. In this respect, they do fit nicely with the framers' "republican solution." On the other hand, if SMDs can be perceived as enhancing the likelihood of locally tyrannical majorities, the framers might have reconsidered their tolerance for them.

The Ends of Representative Government
and the Public Interest

Despite the desires of both Mill and Madison to enhance the number of voices in the governing process, both ultimately advocated majority rule and offered minority groups few, if any, legislative recourses against the will of a popularly elected majority. In fact, both Mill and Madison advocated their visions of government *not* to advance the discrete interests of the factional interests that comprised society but, instead, to promote the *public* interest *despite* the wishes of discrete or, worse, what Mill referred to as "uninstructed" minorities. Accordingly, a key goal of their prescriptions was to create a process by which the governing majority would be least likely to represent one discrete or uninformed interest. Furthermore, both sought to ensure that, ultimately, elites (presumably enlightened ones) would be insulated somewhat from the masses in order to be free to govern in the public interest (see Hamilton et al. 1961, 350).

Madison and Mill both feared the influence of the masses and advocated visions of government that would temper their impact. Whereas Mill hoped that the presence of an instructed minority in the legislature would enhance the quality of discourse, Madison's view was that republican government would ensure that the untempered opinions and factional impulses of the masses would be filtered and refined by the election of representatives who, he assumed, would be less disposed to factional impulses because, by virtue of their standing for election, they had to appeal to a broad spectrum of voters (Hamilton et al. 1961, 82–83; see also Mill 1994, 317–18). Mill, on the other hand, sought not only to ensure that the instructed minority would have a legislative presence but also advocated augmenting the suffrage to provide multiple votes for the more educated members of the polity (1994, 309).

Mill distinguished representation from governing. While the people were entitled to be *heard* in the legislative process, they were not entitled to have an active hand in the day-to-day processes of governing. The legislature, he said, should be

> an arena in which not only the general opinion of the nation, but that of every section of it, and as far as possible of every eminent individual whom it contains, can produce itself in full light and challenge discussion; where every person in the country may count upon finding somebody who speaks his mind, as well or better than he could speak it himself—not to friends and partisans exclusively,

but in the face of opponents, to be tested by adverse controversy; where those whose opinion is overruled, feel satisfied that it is heard, and set aside not by a mere act of will, but for what are thought superior reasons, and commend themselves as such to the representatives of the majority of the nation.

[It is a] place where every interest and shade of opinion in the country can have its cause even passionately pleaded, in the face of the government and of all other interests and opinions, can compel them to listen, and either comply, or state clearly why they do not. (1994, 258–59)

Thus, for Mill, the parliament was supposed to be a mirror—a microcosm—of the polity. Elected representatives would be mouthpieces for public opinions, not proactive governors, because they are "not a selection of the greatest political minds in the country . . . but a fair sample of every grade of intellect among the people. . . . Their part is to indicate wants, to be an organ for popular demands, and a place of adverse discussion for all opinions relating to public matters" (260). Ultimately, these legislators should have a final hand in controlling the political process, as well as the power to dismiss the elite "experts" who ran the government if they failed to please or appease the people:

Instead of the function of governing, for which it is radically unfit, the proper office of a representative assembly is to watch and control the government: to throw the light of publicity on its acts: to compel a full exposition and justification of all of them which any one considers questionable; to censure them if found condemnable, and, if the men who compose the government abuse their trust, or fulfil it in a manner which conflicts with the deliberate sense of the nation, to expel them from office and either expressly or virtually appoint their successors. (258)

The multiplication of legislative voices was expected to enhance the quality of public debate and thereby increase the likelihood of attaining the truly *public* interest. Therefore, all discrete interests were entitled to a legislative *voice* but were still rendered inferior to the public interest, which was most closely approximated by the majority's voice. Accordingly, Mill went so far as to advocate public voting to ensure that those who voted selfishly might be subject to challenge (325–26).

The problem with both Madison's and Mill's prescriptions is that they beg the question, What is the *public* interest? Early on in *Federalist* 10, Madison tells us that a principal motivation for the new constitution was the commonly held belief that the public interest was not being served under the Articles of Confederation. Instead, the national government tended to cater to whatever group formed a temporal majority.

Complaints are everywhere heard from our most considerate and virtuous citizens, equally the friends of public and private faith and of public and personal

liberty, that our governments are too unstable, that the public good is disregarded in the conflicts of rival parties, and that measures are too often decided, not
according to the rules of justice and the rights of the minor party, but by the superior force of an interested and overbearing majority. (Hamilton et al. 1961, 77)

Despite this, Madison is silent regarding the scope and definition of the public
interest. He takes pains to tell us what the public interest is not. The reader of
the *Federalist* is reminded often that the public interest *is not* the interest of
any given faction or a cabal of discrete factions. Yet, Madison either could not
or would not define *the* public interest. He therefore set his sights lower and
justified his advocacy of a large republic by contending that the pluralism that
would arise from our factional impulses would, at least, prevent factional
tyranny. It might never drive us toward a truly national public interest, but it
would keep us from doing too much harm to any one group.

Madison was not concerned as much with the outputs of government as with
its creation and function. He actually *feared* a government that would be too
capable of activism; accordingly, his notions of representation focused clearly
on access to, not success within, the government. As Hanna Pitkin notes, in
Madison's system, "the danger is action and the safeguard is stalemate, or, as
he would have it, balance." For Madison, "representation is a means of
stalemating action in the legislature, and thus in society, until wisdom prevails
[over the naturally egoistic factional interests]" (Pitkin 1967, 195–96).

Thus, both Mill and Madison feared that the government could be taken
over by the masses or by specific factional interests. While Mill therefore
sought to separate the legislative (representative) process from the administration of the government, Madison designed the constitutional system to
make it as hard as possible for the government to act in an efficient, coordi-
nated manner. The separation of powers would make it difficult for even a
strong group to consolidate enough power throughout the nation to be able to
push its agenda through the federal government. Even if a group gained such
power, the Constitution—specifically, the Bill of Rights—would serve as a
limit to the governing group's ambitions. Furthermore, he placed the Constitution beyond the reach of temporal, simple majorities. While he praised the
Americans for having developed a new constitution, he feared that periodic
appeals to them for constitutional adjustment would be perilous. As he says
in *Federalist* 49:

The danger of disturbing the public tranquility by interesting too strongly the
public passions is a still more serious objection against a frequent reference of
constitutional questions to the decision of the whole society. Notwithstanding
the success which has attended the revisions of our established forms of government and which does so much honor to the virtue and intelligence of the peo-

ple of America, it must be confessed that the experiments are of too ticklish a nature to be unnecessarily multiplied. (Hamilton et al. 1961, 315)

We see, then, that Madison and Mill were not populists. While seeking to increase the number of voices in the legislative process, they still sought to subjugate discrete interests to the public interest, which would be best approximated by the deliberations of an *informed*, legitimate *majority*. Says Mill: "[O]ne of the greatest dangers, therefore, of democracy . . . is the danger of class legislation; of government intended for (whether really effecting it or not) the immediate benefit of the dominant class, to the lasting detriment of the whole" (1994, 275).[9] In a similar vein, Madison argued that "to secure the *public good* and private rights against the danger of . . . faction and at the same time to preserve the spirit and form of popular government, is then the great object to which our inquiries are directed" (Hamilton et al. 1961, 80, emphasis added; see also Hamilton et al. 1961, 350). Thus, neither discussed the broad governing role for minorities (or majorities) that contemporary voting rights scholars advocate.[10]

This leaves the contemporary discussion about minority rights, vote dilution, and the scope of the voting right adrift in the democratic theory debate. Minority voting rights activists contend that something is wrong when a particular, discrete group is rendered virtually mute by the rules that govern an electoral system. However, the solution to this sort of problem—constant monitoring of the process or tinkering with the rules to enhance the likelihood of particular outcomes—entails less democracy, not more. Minority rights scholars and reform advocates do force democratic theorists to ponder the fates of specific minorities. But, since virtually any electoral system can fall prey to a charge of vote dilution (as it has come to be interpreted in American jurisprudence), the minority rights problem—cast in these terms—is essentially unresolvable.

Minority Rights Notwithstanding, Will PR Improve American Politics?

Despite the tensions that inhere in the jurisprudence concerning the VRA, the question still remains, Would American politics improve if we were to reform the electoral process? American advocates of PR frequently cite European party systems as proof that PR would deliver a better brand of politics (see Amy 1993). The comparison to Europe by reformers is hardly a new phenomenon (see, e.g., Merriam and Overacker 1928; Ostrogorski 1910).[11] Yet, while reformers trumpet the more attractive elements of European politics, they seldom discuss the costs that would be involved in Europeanizing the conduct of American elections.

Perhaps the most important point to note is that while politics is different in other countries, it may not necessarily be any better. Furthermore, the different tenor of politics is not likely to be the result merely of a difference in the method by which votes are translated into seats. The difference in politics results from radically different constitutional and political architecture. Accordingly, when we read calls for the Europeanization of American politics, we should be wary of the ease with which reformers suggest such a transformation could take place.

PR advocates want more than just a system of proportional representation; they want a "better" political system. As Amy notes, a better system would be characterized by several parties that are ideologically distinct, candidates who adhere to party lines and debate issues (not personalities), and a decreased impact of big money on the electoral process (Amy 1993, 1–21). Furthermore, reformers want an electoral system that is governed by rules that minimize the costs of entry so that as many (viable) parties as possible can appeal to voters. Such a conversion would require more than PR; it would also require a radical alteration of the way parties conduct business and the relationship between parties and their members. However, whether the cost of this transformation would justify the ends—and whether those ends could be achieved—remains a matter for debate.

The Spirit of Party Reform in America

To ensure that political parties are strong and issue oriented, we would certainly need to permit them to police their membership and ensure that only loyal supporters of the party line participate in party affairs. But this is exactly the sort of party organization that has been the target of American reform measures for more than the last hundred years. Late-nineteenth- and early-twentieth-century reforms were designed not only to break the power of political machines but also to democratize the process of elections and nominations (see Merriam and Overacker 1928; Rusk 1970). Because of pronounced opposition by the political parties, the enthusiasm for progressive reforms fizzled by the 1920s (see Weaver 1984, 1986). Nonetheless, a similar spirit of reform animated the changes made to the presidential nominating process in the early 1970s when, once again, the power of party elites was undermined (see Ceaser 1982; Polsby 1983).

While parallels between the two reform eras are imperfect (Ceaser 1982, 26), both were informed by an antiparty (that is, "antimachine") spirit that has always festered beneath the surface of American politics. Ironically, the Europeanized vision of politics that PR advocates desire is grounded on a vision of politics that is antithetical to the American antiparty sentiment. In the wake of the reforms of the 1970s, Americans have witnessed skyrocketing campaign costs, a lengthening of the primary campaign season, increased complaints about the absence of any discussion of real issues, and so on—exactly the sorts of problems that PR advocates would like to see resolved.

Antipartyism in the United States

Much of the political reform movement at the end of the nineteenth and beginning of the twentieth centuries was directed at breaking the power of political parties and their machines. Reforms such as the use of the Australian ballot wrested control over elections from the parties and placed it instead in the hands of the state (see Merriam and Overacker 1928; Evans 1917; Fredman 1968; Rusk 1970). Despite reform efforts such as these, the parties still controlled nominations, and popular resentment continued. Accordingly, reformers set their sights on controlling the nomination process in the same manner that they had implemented controls over the elections. In 1903, Wisconsin, under the leadership of the LaFollette Progressives, implemented the first mandatory direct-primary law, which required parties to hold primary elections instead of conventions. The primary not only increased popular participation but also made it easier for more candidates to run for office since opportunities to run were based on the acquisition of petition signatures and so forth. However, it also made it difficult for parties to control their membership and nominees.

Extending state control over nominations clearly weakened the parties. As a result, critics (e.g., Merriam and Overacker 1928) noted that the parties could not be held accountable. The responsibility for policymaking and nominations had been spread too thinly among the electorate. As a result, *voters* were able to alter the rosters of policymakers and executors with impunity, because no one knew who voted for whom.

Parties' associational rights were further weakened as a result of the Supreme Court's declaring white primaries to be unconstitutional in *Smith v. Allwright* (1944). The Court went even further in *Terry v. Adams* (1953), declaring that "private" primaries held by private groups to endorse particular candidates were unconstitutional. Most recently, the Court held that political parties could not charge registration fees for their nominating conventions. Such fees were found to violate the VRA because they could deter African American voters from participating in the nominating process (*Morse v. Republican Party of Virginia* 1994).

While these decisions were predicated on the desire to eradicate racially motivated denial of the right to vote, there is no questioning their impact on the parties' ability to close ranks and present a coherent platform to the voters. The *Morse* decision suggests that virtually any restriction on an individual's participation in the nominating process could be found to violate the VRA. If this is the case, the VRA is currently being read in a manner that would prevent the strengthening of American parties.

Nonetheless, the *Morse* decision is instructive because it should make us stop and ponder just what costs we would be willing to bear in order to make American politics more European. Certainly, converting to some form of PR would be a step in that direction. But PR alone would not be sufficient to Europeanize the parties. For example, would Americans be willing to give up their access to the nominating process (through the direct primary) in exchange for stronger parties and therefore more coherent platforms?

"Perhaps," reformers might assert, but there is a certain irony to this. An impulse that underlies PR advocates' efforts is the desire to make the political process more open and representative of diverse opinions. A conversion to a more European, strong party system would work against that desire. If voters were unhappy with the candidates the established parties were nominating, the voters' options would be either not to vote or to form a rival party. There would be no more Eugene McCarthys, Gary Harts, Jesse Jacksons, or Jerry Browns running in the Democratic primaries. Pat Buchanan could not just declare his intention to challenge President Bush for the nomination. Instead, challengers to the existing party system would have to follow the route taken by Ross Perot and create new parties. Would Americans find this to be a tolerable trade-off? The quality of choices on election day might improve, but popular input into the creation of those choices would be minimized.

So What If Americans Were Willing to Europeanize the Parties?

Perhaps the American public would be willing to make such a trade-off. Still, there is no assurance that politics would improve. In fact, changes occurring in countries that use PR or have strong parties suggest that we might find ourselves right back where we began: with parties avoiding divisive issues and doing what they can to shore themselves up against attacks from nascent reform-minded groups.

Despite Europe's use of PR and its many strong, coherent parties, European politics suffers from many of the same maladies that American reformers lament. Turnout is falling throughout Europe as well as the United States (Lijphart 1997).[12] In addition, Katz and Mair (1994; 1995) point out that European parties are undergoing a transformation that makes them much more similar to their American counterparts than American reformers have acknowledged.

Critics of the American parties contend that the Democrats and Republicans have monopolized power by erecting campaign finance laws that discriminate in their favor (Raskin and Bonifaz 1993) and other hurdles to participation, such as stringent ballot access requirements for third parties (Rosenstone, Behr, and Lazarus 1996; Argersinger 1980). Yet, Katz and Mair point out, European parties are guilty of the same sort of "cartel"-like behavior. Established parties enact legislation that produces state subventions similar to those—such as American campaign finance laws—that make it difficult for nascent parties to compete with established parties.

The manipulation of ballot access thresholds demonstrates the similarities between the United States and Europe despite the latter's use of PR. An effective way to stymie opponents is to erect ballot access thresholds that are high enough to prevent them from getting their candidates' names on the ballot. If you know that your opponent has a certain number of supporters (say, ten thousand), you (if you are a member of one of the parties in power) can amend the voting laws to require, say, twenty thousand petition signatures to get on the ballot. Failing that, you could amend the laws to require parties to garner a certain percentage of the vote in a particular number of elections in order to retain their ballot position.

A good example of such electoral manipulation occurred in Virginia in 1991. As a result of John Warner's running unopposed for reelection to the U.S. Senate, the Democratic Party of Virginia found itself in danger of failing to qualify as a "party" because it failed to garner 10 percent of the vote in "the previous statewide election" (*Virginia Election Laws* sec. 24.1-1 [1991]). In response, the Virginia General Assembly amended the election laws and redefined a political party as "an organization of citizens . . . which, at either of the *two* preceding statewide general elections, received at least ten percent of the total vote cast for any statewide office" (*Virginia Election Laws* sec, 24.2-101 [1996], emphasis added).

This sort of finagling may seem innocuous—unless you are a member of a minor party. More recently, the Reform Party of Virginia lost its status as an official political party because it failed to meet the 10 percent requirement in two consecutive elections (Whitley 1997). The Reform Party had gained automatic ballot access privileges because Ross Perot had surpassed the 10 percent threshold in 1992 and J. Marshall Coleman received 11 percent of the vote for U.S. Senate in 1994. However, Perot garnered only 6.6 percent of the state's presidential vote in 1996, and none of the party's candidates for statewide office in 1997 received even 5 percent of the vote.

Reform Party candidates may still get on the ballot in Virginia. But they must now do so as independent candidates and by collecting (for statewide office) the signatures of at least 0.5 percent of the registered voters in the Commonwealth—including at least two hundred signatures from each congressional district (*Virginia Election Laws* sec, 24.2-506 [1996]). Critics contend that such petition requirements are quite discriminatory because they make it difficult for aspiring parties to establish themselves.

Yet, were a state or the nation to convert to some form of PR, the ballot access issue would not go away. At some point, a limit would need to be set on the number of candidates that could be placed on a ballot, if only to ensure that the ballot was not "cluttered" by parties that had no chance of receiving

Table 2.8 Ballot Access Laws

Country	Law
Austria	A total of 2,600 signatures at the town halls must be obtained in order for a party to place candidates for all parliamentary seats. A fee equivalent to US$450 is also required (this fee covers the entire slate of candidates).
Croatia	If the party has fewer than three members in the old parliament, it must submit between 200 and 400 signatures from each parliamentary district, depending on the size of the district. There are twenty districts.
Finland	Each candidate for the national legislature needs 150 signatures.
Germany	If the party has no members in the old parliament, it must submit 2,000 signatures in each of the sixteen German states and 200 signatures in each of the 328 districts.
Great Britain	Candidates for Parliament must pay £500, which is returned if the candidate polls 5 percent.
Greece	No petition is required, but the party must pay the equivalent of US$180 per candidate and must print and distribute paper ballots bearing the candidates' names.
Ireland	No petition is required, just a deposit of £300 per candidate.
Netherlands	No petition is required, just a deposit of 25,000 guilders (US$12,500) for a full slate.
Norway	Five hundred signatures per district are required.
Poland	Three thousand signatures per district—75,000 signatures for the whole nation—are needed.
Spain	A party merely needs to request a place on the ballot.
Sweden	Neither fee nor petition is required, but a party must print its own ballots and distribute them to its supporters.
Switzerland	Between 100 and 400 signatures are required for each of the 25 cantons.

Source: Ballot Access News, October 1997

enough votes to gain legislative representation. A recent survey of European ballot access laws by Richard Winger of *Ballot Access News* (October 1997) shows that the range of ballot access restrictions is quite broad, even in countries that use PR (see table 2.8).

Thus, a simple change to the method of counting votes would not resolve the controversies that arise as a result of an aspiring political party's failure to get on the ballot in the first place. Nonetheless, how can we distinguish between valid ballot access restrictions and those that are established simply to keep legitimate aspiring parties off the ballot?

Obviously, some restrictions on access to the ballot are necessary in order to preserve the integrity of an election. In the United States, the Supreme Court has acknowledged the need to restrict ballot access but has also expressed suspicion of restrictions enacted by Democrats and Republicans that seem to discriminate too heavily in their favor.

In *Williams v. Rhodes* (1968), for example, the Court struck down an unusually restrictive Ohio ballot access law that had made it virtually impossible for candidates other than those of the Democratic and Republican Parties to get on the ballot. The Court acknowledged that such a lockup (Issacharoff and Pildes 1998) of the political process was suspicious because "the right to vote is heavily burdened if that vote may be cast only for one of two parties at a time when other parties are clamoring for a place on the ballot" (*Williams v. Rhodes* 1968, 31). Despite the limits placed on the choices presented to voters, the Court still maintained that such restrictions were necessary to preserve the integrity of the electoral process. If the ballot were to become "cluttered" and confusing with the names of candidates and parties that had no chance of winning, voters could not cast their ballots effectively (30).

Thresholds can be created either through ballot access hurdles such as the one challenged in *Williams* or by other means, such as prohibiting fusion candidacies (*Timmons v. Twin Cities Area New Party* 1997) or write-in candidacies (*Burdick v. Takushi* 1992). Ironically, in both of these cases, the Supreme Court was much less suspicious of state motivations than it was in *Williams*. In both cases, the Court endorsed the preservation of the two-party system as an important governmental interest. Thus, the restriction on write-in voting in *Burdick* was justified because the state (i.e., the Democrats and Republicans) wished to avoid "the possibility of unrestrained factionalism at the general election" (*Burdick v. Takushi* 1992, 439). In *Timmons*, the Court elaborated:

> States . . . have a strong interest in the stability of their political systems. This interest does not permit a State to completely insulate the two-party system from minor parties' or independent candidates' competition and influence. . . . That said, the States' interest permits them to enact reasonable election regulations that may, in practice, favor the traditional two-party system, and that temper the destabilizing effects of party-splintering and excessive factionalism. (*Timmons v. Twin Cities Area New Party* 1997, 366–67)

create to many parties → caos

moral of story? Thus, electoral reforms would not necessarily alter politics to the extent that their advocates desire. To ensure effective government, it is necessary to establish limits on access to effective representation in that government. This means that some groups will remain without a voice in a legislative body, regardless of their agenda or the intensity of their commitment to it.

effective gov. vs. effective representation

Different Visions of Democracy, Different Democratic Values

In this chapter, I have shown that no electoral arrangement is beyond criticism and that all electoral systems have their drawbacks. In some situations, one electoral arrangement may be clearly preferable to another. There is, for example, no question that alternative electoral arrangements such as PR or the creation of majority-minority districts have enhanced opportunities for minority representation in the United States. Nonetheless, the history of PR in the United States manifests a record of mixed successes at best. It has endured in a few spots such as Cambridge, Massachusetts, but it has also disappeared in other spots such as Ohio and New York City (see, e.g., Barber 1995; Zeller and Bone 1948; Weaver 1986).

It is clear that SMP and the two-party system mute some voices that might have more of an impact in a multiparty system. But all institutions are criticized by those who are dissatisfied or frustrated with their performance. As Nelson Polsby notes, "It is not much of a criticism to point out that a given set of decisionmaking processes (like first past the post) denies some people the outcomes they want. All decisionmaking processes, operating in the absence of unanimity, do that" (Brinkley, Polsby, and Sullivan 1997, 42).

Without additional, systemwide changes to how elections are conducted, discrete electoral reforms won't necessarily deliver upon the promises made by their proponents. They won't necessarily enhance minority representation unless we can be assured that minority voters and candidates behave strategically. For the same reasons, a new electoral system will not eradicate vote dilution; it will simply manifest it differently. PR won't necessarily enhance turnout, because turnout is dropping worldwide, even in PR systems. While an alternative electoral system will put an end to redistricting-based gerrymandering controversies, it will replace them with quota controversies.

But, reformers argue, an alternative electoral system would at least ensure more legitimate governing majorities that are not "manufactured" or unfairly magnified by the idiosyncrasies of the SMP system. While examples such as Amy's (table 2.1) indicate that SMP may turn slim majorities into overwhelming ones or convert majorities to minorities or vice versa, PR systems can do so as well.

The SMP system may have its quirks, but at least at the congressional level, it has not in recent years ever produced a minority government. As table 2.9 indicates, congressional majorities in the United States have always been able to claim that they represent a majority of the people, even though the majority party's percentage of seats might be much larger than its percentage of the vote.

In PR systems, this is not always the case. In the 1998 German federal elections, for example, no party received a majority of the seats in the Bundestag. As a result, the various parties had to negotiate after the election until

Table 2.9 Democratic Congressional Vote and Seat Percentages, 1954–1998

	1954	1956	1958	1960	1962	1964	1966	1968
% of Vote	52.5	51.1	56.3	54.2	52.3	57.4	50.9	50.2
% of Seats	53.3	53.8	64.8	50.2	59.3	67.8	57.0	55.9
Difference (%)	-0.8	-2.7	-8.5	4	-7	-10.4	-6.1	-5.7

	1970	1972	1974	1976	1978	1980	1982	1984
% of Vote	53.4	51.7	57.6	56.2	53.4	50.4	55.6	52.1
% of Seats	58.6	55.9	66.9	67.1	63.7	55.9	61.8	58.2
Difference (%)	-5.2	-4.2	-9.3	-10.9	-10.3	-5.5	-6.2	-6.1

	1986	1988	1990	1992	1994	1996	1998	
% of Vote	54.5	53.3	52.9	50.8	45.4	48.5	47.8	
% of Seats	59.3	59.8	61.4	59.3	46.7	47.6	48.5	
Difference (%)	-4.8	-6.5	-8.5	-8.5	-1.3	0.9	-0.7	

Sources: 1952–1996 results: Stanley and Niemi 2000, 41–43

a governing coalition was formed. Unless it is a minority government, a coalition needs at least 335 seats to govern the Bundestag. The SPD and Green Party formed a coalition and together controlled 345 seats. Nonetheless, as table 2.10 shows, these two parties represented only 47.6 percent of the electorate.

This is not an uncommon occurrence. In his survey of 309 elections, Katz (1997, 164) found that SMP and PR systems produced true majority governments at comparable rates. In the 110 elections held under SMP, 52.7 percent produced governments that had the support of an electoral majority. In PR systems, the figure was 57.2 percent. In recent national elections, the governing parties or coalitions in Denmark (1998), Germany (1998), Greece (1996), Ireland (1997), Italy (1996), New Zealand (1996), Norway (1997), Portugal (1995), and Spain (1996) all represented less than a majority of the voters.[13]

In addition, while PR's supporters emphasize the diversity that it brings to legislatures, they overlook the extent to which it may minimize governmental change. Pinto-Duschinsky (1998) argues that while PR may produce more diverse legislatures, it does not result in much change in governmental composition. He notes that in Great Britain, India, Canada, and New Zealand "sitting governments were ousted by the voters in twenty-five out of fifty-eight elections . . . held in the fifty years after the Second World War." In contrast, the governing parties in Germany, Italy, Japan, and Switzerland (all of which use PR) were never ousted (Pinto-Duschinsky 1999a, 1999b).[14]

In sum, it remains clear that electoral reform—specifically, the choice of

Table 2.10 A Manufactured Majority in Germany, October 1998

	% of Vote	Seats Number*	%
Social Democrats (SPD)	**40.9****	**298**	**44.5**
Christian Democrats (CDU)	28.4	198	29.5
Christian Social Union (CSU)	6.7	47	7
Green Party	**6.7**	**47**	**7**
Free Democrats (FDP)	6.2	43	6.4
Democratic Socialists (PDS, Partei des Demokratischen Sozialismus)	5.1	36	5.4

Source: Inter-Parliamentary Union, www.ipu.org.
*Total seats: 669.
**Bold type indicates figures for parties that formed majority.

electoral systems—involves choices among competing models of democracy. Unfortunately, the best or fairest method of counting votes from a systemic point of view may not be the best or fairest method from the point of view of any particular political group, especially if that group has a hard time winning elections. In the United States, the commitment of the Voting Rights Act to ensuring representational opportunities for racial and ethnic minorities constrains attempts to convert to some form of proportional representation. While the vision of democracy enshrined in the VRA is grounded on minority rights, the vision of democracy underpinning PR is grounded on more systemic concerns such as accurate translation of votes into seats. By itself, PR may promise a different—even a better—form of democracy. However, so long as the VRA controls the administration of American electoral change, the promise of PR will not be fulfilled.

Conclusion

If we step back from the constitutional concerns, the legal arguments, and the political science analysis of electoral systems, it is possible to view the question of minority representation rights (or, if you will, minority representation opportunities) in a much less contentious light.

Critics of the VRA and the Supreme Court decisions that have advanced the cause of minority voting rights contend that *any* racially motivated attempt (even a benign one) to tinker with electoral system violates the Fourteenth Amendment's guarantee of equal protection (see, e.g., Thernstrom

1987). They have a point. If it is constitutionally repugnant to gerrymander minority groups out of power, how can it be acceptable to gerrymander them into power? One person's benign attempt to help a historically disadvantaged racial group is another's racially motivated attempt to condition electoral outcomes.

I suggest that the real problem underlying minority voting rights and attempts to reform the electoral system to enhance them lies, in of all places, the Constitution itself. Furthermore, I suggest that the controversy surrounding minority representational opportunities has been exacerbated, ironically, by the Voting Rights Act.

More liberal critics of the Supreme Court's post–*Shaw v. Reno* decisions, such as Morgan Kousser and Jamin Raskin, argue that the Court employs a double standard when it limits the extent to which race may be taken into account when redrawing legislative or congressional districts (see generally Kousser 1999; Raskin 1998). When it comes to voting rights, they argue, a color-blind or racially neutral approach to organizing the electorate is, in fact, devastatingly insensitive to the needs of minority voters. As a result, "color-blind" is not racially neutral.

In fact, liberal critics of the Court's recent decisions offer a very strong, principled rebuttal to conservative critics of electoral reform: If it is all right to gerrymander legislative districts to help incumbents or to protect urban enclaves or what have you, why is it so repugnant to do the same to help out African American and Hispanic voters? There is no gainsaying the importance of this criticism. If the Court really seeks to purify the electoral process, why stop at (or, perhaps more accurately, why single out) benign racial gerrymandering when we ignore other kinds? Congress and the states pass all sorts of legislation designed to help particular or discrete interests. If aid to farmers or families with dependent children is permissible, why isn't aid to minority voters?

The problem is that critics such as Kousser and Raskin ask the wrong question. If we seek a consistent political principle, we are unlikely to find it in the Supreme Court's voting rights jurisprudence or, for that matter, in the Voting Rights Act. The VRA—especially the amended section 2—is inherently contradictory. Subsection 2(a) states: "No voting qualification or prerequisite to voting or standard, practice, or procedure shall be imposed or applied by any State or political subdivision in a manner which *results in a denial or abridgement of the right of any citizen of the United States to vote on account of race or color*." This language describes the franchise in terms of an individual's right to vote.

Subsection b states in part that a violation of subsection a occurs if members of a racial or ethnic group "have less opportunity than other members of the electorate to participate in the political process and to elect representatives of their choice." This clearly describes a group-based voting right. Finally, section 2(b) states that "nothing in this section establishes a right to have members of a protected class elected in numbers equal to their proportion in the population." (42 USCS sec. 1973 [1997], emphasis added). Looking at the section as a whole, one would be hard-pressed to state exactly what Congress had in mind when it passed the amended section 2.

The Court's jurisprudence is quite confused and contradictory because issues of voting rights and representation are inherently complex, and the Voting Rights Act has exacerbated this complexity. Early on, the Court supported Congress's authority to pass the VRA *(South Carolina v. Katzenbach* 1966). But recently various members of the Court have suggested that the VRA may in fact actually conflict with the Fourteenth Amendment. The Court has condemned gerrymandering at the expense of racial minorities *(Gomillion v. Lightfoot)* while allowing some leeway for states to gerrymander in order to help them. It has permitted bipartisan sweetheart gerrymanders that discriminate against third parties *(Gaffney v. Cummings)* while condemning partisan gerrymanders *(Davis v. Bandemer)* that are perpetrated at the expense of one of the major parties.

Accordingly, the Court is caught in a conundrum: The Fourteenth Amendment calls for evenhandedness, yet the public interest—as conceived by Congress in the VRA—demands that the electoral system be designed consciously to protect specific minority groups. As Dick Engstrom notes, the Court's attempts to codify "traditional districting principles" has resulted in nothing but failure and more confusion. In part, this may be due to the irreconcilable agendas of the various justices. In truth, however, it is due to the contradictory values that are embodied in the Court's case law, legal scholarship, and congressional legislation.

In *Bush v. Vera* (1996), Justice Sandra Day O'Connor attempted to summarize coherently the Court's rules for assessing the fairness of a redistricting plan. A fair plan that was sensitive to minority voting rights would have to adhere to the following criteria:

1. Majority-minority districts will survive judicial scrutiny so long as they don't subordinate "traditional districting principles" to the use of race "for its own sake."
2. Section 2 of the Voting Rights Act essentially compels creation of majority-minority districts where the three *Gingles* factors are present.
3. States have a compelling interest to draw majority-minority districts in order to avoid section 2 liability.
4. But this compelling interest does not justify deviating from traditional districting principles.
5. But in any event, bizarre, noncompact districts drawn for racial reasons are unconstitutional.

Essentially, O'Connor's summary restates the *Gingles* test: geographically compact minority groups are entitled to enhanced representational opportunities, but geographically dispersed ones are not. Clearly, however, these criteria are not truly fair because geography does not necessarily determine common political interest. But so long as the United States remains committed to its tradition of single-member districts, *all* geographically dispersed interests (not just racial ones) will be disadvantaged.

Alternative electoral systems offer a way out of this controversy because they would allow for (without guaranteeing) political results that would accommodate minority representational opportunities. Generally speaking, the alternative electoral arrangements advocated by reformers such as Dick Engstrom are *candidate centered*. That is, they allow voters to pick and choose among individual candidates without being forced to choose among party lists. In this respect, alternative systems such as cumulative voting and the single transferable vote cut a path midway between the American SMP system and full-blown European PR systems. Accordingly, their impact might not be as drastic as a conversion to PR.

Nonetheless, any electoral reform will bring with it a new host of questions and controversies about its inherent fairness. To work well, a new electoral system may work at the expense of values that, while not the object of reformers' wrath, may nonetheless be casualties of the reformers' crusades.

Notes

1. Alternative electoral systems take on many forms, some of which are more proportional than others. For the sake of simplicity, I will refer generally to these alternative electoral arrangements as proportional representation (PR) systems.

2. To be more accurate, Hodgkiss should have stated that the Justice Department's support depended on H.R. 1173's compliance with *the department's interpretation* of the Voting Rights Act. The Supreme Court has, on several recent occasions, rejected the Justice Department's expansive interpretation of the Voting Rights Act.

3. In fact, some critics have argued that such nonideological behavior on the part of individual candidates makes absolute sense in a democracy. See, e.g., Downs 1957.

4. This first example is drawn from Reynolds and Reilly 1997, 156. The ensuing discussion is drawn from Rush 1998.

5. While some observers—especially Americans—might think that this is rather unimportant, it actually has always been an extremely important question. Allocating congressional seats among the states proportionally according to population has always been laden with potential controversy because the formula used can shortchange some states. After the census of 1880, for example, it was found that if the membership of the House were increased from 299 to 300, Alabama would actually have *lost* a seat (see Carstairs 1980, 24, 29; Brams 1976, 137–66; Balinski and Young 1982). Most recently, in 1992 the State of Montana went to the Supreme Court to challenge the method by which congressional seats had been apportioned among the states (*U.S. Department of Commerce v. Montana* 1992).

6. STV is a simple system for voters. They simply rank candidates in order of their preference. A quota is then established on the basis of the number of votes cast and seats being contested. Winning candidates are those who receive a quota's worth of first-preference votes or who obtain a quota as a result of the transfer of subsequent preference votes. There are several formulas for transferring preferences. For an explanation of the transfer process, see Taagepera and Shugart 1989, 26–27.

7. In this respect, he echoed Justice Frankfurter's admonition in *Colegrove v. Green* 1946.

8. Mill went so far as to advocate plural voting for university graduates. See Mill 1994, xxxvi–xxxviii.

9. Ironically, despite assertions to the contrary, the search for the public interest ultimately unites Mill with Edmund Burke, who is frequently presented as Mill's antithesis (Lakeman 1984, 23). Mill is described by PR advocates as rebelling against the notion that elections were little more than opportunities for voters to express approval or disapproval of their legislators' performance. Yet, to the extent that Mill would limit the representatives' (and by extension, the electors') role, he echoes the thoughts of Edmund Burke, who, in his speech to the electors of Bristol, contended, that

> Parliament is not a *congress* of ambassadors from different and hostile interests, which interests each must maintain, as an agent and advocate, against other agents and advocates; but Parliament is a *deliberative* assembly of *one* nation, with *one* interest, that of the whole—where, not local purposes, not local prejudices, ought to guide, but the general good, resulting from the general reason of the whole. You choose a member indeed; but when you have chosen him, he is not a member of Bristol, but he is a member of *Parliament*. If the local constituent should have an interest, or should form a hasty opinion, evidently opposite to the real good of the rest of the community, the member for that place ought to be as far, as any other, from any endeavor to give it effect. (Pitkin 1969, 175–76)

10. Pitkin also concludes that the representative is bound to pursue the public interest: "The representative system must look after the public interest and be responsive to public opinion, except insofar as unresponsiveness can be justified in terms of the public interest" (1967, 224).

11. Ostrogorski did not compare European parties favorably to their American counterparts. Nonetheless, he offered a piercing criticism of the American party system.

12. In fact, voter apathy was widespread in the latest round of elections to the European Parliament. See "Europe's Voters" 1999.

13. These data are drawn from the Inter-Parliamentary Union's Web site, www.ipu.org, accessed October 2000.

14. Pinto-Duschinsky's analysis has raised several challenges. See Lijphart 1999a, Powell 1999, Shugart 1999, and Vowles 1999.

References

Abramson, Paul R., John H. Aldrich, and David W. Rohde. 1999. *Change and Continuity in the 1996 and 1998 Elections*. Washington, D.C.: CQ Press.

Adams, Greg D. 1996. "Legislative Effects of Single-Member vs. Multi-Member Districts." *American Journal of Political Science* 40 (February): 129–44.

Aguilar, Javier. 1998. "Congressional Redistricting in Texas: Time for a Change." *Stetson Law Review* 27 (Winter): 781–811.

Aleinikoff, T. Alexander, and Samuel Issacharoff. 1993. "Race and Redistricting: Drawing Constitutional Lines after *Shaw v. Reno*." *Michigan Law Review* 92 (December): 588–651.

Allen v. State Board of Elections. 1969. 393 U.S. 544.

Amy, Douglas J. 1993. *Real Choices/New Voices: The Case for Proportional Representation Elections in the United States*. New York: Columbia University Press.

———. 1996/1997. "The Forgotten History of the Single Transferable Vote in the United States." *Representation* 34 (Winter): 13–20.

Ansolabehere, Stephen, and Shanto Iyengar. 1995. *Going Negative: How Political Advertisements Shrink and Polarize the Electorate*. New York: Free Press.

Arden, Wayne, Bernard Grofman, and Lisa Handley. 1997. "The Impact of Redistricting on African-American Representation in the U.S. Congress and State Legislatures in the 1990s." *National Political Science Review* 6: 35–43.

Argersinger, Peter H. 1980. "'A Place on the Ballot': Fusion Politics and Antifusion Laws." *American Historical Review* 85: 287–306.

Arrington, Theodore S., and Gerald L. Ingalls. 1998. "The Limited Vote Alternative to Affirmative Districting." *Political Geography* 17 (August): 701–28.

Aspin, Larry T., and William K. Hall. 1996. "Cumulative Voting and Minority Candidates: An Analysis of the 1991 Peoria City Council Elections." *American Review of Politics* 17 (Fall): 225–44.

Attlesey, Sam. 1996. "David and Goliath Both Drive Pickup Trucks: Gramm, Morales Duel over Who's the Underdog." *Dallas Morning News,* July 7, 44A.

Australian Electoral Commission. 1985. *Community of Interest*. Research Report 3. Canberra: Australian Electoral Commission.

Avery v. Midland County. 1968. 390 U.S. 474.

Backstrom, Charles, Leonard Robins, and Scott Eller. 1990. "Establishing a Statewide

Electoral Effects Baseline." In *Political Gerrymandering and the Courts,* ed. Bernard Grofman. New York: Agathon Press.

Baker v. Carr. 1962. 369 U.S. 186.

Balinski, Michel, and H. Peyton Young. 1982. *Fair Representation.* New Haven: Yale University Press.

Ballot Access News. www.ballot-access.org/. Accessed October 2000.

Barber, Kathleen L. 1995. *Proportional Representation and Electoral Reform in Ohio.* Columbus: Ohio State University Press.

Barnett v. City of Chicago. 1998. 17 F. Supp. 2d 753 (N.D. Ill.).

———. 2000. __ F. Supp. 2d ___ (N.D. Ill.).

Beer v. United States. 1976. 425 U.S. 130.

Benoit, Kenneth, and Kenneth A. Shepsle. 1995. "Electoral Systems and Minority Representation." In *Classifying by Race,* ed. Paul E. Peterson. Princeton, N.J.: Princeton University Press.

Bibby, John F., and Thomas M. Holbrook. 1999. "Parties and Elections." In *Politics in the American States: A Comparative Analysis,* ed. Virginia Gray, Russell L. Hanson, and Herbert Jacob. Washington, D.C.: CQ Press.

Blair, George S. 1960. *Cumulative Voting: An Effective Electoral Device in Illinois Politics.* Urbana: University of Illinois Press.

Blais, André, and R. Kenneth Carty. 1990. "Does Proportional Representation Foster Voter Turnout?" *European Journal of Political Research* 18: 167–81.

Blais, André, and Louis Massicotte. 1996. "Electoral Systems." In *Comparing Democracies: Elections and Voting in Global Perspective,* ed. Lawrence LeDuc, Richard Niemi, and Pippa Norris. Thousand Oaks, Calif.: Sage.

Bloch, Stephen. 1998. "Cumulative Voting and the Religious Right: In the Best Interest of Democracy?" *Journal of Contemporary Law* 24: 1–34.

Boeckelman, Keith, William Arp III, and Bernard Terradot. 1995. "Messenger or Message? David Duke in the Louisiana Legislature." In *David Duke and the Politics of Race in the South,* ed. John C. Kuzenski, Charles S. Bullock III, and Ronald Keith Gaddie. Nashville, Tenn.: Vanderbilt University Press.

Bowden, Beth, and Lloyd Falck. 1996. "Redistribution and Representation: New Zealand's New Electoral System and the Role of the Political Commissioners." In *Fixing the Boundaries: Defining and Redefining Single-Member Electoral Districts,* ed. Iain McLean and David Butler. Aldershot, England: Dartmouth Publishing.

Brams, Steven J. 1976. *Paradoxes in Politics.* New York: Free Press.

Briffault, Richard. 1995. "Lani Guinier and the Dilemmas of American Democracy." *Columbia Law Review* 95 (March): 418–72.

Brinkley, Alan, Nelson W. Polsby, and Kathleen Sullivan. 1997. *New Federalist Papers: Essays in Defense of the Constitution.* New York: Norton.

Brischetto, Robert R. 1998. "Latino Voters and Redistricting in the New Millennium." In *Redistricting and Minority Representation: Learning from the Past, Preparing for the Future,* ed. David A. Bositis. Lanham, Md.: University Press of America.

Brischetto, Robert R., and Richard L. Engstrom. 1997. "Cumulative Voting and Latino Representation: Exit Surveys in 15 Texas Communities." *Social Science Quarterly* 78 (December): 973–91.

Brockington, David, Todd Donovan, Shaun Bowler, and Robert Brischetto. 1998.

"Minority Representation under Limited and Cumulative Voting." *Journal of Politics* 60 (November): 1108–25.

Buery, Richard R., Jr. 1999. "'Bizarre' Districts' Double Standard." *National Law Journal,* February 15, p. A21.

Burdick v. Takushi. 1992. 504 U.S. 428.

Bureau of the Census. 1995. *1992 Census of Governments. Vol. 1. Government Organization, No. 2. Popularly Elected Officials.* Washington, D.C.: U.S. Department of Commerce.

Burnham, R. A. 1997. "Reform, Politics, and Race in Cincinnati: Proportional Representation and the City Charter Committee, 1924–1959." *Journal of Urban History* 23 (January): 131–63.

Burton v. Sheheen. 1992. 793 F. Supp. 1329 (D. S.C.)

Busch, Andrew E. 1999. Prepared Statement Concerning H.R. 1173, States' Choice of Voting Systems Act, before the Subcommittee on the Constitution, Committee on the Judiciary, U.S. House of Representatives, Washington, D.C., September 23. Available at www.house.gov/judiciary/busc0923.htm.

Bush v. Vera. 1996. 517 U.S. 952.

Butler, David, and Bruce E. Cain. 1992. *Congressional Redistricting: Comparative and Theoretical Perspectives.* New York: Macmillan.

Butler, David, and Iain McLean. 1996. "The Redrawing of Parliamentary Boundaries in Britain." In *Fixing the Boundaries: Defining and Redefining Single-Member Electoral Districts,* ed. Iain McLean and David Butler. Aldershot, England: Dartmouth Publishing.

Bybee, Keith J. 1998. *Mistaken Identities: The Supreme Court and the Politics of Minority Representation.* Princeton, N.J.: Princeton University Press.

Cain, Bruce E., and Kenneth P. Miller. 1998. "Voting Rights Mismatch: The Challenge of Applying the Voting Rights Act to 'Other Minorities.'" In *Voting Rights and Redistricting in the United States,* ed. Mark E. Rush. Westport, Conn.: Greenwood Press.

Campbell, James E. 1996. *Cheap Seats: The Democratic Party's Advantage in U.S. House Elections.* Columbus: Ohio State University Press.

Canady, Charles T. 1999. Statement of Chairman Charles T. Canady, Hearing on H.R. 1173: The States' Choice of Voting Systems Act, September 23. Available at www.house.gov/judiciary/cana0923.htm.

Canon, David T. 1999a. "Electoral Systems and the Representation of Minority Interests in Legislatures." *Legislative Studies Quarterly* 24 (August): 331–85.

———. 1999b. *Race, Redistricting, and Representation: The Unintended Consequences of Black Majority Districts.* Chicago: University of Chicago Press.

Carstairs, Andrew M. 1980. *A Short History of Electoral Systems in Western Europe.* Boston: George Allen & Unwin.

Ceaser, James. 1982. *Reforming the Reforms.* Cambridge, Mass.: Ballinger.

Chen v. City of Houston. 2000. 206 F. 3d 502 (5th Cir.).

Cirincione, Carmen, Thomas A. Darling, and Timothy G. O'Rourke. 2000. "Assessing South Carolina's 1990s Congressional Districting." *Political Geography* 19 (February): 189–211.

City of Mobile v. Bolden. 1980. 446 U.S. 55.

Clegg, Roger. 1999. Prepared Statement Concerning H.R. 1173, States' Choice of Voting Systems Act, before the Subcommittee on the Constitution, Committee on the Judiciary, U.S. House of Representatives, Washington, D.C., September 23.

Cleveland County Association for Government by the People v. Cleveland County Board of Commissioners. 1997. 965 F. Supp. 72 (D.C. D.C.).

———. 142 F. 3d 468 (D.C. Cir.).

Clymer, Adam. 1991. "Republicans Gain as States Battle over Redistricting." *New York Times,* December 30, A1, A13.

Cole, Richard L., and Delbert A. Taebel. 1992. "Cumulative Voting in Local Elections: Lessons from the Alamogordo Experience." *Social Science Quarterly* 73 (March): 194–201.

Cole, Richard L., Richard L. Engstrom, and Delbert A. Taebel. 1990. "Cumulative Voting in a Municipal Election: A Note on Voter Reactions and Electoral Consequences." *Western Political Quarterly* 43 (March): 191–99.

Colegrove v. Green. 1946. 328 U.S. 549.

Collet, Christian, and Jerrold Hansen. 1996. "Minor Parties and Candidates in Sub-Presidential Elections." In *The State of the Parties: The Changing Role of Contemporary American Parties,* ed. John C. Green and Daniel M. Shea. 2d ed. Lanham, Md.: Rowman & Littlefield.

Cromartie v. Hunt. 1998. U.S. Dist. LEXIS 7767 (E.D. N.C.).

———. 2000. __ F. Supp. 2d __ (E.D. N.C.)

Cummings v. Meskill. 1972. 341 F. Supp. 139 (D. Conn.).

Davidson, Chandler. 1989. *Minority Vote Dilution.* Washington, D.C.: Howard University Press.

Davidson, Chandler, and Luis Fraga. 1989. "Nonpartisan Slating Groups in an At-Large Setting." In *Minority Vote Dilution,* ed. Chandler Davidson. Washington, D.C.: Howard University Press.

Davidson, Chandler, and George Korbel. 1989. "At-Large Elections and Minority Group Representation." In *Minority Vote Dilution,* ed. Chandler Davidson. Washington, D.C.: Howard University Press.

Davis v. Bandemer. 1986. 478 U.S. 109.

De la Garza, Rudolfo O., Louis DeSipio, F. Chris Garcia, John Garcia, and Angelo Falcon. 1992. *Latino Voices: Mexican, Puerto Rican, and Cuban Perspectives on American Politics.* Boulder, Colo.: Westview Press.

DeLeon, Richard E., Lisel Blash, and Steven Hill. 1997. "The Politics of Electoral Reform in San Francisco: Preference Voting versus Districts versus Plurality At-Large." Paper presented at the 1977 Annual Meeting of the Western Political Science Association, March 13–15, Tucson, Ariz.

DeLeon, Richard E., Steven Hill, and Lisel Blash. 1998. "The Campaign for Proposition H and Preference Voting in San Francisco, 1996." *Representation* 35 (Winter): 265–74.

DeSipio, Louis. 1996. *Counting on the Latino Vote: Latinos as a New Electorate.* Charlottesville: University of Virginia Press.

DeWitt v. Wilson. 1994. 856 F. Supp. 1409 (E.D. Cal.).

———. 1995. 515 U.S. 1170.

Diaz v. Silver. 1997. 978 F. Supp. 96 (E.D. N.Y.).

Dillard v. Chilton County Board of Education. 1988. 699 F. Supp. 870 (M.D. Ala.)

Dixon, Robert G., Jr. 1968. *Democratic Representation: Reapportionment in Law and Politics.* New York: Oxford University Press.

———. 1971a. "The Court, the People, and 'One Man, One Vote.'" In *Reapportionment in the 1970s,* ed. Nelson W. Polsby. Berkeley and Los Angeles: University of California Press.

———. 1971b. "Rejoinder." In *Reapportionment in the 1970s,* ed. Nelson W. Polsby. Berkeley and Los Angeles: University of California Press.

Donze, Frank. 1999. "Boissiere, Cade Get Down and Dirty." *New Orleans Times-Picayune,* March 3, B1–B2.

Downs, Anthony. 1957. "An Economic Theory of Political Action in a Democracy." *Journal of Political Economy* 65: 135–50.

Duke v. Massey. 1996. 87 F. 3d 1226.

Dunn, Charles W. 1972. "Cumulative Voting Problems in Illinois Legislative Elections." *Harvard Journal of Legislation* 9 (May): 627–65.

Duverger, Maurice. 1984. "Which Is the Best Electoral System?" In *Choosing an Electoral System,* ed. Arend Lijphart and Bernard Grofman. New York: Praeger.

———. 1986. "Duverger's Law: Forty Years Later." In *Electoral Laws and Their Political Consequences,* ed. Bernard Grofman and Arend Lijphart.

Eagles, Munroe, Richard S. Katz, and David Mark. 1999. "GIS and Redistricting: Emergent Technologies, Social Geography, and Political Sensibilities." *Social Science Computer Review* 17 (Spring): 5–9.

———. 2000. "Controversies in Political Redistricting: GIS, Geography, and Society." *Political Geography* 19 (February): 135–39.

Electoral Reform Society. 1996. *Report on the San Francisco Voting Reform Referendum 96.* London: Electoral Reform Society.

Ellison, Mary. 1991. "David Duke and the Race for the Governor's Mansion." *Race and Class* 33 (October–December): 71–79.

Engstrom, Richard L. 1977. "The Supreme Court and Equi-Populous Gerrymandering: A Remaining Obstacle in the Quest for Fair and Effective Representation." *Arizona State Law Journal* 1976 (2): 277–319.

———. 1980. "The Hale Boggs Gerrymander: Congressional Redistricting, 1969." *Louisiana History* 21 (Winter): 59–66.

———. 1990. "Cincinnati's Proportional Representation Initiative." *Electoral Studies* 9 (September): 217–25.

———. 1992a. "Modified Multi-Seat Election Systems as Remedies for Minority Vote Dilution." *Stetson Law Review* 21 (Summer): 743–70.

———. 1992b. "Councilmanic Redistricting Conflicts: The Dallas Experience." *Urban News* 6 (Fall): 1, 4–8.

———. 1993. "The Single Transferable Vote: An Alternative Remedy for Minority Vote Dilution." *University of San Francisco Law Review* 27 (Summer): 781–813.

———. 1994. "The Voting Rights Act: Disfranchisement, Dilution, and Alternative Election Systems." *P.S.: Political Science and Politics* 27 (December): 685–88.

———. 1995a. "Voting Rights Districts: Debunking the Myths." *Campaigns and Elections* 16 (April): 24, 46.

————. 1995b. "*Shaw, Miller,* and the Districting Thicket." *National Civic Review* 84 (Fall–Winter): 323–36.

————. 1998. "Minority Electoral Opportunities and Alternative Election Systems in the United States." In *Voting Rights and Redistricting in the United States,* ed. Mark E. Rush. Westport, Conn.: Greenwood Press.

————. 1999. Review of *Race, Redistricting, and Representation,* by David T. Canon. *Law and Politics Book Review* 9 (October): 467–71.

————. 2000. "Electoral Arrangements and Minority Political Incorporation." In *Minority Politics at the Millennium,* ed. Richard Kaiser and Katherine Underwood. New York: Garland Publishing.

Engstrom, Richard L., and Charles J. Barrilleaux. 1991. "Native Americans and Cumulative Voting: The Sisseton Wahpeton Sioux." *Social Science Quarterly* 72 (June): 388–93.

Engstrom, Richard L., and Robert R. Brischetto. 1998. "Is Cumulative Voting Too Complex? Evidence from Exit Polls." *Stetson Law Review* 27 (Winter): 813–34.

Engstrom, Richard L., and Jason F. Kirksey. 1998. "Race and Representational Redistricting in Louisiana." In *Race and Redistricting in the 1990s,* ed. Bernard Grofman. New York: Agathon Press.

Engstrom, Richard L., and Michael D. McDonald. 1987. "The Election of Blacks to Southern City Councils: The Dominant Impact of Election Arrangements." In *Blacks in Southern Politics,* ed. Robert P. Steed, Laurence W. Moreland, and Todd A. Baker. New York: Praeger.

————. 1993. "'Enhancing' Factors in At Large Plurality and Majority Systems: A Reconsideration." *Electoral Studies* 12: 385–401.

Engstrom, Richard L., Jason F. Kirksey, and Edward Still. 1997a. "Limited and Cumulative Voting in Alabama: An Assessment after Two Rounds of Elections." *National Political Science Review* 6: 180–91.

————. 1997b. "One Person, Seven Votes: The Cumulative Voting Experience in Chilton County, Alabama." In *Affirmative Action and Representation: Shaw v. Reno and the Future of Voting Rights,* ed. Anthony A. Peacock. Durham, N.C.: Carolina Academic Press.

Engstrom, Richard L., Delbert A. Taebel, and Richard L. Cole. 1989. "Cumulative Voting as a Remedy for Minority Vote Dilution: The Case of Alamogordo, New Mexico." *Journal of Law and Politics* 5 (Spring): 469–97.

Erie, Stephen P. 1988. *Rainbow's End: Irish-Americans and the Dilemmas of Urban Machine Politics, 1840–1985.* Berkeley and Los Angeles: University of California Press.

"Europe's Voters Stay at Home." 1999. *Economist,* June 19, 1999, 51–52.

Evans, Eldon Cobb. 1917. *A History of the Australian Ballot System in the United States.* Chicago: University of Chicago Press.

Everett, H. Robinson. 1999. Prepared Statement Concerning H.R. 1173, States' Choice of Voting Systems Act, before the Subcommittee on the Constitution, Committee on the Judiciary, U.S. House of Representatives, Washington, D.C., September 23. Available at www.house.gov/judiciary/ever0923.htm.

Everson, David H. 1992. "The Impact of Term Limitations on the States: Cutting the

Underbrush or Chopping Down the Tall Timber?" In *Limiting Legislative Terms,* ed. Gerald Benjamin and Michael Malbin. Washington, D.C.: CQ Press.

Everson, David H., Joan A. Parker, William L. Day, Rita A. Harmony, and Kent D. Redfield. 1982. *The Cutback Amendment.* Illinois Issues Special Report. Sangamon State University, Springfield, Ill.

Farrell, David M. 1997. *Comparing Electoral Systems.* London: Prentice Hall/Harvester Wheatsheaf.

Farrell, David M., and Michael Gallagher. 1999. "British Voters and Their Criteria for Evaluating Electoral Systems." *British Journal of Politics and International Relations* 1 (October): 293–316.

Fenno, Richard. 1978. *Homestyle: House Members in Their Districts.* Boston: Little, Brown.

Fiorina, Morris. 1989. *Congress: Keystone of the Washington Establishment.* 2d ed. New Haven: Yale University Press.

Fleischmann, Arnold. 2000. "Can Cities Be Elastic and Democratic, Too?" In *Minority Politics at the Millennium,* ed. Richard A. Keiser and Katherine Underwood. New York: Garland Publishing.

Franklin, Mark. 1996. "Electoral Participation," In *Comparing Democracies: Elections and Voting in Global Perspective,* ed. Lawrence LeDuc, Richard Niemi, and Pippa Norris,Thousand Oaks, Calif.: Sage.

Fredman, L. E. 1968. *The Australian Ballot: The Story of an American Reform.* Lansing: Michigan State University Press.

Frymer, Paul. 1999. *Uneasy Alliances: Race and Party Competition in America.* Princeton, N.J.: Princeton University Press.

Gaffney v. Cummings. 1973. 412 U.S. 735.

Gelman, Andrew, and Gary King. 1996. "Advantages of Conflictual Redistricting." In *Fixing the Boundaries: Defining and Redefining Single-Member Electoral Districts,* ed. Iain McLean and David Butler. Aldershot, England: Dartmouth Publishing.

Gerber, Elisabeth, Rebecca B. Morton, and Thomas A. Rietz. 1998. "Minority Representation in Multimember Districts." *American Political Science Review* 92 (March): 127–44.

Gomillion v. Lightfoot. 1960. 364 U.S. 339.

Griffith, Elmer C. 1907. *The Rise and Development of the Gerrymander.* Chicago: Scott, Foresman.

Grofman, Bernard. 1985. "Criteria for Districting: A Social Science Perspective." *UCLA Law Review* 33 (October): 77–184.

Grofman, Bernard, and Chandler Davidson. 1994. "The Effect of Municipal Election Structure on Black Representation in Eight Southern States." In *Quiet Revolution in the South: The Impact of the Voting Rights Act, 1965–1990,* ed. Chandler Davidson and Bernard Grofman. Princeton, N.J.: Princeton University Press.

Grofman, Bernard, and Lisa Handley. 1992. "Preconditions for Black and Hispanic Congressional Success." In *United States Electoral Systems: Their Impact on Women and Minorities,* ed. Wilma Rule and Joseph F. Zimmerman. New York: Greenwood Press.

Gronke, Paul, and J. Matthew Wilson. 1999. "Competing Redistricting Plans as Evidence of Political Motives: The North Carolina Case." *American Politics Quarterly* 27 (April): 147–76.

Growe v. Emison. 1993. 507 U.S. 25.

Guinier, Lani. 1991. "The Triumph of Tokenism: The Voting Rights Act and the Theory of Black Electoral Success."*Michigan Law Review* 89: 1077–1154.

———. 1994a. "Erasing Democracy: The Voting Rights Cases."*Harvard Law Review* 108: 109–37.

———. 1994b. *The Tyranny of the Majority: Fundamental Fairness in Representative Democracy.* New York: Free Press.

———. 1998. *Lift Every Voice: Turning a Civil Rights Setback into a New Vision of Social Justice.* New York: Simon & Schuster.

———. 1999. Foreword to *Reflecting All of Us: The Case for Proportional Representation,* ed. Robert Richie and Steven Hill. Boston: Beacon Press.

Hadley v. Junior College District of Metropolitan Kansas City. 1970. 397 U.S. 50.

Hamilton, Alexander, et al. 1961. *The Federalist Papers,* ed. Clinton Rossiter. New York: Mentor.

Handley, Lisa, and Bernard Grofman. 1994. "The Impact of the Voting Rights Act on Minority Representation: Black Officeholding in Southern State Legislatures and Congressional Delegations." In *Quiet Revolution in the South: The Impact of the Voting Rights Act, 1965–1990,* ed. Chandler Davidson and Bernard Grofman. Princeton, N.J.: Princeton University Press.

Handley, Lisa, Bernard Grofman, and Wayne Arden. 1998. "Electing Minority-Preferred Candidates to Legislative Office: The Relationship between Minority Percentages in Districts and the Election of Minority-Preferred Candidates." In *Race and Redistricting in the 1990s,* ed. Bernard Grofman. New York: Agathon Press.

Hanson, Royce. 1966. *The Political Thicket: Reapportionment and Constitutional Democracy.* Englewood Cliffs, N.J.: Prentice-Hall.

Hardy-Fanta, Carol. 1993. *Latina Politics, Latino Politics: Gender, Culture, and Political Participation in Boston.* Philadelphia: Temple University Press.

Hare, Thomas. 1857. *The Machinery of Representation.* London: W. Maxwell.

Harper v. City of Chicago Heights and the Chicago Heights Election Commission. 2000. 223 F. 3d 593 (7th Cir.)

Hasen, Richard L. 1999. "Election Law at Puberty: Optimism and Words of Caution." *Loyola of Los Angeles Law Review* 32 (June): 1095–1103.

Hastert v. State Board of Elections. 1991. 777 F. Supp. 634 (N.D. Ill.).

Hays v. State of Louisiana. 1993. 839 F. Supp. 1188 (W.D. La.).

———. 1994. 862 F. Supp. 119 (W.D. La.).

———. 1996. 936 F. Supp. 360 (W.D. La.).

Hebert, J. Gerald, Donald B. Verrilli Jr., Paul M. Smith, Sam Hirsch, and Heather K. Gerken. 1998. "The Realist's Guide to Redistricting: Avoiding the Legal Pitfalls." In *Redistricting and Minority Representation: Learning from the Past, Preparing for the Future,* ed. David A. Bositis. Lanham, Md.: University Press of America.

Hill, Lance. 1992. "Nazi Race Doctrine in the Political Thought of David Duke." In *The Emergence of David Duke and the Politics of Race,* ed. Douglas Rose. Chapel Hill: University of North Carolina Press.

Hirczy de Mino, Wolfgang. 1996. "Malta: STV in a Two-Party System." Paper presented at the Conference on Elections in Australia, Ireland, and Malta under the Single Transferable Vote, sponsored by the University of California at Irvine Center for the Study of Democracy, Laguna Beach, Calif., December 14–15.

Hodgkiss, Anita. 1999. Prepared Statement Concerning H.R. 1173, States' Choice of Voting Systems Act, before the Subcommittee on the Constitution, Committee on the Judiciary, U.S. House of Representatives, Washington, D.C., September 23. Available at www.house.gov/judiciary/hodg0923.htm.

Holder v. Hall. 1994. 512 U.S. 874.

Holmes, Robert A. 1998. "Reapportionment Strategies in the 1990s: The Case of Georgia." In *Race and Redistricting in the 1990s,* ed. Bernard Grofman. New York: Agathon Press.

Horowitz, Donald L. 1994. Affidavit. *Cane, et al. v. Worcester County, Md., et al.* Case No. Y92-3226 (D.C. Md.).

Hosler, Karen. 1999. "State Elections Could Reshape Congress." *New Orleans Times-Picayune.* December 30, A3.

Hunt v. Cromartie. 1999. 562 U.S. 541.

———. 2000. __ U.S. __.

Inman, Mary A. 1993. "C.P.R. (Change through Proportional Representation): Resuscitating a Federal Electoral System." *University of Pennsylvania Law Review* 141 (May): 1991–2053.

In re: Constitutionality of S.J.R. 2G. 1992. 597 So. 2d 576 (Fla.).

Issacharoff, Samuel. 1995. "The Constitutional Contours of Race and Politics." In *The Supreme Court Review 1995,* ed. Dennis J. Hutchinson, David A. Strauss, and Geoffrey R. Stone. Chicago: University of Chicago Press.

Issacharoff, Samuel, and Richard H. Pildes. 1998. "Politics as Markets: Partisan Lock-ups of the Democratic Process." *Stanford Law Review* 50: 643–717.

Jackman, Robert W. 1987. "Political Institutions and Turnout in the Industrialized Democracies." *American Political Science Review* 81: 405–24.

Jennings, Keith, and Clarence Lusane. 1994. "The State and Future of Black/Latino Relations in Washington, D.C.: A Bridge in Need of Repair." In *Blacks, Latinos, and Asians in Urban America: Status and Prospects for Politics and Activism,* ed. James Jennings. Westport, Conn.: Praeger.

Jewell, Malcolm E. 1955. "Constitutional Provisions for State Legislative Apportionment." *Western Political Quarterly* 8 (June): 271–79.

Jewett, Aubrey. 2000. "Republican Strength in a Southern Legislature: The Impact of 'One Person, One Vote' Redistricting in Florida." *American Review of Politics* 21 (Spring): 1–18.

Johnson v. DeGrandy. 1994. 512 U.S. 997.

Johnson v. Knowles. 1997. 522 U.S. 1996.

Johnson v. Miller. 1994. Civil Action No. 194-008 (S.D. Ga.).

———. 1994. 864 F. Supp. 1354 (S.D. Ga.).

———. 1995. 922 F. Supp. 1556 (S.D. Ga.)

Johnson v. Mortham. 1996. 926 F. Supp. 1460 (N.D. Fla.).

Johnston, R. J., D. J. Rossiter, and C. J. Pattie. 1996. "How Well Did They Do? The Boundary Commissions at the Third and Fourth Periodic Reviews." In *Fixing the*

Boundaries: Defining and Redefining Single-Member Electoral Districts, ed. Iain McLean and David Butler. Aldershot, England: Dartmouth Publishing.

Kaelin v. Warden. 1971. 334 F. Supp. 602 (E.D. Pa.).

Karlan, Pamela S. 1989. "Maps and Misreadings: The Role of Geographical Compactness in Racial Vote Dilution Litigation." *Harvard Civil Rights–Civil Liberties Law Review* 24 (1): 173–248.

———. 1993. "The Rights to Vote: Some Pessimism about Formalism." *Texas Law Review* 71: 1705–1740.

———. 1998. "The Fire Next Time: Reapportionment after the 2000 Census." *Stanford Law Review* 50 (February): 729–63.

Katz, Joseph L. 1994. Report of Dr. Joseph L. Katz in *Johnson v. Miller,* Civil Action No. 194-008 (S.D. Ga.).

Katz, Richard S. 1986. "Intraparty Preference Voting." In *Electoral Laws and Their Political Consequences,* ed. Bernard Grofman and Arend Lijphart. New York: Agathon Press.

———. 1997. *Democracy and Elections.* New York: Oxford University Press.

———. 1998. "Malapportionment and Gerrymandering in Other Countries and Alternative Electoral Systems." In *Voting Rights and Redistricting in the United States,* ed. Mark E. Rush. Westport, Conn.: Greenwood Press.

———. 1999. "Electoral Reform Is Not as Simple As It Looks." In *Making Every Vote Count: Reassessing Canada's Electoral System,* ed. Henry Milner. Peterborough, Ont.: Broadview Press.

Katz, Richard S., and Robin Kolodny. 1994. "Party Organizations as an Empty Vessel: Parties in American Politics." In *How Parties Organize: Change and Adaptation in Party Organizations in Western Democracies,* ed. Richard S. Katz and Peter Mair. Thousand Oaks, Calif.: Sage.

Katz, Richard S., and Peter Mair, eds. 1994. *How Parties Organize: Change and Adaptation in Party Organizations in Western Democracies.* Thousand Oaks, Calif.: Sage, 1994.

———. 1995. "Changing Models of Party Organization and Party Democracy: The Emergence of the Cartel Party." *Party Politics* 1: 5–28.

Kelly, Lisa A. 1996. "Race and Place: Geographic and Transcendent Community in the Post-*Shaw* Era." *Vanderbilt Law Review* 49 (March): 227–308.

King v. Illinois Board of Elections. 1998. 522 U.S. 1087.

King v. State Board of Elections. 1996. 979 F. Supp. 582 (N.D. Ill.).

———. 1997. 979 F. Supp. 619 (N.D. Ill.).

Kousser, J. Morgan. 1998. "Reapportionment Wars: Party, Race, and Redistricting in California, 1971–1992." In *Race and Redistricting in the 1990s,* ed. Bernard Grofman. New York: Agathon Press.

———. 1999. *Colorblind Injustice: Minority Voting Rights and the Undoing of the Second Reconstruction.* Chapel Hill: University of North Carolina Press.

Kubin, Jeffrey C. 1997. "The Case for Redistricting Commissions." *Texas Law Review* 75 (March): 837–72.

Kuklinski, James. 1973. "Cumulative and Plurality Voting: An Analysis of Illinois' Unique Electoral System." *Western Political Quarterly* 26 (December): 726–46.

LaComb v. Growe. 1982. 541 F. Supp. 145.

Lakeman, Enid. 1984. "The Case for Proportional Representation." In *Choosing an Electoral System,* ed. Arend Lijphart and Bernard Grofman. New York: Praeger.

Lawyer v. Department of Justice. 1997. 521 U.S. 567.

Leib, Jonathan. 1998. "Communities of Interest and Minority Districting after *Miller v. Johnson.*" *Political Geography* 17 (6): 683–99.

Lennertz, James E. 2000. "Back in Their Proper Place: Racial Gerrymandering in Georgia." *Political Geography* 19 (February): 163–88.

Lewyn, Michael E. 1995. "When Is Cumulative Voting Preferable to Single Member Districting?" *New Mexico Law Review* 25: 197–227.

Lichtman, Allan J. 1994a. *Report on Issues Relating to Georgia Congressional Districts.* Johnson v. Miller, Civil Action No. 194-008 (S.D. Ga.).

———. 1994b. *Supplemental Report: Issues Relating to Georgia Congressional Districts.* Johnson v. Miller, Civil Action No. 194-008 (S.D. Ga.).

Lijphart, Arend. 1991. "Constitutional Choices for New Democracies." *Journal of Democracy* 2 (Winter): 72–84.

———. 1997. "Unequal Participation: Democracy's Unresolved Dilemma." *American Political Science Review* 91 (March): 1–14.

———. 1999a. "First-Past-the-Post, PR, and the Empirical Evidence." *Representation* 36 (Summer): 133–36.

———. 1999b. *Patterns of Democracy: Government Forms and Performance in Thirty-six Countries.* New Haven: Yale University Press.

Lilley, William III, Laurence J. DeFranco, and William M. Diefenderfer III. 1994. *The Almanac of State Legislatures.* Washington, D.C.: Congressional Quarterly.

LoFrisco v. Schaffer. 1972. 341 F. Supp. 743 (D. Conn.).

Lowi, Theodore J. 1999. "Toward a Responsible Three-Party System: Plan or Obituary?" In *The State of the Parties: The Changing Role of Contemporary American Parties,* ed. John C. Green and Daniel M. Shea. 3d ed. Lanham, Md.: Rowman & Littlefield.

Lublin, David. 1997. "The Election of African Americans and Latinos to the U.S. House of Representatives, 1972–1994." *American Politics Quarterly* 25 (July): 269–86.

Lublin, David, and D. Stephen Voss. 2000. "Racial Redistricting and Realignment in Southern State Legislatures." *American Journal of Political Science* 44 (October): 792–810.

Lucas v. The Forty Fourth General Assembly District of the State of Colorado. 1964. 377 U.S. 713.

Lyons, Michael, and Peter F. Galderisi. 1995. "Incumbency, Reapportionment, and U.S. House Redistricting." *Political Research Quarterly* 48 (December): 857–71.

Lyons, W. E. 1970. *One Man, One Vote.* Toronto: McGraw-Hill.

Lyons, W. E., and Malcolm E. Jewell. 1986. "Redrawing Council Districts in American Cities." *State and Local Government Review* 18 (Spring): 71–81.

Macchiarola, Frank J., and Joseph G. Diaz. 1993. "The 1990 New York City Districting Commission: Renewed Opportunity for Participation in Local Government or Race-Based Gerrymandering?" *Cardozo Law Review* 14 (April): 1175–1235.

MacIver, Heather. 1999. "A Brief Introduction to Electoral Reform." In *Making Every Vote Count: Reassessing Canada's Electoral System,* ed. Henry Milner. Peterborough, Ont.: Broadview Press.

Magleby, David B. 2000. *Outside Money: Soft Money and Issue Advocacy in the 1998 Congressional Elections.* Lanham, Md.: Rowman & Littlefield.

Maley, Michael, Trevor Morling, and Robin Bell. 1996. "Alternative Ways of Redistricting with Single-Member Seats: The Case of Australia." In *Fixing the Boundaries: Defining and Redefining Single-Member Electoral Districts,* ed. Iain McLean and David Butler. Aldershot, England: Dartmouth Publishing.

Malone, Stephen J. 1997. "Recognizing Communities of Interest in a Legislative Apportionment Plan." *Virginia Law Review* 83 (March): 461–92.

Marable, Manning. 1994. "Building Coalitions among Communities of Color: Beyond Racial Identity Politics." In *Blacks, Latinos, and Asians in Urban America: Status and Prospects for Politics and Activism,* ed. James Jennings. Westport, Conn.: Praeger.

McClain, Paula D. 1996. "Coalition and Competition: Patterns of Black–Latino Relations in Urban Politics." In *The Politics of Minority Coalitions: Race, Ethnicity, and Shared Uncertainties,* ed. Wilbur Rich. Westport, Conn.: Praeger.

McCoy v. Chicago Heights. 1998. 6 F. Supp. 2d 973 (N.D. Ill.).

McDonald, Michael D., and Richard L. Engstrom. 1992. "Minority Representation and City Council Electoral Systems: A Black and Hispanic Comparison." In *Ethnic and Racial Minorities in Advanced Industrial Democracies,* ed. Anthony M. Messina, Luis R. Fraga, Laurie A. Rhodebeck, and Frederick D. Wright. New York: Greenwood Press.

McKaskle, Paul L. 1995. "The Voting Rights Act and the 'Conscientious Redistricter.'" *University of San Francisco Law Review* 30 (Fall): 1–94.

————. 1998. "Of Wasted Votes and No Influence: An Essay on Voting Systems in the United States." *Houston Law Review* 35 (Winter): 1119–1205.

McKinney, Cynthia. 1999. "Keep It Simple." In *Reflecting All of Us: The Case for Proportional Representation,* ed. Robert Richie and Steven Hill. Boston: Beacon Press.

Merriam, Charles W., and Louise Overacker. 1928. *Primary Elections.* Chicago: University of Chicago Press.

Mill, John Stuart. 1994. *Utilitarianism, On Liberty, Considerations on Representative Government,* ed. Geraint Williams. London: Everyman.

Miller v. Johnson. 1995. 515 U.S. 900.

Milner, Henry. 1999. "The Case for Proportional Representation." In *Making Every Vote Count: Reassessing Canada's Electoral System,* ed. Henry Milner. Peterborough, Ont.: Broadview Press.

Morrill, Richard L. 1990. "A Geographer's Perspective." In *Political Gerrymandering and the Courts,* ed. Bernard Grofman. New York: Agathon Press.

————. 1994. "Electoral Geography and Gerrymandering: Space and Politics." In *Reordering the World: Geopolitical Perspectives,* ed. G. J. Demko and W. B. Wood. Boulder,Colo.: Westview Press.

————. 1996a. "Territory, Community, and Collective Representation." *Social Science Quarterly* 77 (March): 3-5.

————. 1996b. "Spatial Engineering and Geographical Integrity." *Political Geography* 15 (1): 95–97.

Morse v. Republican Party of Virginia. 1994. 517 U.S. 186.

Mulroy, Steven J. 1995. "Limited, Cumulative Evidence: Divining Justice Department Positions on Alternative Electoral Systems." *National Civic Review* 84 (Winter): 66–71.

————. 1998. "The Way Out: A Legal Standard for Imposing Alternative Electoral Systems as Voting Rights Remedies." *Harvard Civil Rights–Civil Liberties Law Review* 33 (Summer): 333–80.

————. 1999. "Alternative Ways Out: A Remedial Road Map for the Use of Alternative Electoral Systems as Voting Rights Remedies." *North Carolina Law Review* 77 (June): 1867–1924.

Niemi, Richard G., Bernard Grofman, Carl Carlucci, and Thomas Hofeller. 1990. "Measuring Compactness and the Role of a Compactness Standard in a Test for Partisan and Racial Gerrymandering." *Journal of Politics* 52 (November): 1155–81.

Niemi, Richard G., Simon Jackman, and Laura R. Winsky. 1991. "Candidacies and Competitiveness in Multimember Districts." *Legislative Studies Quarterly* 16 (February): 91–109.

Note. 1966. "Reapportionment." *Harvard Law Review* 79 (April): 1228–87.

Note. 1981. "Affirmative Action and Electoral Reform." *Yale Law Journal* 90 (July): 1811–32.

Note. 1982. "Alternative Voting Systems as Remedies for Unlawful At-Large Systems." *Yale Law Journal* 92 (November): 144–60.

Oren v. Foster. 1999. CIV No. 96-3130 (M.D. La.).

Orloski v. Davis. 1983. 564 F. Supp. 526 (M.D. Pa.).

O'Rourke, Timothy G. 1995. "*Shaw v. Reno:* The Shape of Things to Come." *Rutgers Law Review* (Spring): 723–73.

————. 1998. "The Impact of Reapportionment on Congress and State Legislatures." In *Voting Rights and Redistricting in the United States,* ed. Mark E. Rush. Westport, Conn.: Greenwood Press.

Ostrogorski, Moise. 1910. *Democracy and the Party System in the United States: A Study in Extra-constitutional Government.* New York: Macmillan.

Partridge, Hilary. 1998. *Italian Politics Today.* Manchester: Manchester University Press.

Peretz, Don, and Gideon Doron. 1997. *The Government and Politics of Israel.* 3d ed. Boulder, Colo.: Westview Press.

Persily, Nathaniel. 1999. Prepared Statement Concerning H.R. 1173, States' Choice of Voting Systems Act, before the Subcommittee on the Constitution, Committee on the Judiciary, U.S. House of Representatives, Washington, D.C., September 23. Available at www.house.gov/judiciary/pers0923.htm.

Petrocik, John R., and Scott W. Desposato. 1998. "The Partisan Consequences of Majority-Minority Redistricting in the South, 1992 and 1994." *Journal of Politics* 60 (August): 613–33.

Pildes, Richard H., and Kristen A. Donoghue. 1995. "Cumulative Voting in the United States." *University of Chicago Legal Forum* (1995): 241–313.

Pildes, Richard H., and Richard G. Niemi. 1993. "Expressive Harms, 'Bizarre Districts,' and Voting Rights: Evaluating Election-District Appearances after *Shaw v. Reno.*" *Michigan Law Review* 92 (December): 483–587.

Pinto-Duschinsky, Michael. 1999a. "Send the Rascals Packing: Defects of Proportional Representation and the Virtues of the Westminster Model." *Representation* 36 (Summer): 117–26.

———. 1999b. "A Reply to the Critics." *Representation* 36 (Summer): 148–55.

Pitkin, Hanna. 1967. *The Concept of Representation.* Berkeley and Los Angeles: University of California Press.

———. 1969. *Representation.* New York: Atherton Press.

Polsby, Daniel D., and Robert D. Popper. 1993. "Ugly: An Inquiry into the Problem of Racial Gerrymandering under the Voting Rights Act." *Michigan Law Review* 92: 652–82.

Polsby, Nelson W. 1983. *The Consequences of Party Reform.* New York: Oxford University Press.

Pope v. Blue. 1992. 809 F. Supp. 392 (W.D. N.C.).

Powell, G. Bingham. 1986. "American Voter Turnout in Comparative Perspective." *American Political Science Review* 80: 17–43.

———. 1999. "Westminster Model versus PR: Normative and Empirical Assessments." *Representation* 36 (Summer): 127–32.

Powell, Lawrence N. 1992. "Slouching toward Baton Rouge: The 1989 Legislative Election of David Duke." In *The Emergence of David Duke and the Politics of Race,* ed. Douglas Rose. Chapel Hill: University of North Carolina Press.

Rae, Douglas W. 1971. *The Political Consequences of Electoral Laws.* 2d ed. New Haven: Yale University Press.

Rae, Douglas W., Victor Hanby, and John Loosemore. 1971. "Thresholds of Representation and Thresholds of Exclusion: An Analytic Note on Electoral Systems." *Comparative Political Studies* 3 (January): 479–88.

Ramirez, Deborah. 1995. "Multicultural Empowerment: It's Not Just Black and White Anymore." *Stanford Law Review* 47 (May): 957–92.

Raskin, Jamin. 1998. "The Supreme Court's Racial Double Standard in Redistricting: Unequal Protection in Politics and the Scholarship that Defends It." *Journal of Law and Politics* 14: 591–665.

Raskin, Jamin, and John Bonifaz. 1993. "Equal Protection and the Wealth Primary." *Yale Law and Policy Review* 11: 273–332.

Reed, Judith. 1992. "Of Boroughs, Boundaries, and Bullwinkles: The Limitations of Single-Member Districts in a Multiracial Context." *Fordham Urban Law Journal* 19 (Spring): 759–80.

Reichley, A. James. 1999. "The Future of the American Two-Party System after 1996." In *The State of the Parties: The Changing Role of Contemporary American Parties,* ed. John C. Green and Daniel M. Shea. 3d ed. Lanham, Md.: Rowman & Littlefield.

Reilly, Ben, and Andrew Reynolds. 1999. *Electoral Systems and Conflict in Divided Societies.* Washington, D.C.: National Academy Press.

Reno v. Bossier Parish School Board. 1997. 520 U.S. 471.

———. 2000. 528 U.S. 320.

Republican Party of Texas v. Dietz. 1997. 940 S.W. 2d 86.

Reynolds, Andrew, and Ben Reilly 1997. *The International IDEA Handbook of Electoral System Design.* Stockholm: International Institute for Democracy and Electoral Assistance.

Reynolds v. Sims. 1964. 377 U.S. 533.

Richie, Robert, and Steven Hill. 1999a. "The Case for Proportional Representation." In *Reflecting All of Us: The Case for Proportional Representation,* ed. Joshua Cohen and Joel Rogers. Boston: Beacon Press.

———. 1999b. "This Time Let the Voters Decide: The Proportional Representation Movement in the United States." In *Making Every Vote Count: Reassessing Canada's Electoral System,* ed. Henry Milner. Peterborough, Ont.: Broadview Press.

Riker, William. 1984. "Electoral Systems and Constitutional Restraints." In *Choosing an Electoral System,* ed. Arend Lijphart and Bernard Grofman. New York: Praeger.

———. 1986. "Duverger's Law Revisited." In *Electoral Laws and Their Political Consequences,* ed. Bernard Grofman and Arend Lijphart.

Rosario v. Rockefeller. 1973. 410 U.S. 752.

Rosenblum, Darren. 1996. "Geographically Sexual? Advancing Lesbian and Gay Interests through Proportional Representation." *Harvard Civil Rights–Civil Liberties Law Review* 31 (Spring): 119–54.

Rosenstone, Steven J., Roy L. Behr, and Edward H. Lazarus. 1996. *Third Parties in America.* 2d ed. Princeton, N.J.: Princeton University Press.

Rossiter, D. J., R. J. Johnston, and C. J. Pattie. 1999. *The Boundary Commissions: Redrawing the UK's Map of Parliamentary Constituencies.* Manchester: Manchester University Press.

Rule, Wilma, and Joseph F. Zimmerman. 1992. *United States Electoral Systems: Their Impact on Women and Minorities.* New York: Greenwood Press.

———, eds. 1994. *Electoral Systems in Comparative Perspective: Their Impact on Women and Minorities.* Westport, Conn.: Greenwood Press.

Rush, Mark E. 1993. "The Variability of Partisanship and Turnout: Implications for Gerrymandering Analysis and Representation Theory." *American Politics Quarterly* 20: 99–122.

———. 1994. *Does Redistricting Make a Difference?* Baltimore: Johns Hopkins University Press.

———. 1998. *Voting Rights and Redistricting in the United States.* Westport, Conn.: Greenwood Press.

———. 1999. Prepared Statement Concerning H.R. 1173, States' Choice of Voting Systems Act, before the Subcommittee on the Constitution, Committee on the Judiciary, U.S. House of Representatives, Washington, D.C., September 23. Available at www.house.gov/judiciary/rush0923.htm.

———. 2000. "Redistricting and Partisan Fluidity: Do We Really Know a Gerrymander When We See One?" *Political Geography* 19: 249–60.

Rusk, Jerrold G. 1970. "The Effect of the Australian Ballot on Split Ticket Voting." *American Political Science Review* 64: 1220–38.

Scher, Richard K., Jon L. Mills, and John J. Hotaling. 1997. *Voting Rights and Democracy: The Law and Politics of Districting.* Chicago: Nelson-Hall.

Scott v. United States Department of Justice. 1996. 920 F. Supp. 1248 (M.D. Fla.).

Sellers, Patrick J., David T. Canon, and Matthew M. Schousen. 1998. "Congressional

Redistricting in North Carolina." In *Race and Redistricting in the 1990s,* ed. Bernard Grofman. New York: Agathon Press.

Shaw v. Barr. 1992. 808 F. Supp. 461 (E.D. N.C.).

Shaw v. Hunt. 1994. 861 F. Supp. 408 (E.D. N.C.).

———. 1996. 517 U.S. 899.

Shaw v. Reno. 1993. 509 U.S. 630.

Shea, Daniel M. 1999. "The Passing of Realignment and the Advent of the 'Base-Less' Party System." *American Politics Quarterly* 27 (January): 33–57.

Shugart, Matthew Soberg. 1999. "The Jenkins Paradox: A Complex System Yet Only a Timid Step towards PR." *Representation* 36 (Summer): 143–47.

Silverberg, Kristen. 1996. "The Illegitimacy of the Incumbent Protection Gerrymander." *Texas Law Review* 74 (March): 913–41.

Simpson, Cam. 1999. "City's Remap Fight to Cost $20 Million." *Chicago Sun-Times* (March 29): 8.

Smith v. Allwright. 1944. 321 U.S. 649.

South Carolina v. Katzenbach. 1966. 383 U.S. 301.

Stanley, Harold W., and Richard Niemi. 2000. *Vital Statistics on American Politics, 1999–2000.* Washington, D.C.: CQ Press.

Still, Edward. 1984. "Alternatives to Single-Member Districts." In *Minority Vote Dilution,* ed. Chandler Davidson. Washington, D.C.: Howard University Press.

———. 1991. "Voluntary Constituencies: Modified At-Large Voting as a Remedy for Minority Vote Dilution in Judicial Elections." *Yale Law and Policy Review* 9 (2): 354–69.

———. 1992. "Cumulative and Limited Voting in Alabama." In *United States Electoral Systems: Their Impact on Women and Minorities,* ed. Wilma Rule and Joseph F. Zimmerman. New York: Greenwood Press.

Still, Edward, and Pamela Karlan. 1995. "Cumulative Voting as a Remedy in Voting Rights Cases." *National Civic Review* 84 (Winter): 337–46.

Taagepera, Rein. 1998. "How Electoral Systems Matter for Democratization." *Democratization* 5 (Autumn): 68–91.

Taagepera, Rein, and Matthew Soberg Shugart. 1989. *Seats and Votes: The Effects and Determinants of Electoral Systems.* New Haven: Yale University Press.

Teixeira, Ruy. 1992. *The Disappearing American Voter.* Washington, D.C.: Brookings Institute.

Terry v. Adams. 1953. 345 U.S. 461.

Theriot v. Parish of Jefferson. 1999. 185 F. 3d 477 (5th Cir.).

Thernstrom, Abigail. 1987. *Whose Votes Count? Affirmative Action and Minority Voting Rights.* Cambridge: Harvard University Press.

———. 1999. Prepared Statement Concerning H.R. 1173, States' Choice of Voting Systems Act, before the Subcommittee on the Constitution, Committee on the Judiciary, U.S. House of Representatives, Washington, D.C., September 23.

Thernstrom, Stephen, and Abigail Thernstrom. 1997. *America in Black and White: One Nation, Indivisible.* New York: Simon & Schuster.

Thornburg v. Gingles. 1986. 478 U.S. 30.

Thurber, James A., Candice J. Nelson, and David A. Dulio, eds. 2000. *Crowded Air-*

waves: Campaign Advertising in Elections. Washington, D.C.: Brookings Institution Press.

Timmons v. Twin Cities Area New Party. 1997. 520 U.S. 351.

United Jewish Organizations of Williamsburgh v. Carey. 1973. 430 U.S. 144.

United States v. Hays. 1995. 515 U.S. 737.

U.S. Department of Commerce v. Montana. 1992. 503 U.S. 442.

Vera v. Richards. 1994. 861 F. Supp. 1304 (S.D. Tex.).

Viteritti, Joseph P. 1994. "Unapportioned Justice: Local Elections, Social Science, and the Evolution of the Voting Rights Act." *Cornell Journal of Law and Public Policy* 4 (Fall): 199–271.

Vowles, Jack. 1999. "Rascals and PR: How Pinto-Duschinsky Stacked the Decks." *Representation* 36 (Summer): 137–42.

Weaver, Leon. 1984. "Semi-Proportional and Proportional Representation Systems in the United States." In *Choosing an Electoral System: Issues and Alternatives,* ed. Arend Lijphart and Bernard Grofman. New York: Praeger.

———. 1986. "The Rise, Decline, and Resurrection of Proportional Representation in Local Governments in the United States." In *Electoral Laws and Their Political Consequences*, ed. Bernard Grofman and Arend Lijphart. New York: Agathon Press.

Weber, Ronald E. 1994. *Revised Report of Ronald E. Weber.* Johnson v. Miller, Civil Action No. 194-008 (S.D. Ga.).

———. 1995. "Redistricting and the Courts: Judicial Activism in the 1990s." *American Politics Quarterly* 23 (April): 204–28.

———. 2000. "Race-Based Districting: Does It Help or Hinder Legislative Representation?" *Political Geography* 19 (February): 213–47.

Webster, Gerald R. 1997. "Geography and the Decennial Task of Redistricting." *Journal of Geography* 96 (March/April): 61–68.

———. 2000. "Playing a Game with Changing Rules: Geography, Politics, and Redistricting in the 1990s." *Political Geography* 19 (February): 141–61.

Welch, Susan. 1990. "The Impact of At-Large Elections on the Representation of Blacks and Hispanics." *Journal of Politics* 52 (November): 1050–76.

Welch, Susan, and Timothy Bledsoe 1988. *Urban Reform and Its Consequences: A Study in Representation.* Chicago: University of Chicago Press.

Wells, David I. 1979. "The Reapportionment Game." *Empire State Review* (February): 8–14.

Wesberry v. Sanders. 1964. 376 U.S. 1.

Whitby, Kenny J. 1997. *The Color of Representation: Congressional Behavior and Black Interests.* Ann Arbor: University of Michigan Press.

White v. Regester. 1973. 412 U.S. 755.

Whitley, Tyler. 1997. "Reform Party Loses Standing in Virginia." *Richmond Times-Dispatch*, November 25.

Wiggins, Charles W., and Janice Petty. 1979. "Cumulative Voting and Electoral Competition: The Illinois House." *American Politics Quarterly* 7 (July): 345–65.

Wildgen, John K., and Richard L. Engstrom. 1980. "Spatial Distribution of Partisan Support and the Seats/Votes Relationship." *Legislative Studies Quarterly* 5 (August): 423–35.

Williams, Jackson. 1994. "The Courts and Partisan Gerrymandering: Recent Cases on

Legislative Apportionment." *Southern Illinois University Law Review* 18 (Spring): 563–602.

Williams v. Rhodes. 1968. 393 U.S. 23.

Young, H. P. 1988. "Measuring the Compactness of Legislative Districts." *Legislative Studies Quarterly* 13 (February): 105–15.

Zeller, B., and H. A. Bone. 1948. "The Repeal of P.R. in New York City: Ten Years in Retrospect." *American Political Science Review* 42: 1127–48.

Zimmerman, Joseph F. 1978. "The Federal Voting Rights Act and Alternative Election Systems." *William and Mary Law Review* 19 (Summer): 621–60.

II

READINGS

The Supreme Court has decided numerous cases concerning representation and the Voting Rights Act. We present here a series of excerpts from decisions that played a key role in developing the Court's voting rights jurisprudence. It will become clear that the Court's jurisprudence involves several apparent contradictions and inconsistencies. In part, these can be attributed to the impact of the 1982 amendments to the Voting Rights Act.

Throughout the following excerpts, we see the Supreme Court wrestling with several issues. On the one hand, the Court asserts throughout that *individuals* must be treated fairly and equally. On the other, the Court also acknowledges that a strictly color-blind focus on the equality of individual voters will result in a disparate impact on political groups. To avoid such an impact, state legislatures must take into account the fate of political groups when drawing legislative and congressional district lines. The problem, however, is that this approach to line drawing is also known as *gerrymandering*—organizing electoral arrangements to benefit some groups at the expense of others.

Thus, in cases such as *Gomillion v. Lightfoot* the Court has lashed out against clearly malicious attempts to gerrymander minorities out of power.. Since that decision, the Court has divided concerning the fairness and constitutionality of gerrymandering minorities *into* power, in cases such as *Wright v. Rockefeller, United Jewish Organizations of Williamsburgh v. Carey,* and *Shaw v. Reno.*

These cases all involved charges of conscious, intentional gerrymandering by state legislatures. In other cases, minority groups challenged electoral arrangements because they had an unfair impact on minority voters—intentions and motivations of legislators notwithstanding. In *Mobile v. Bolden,* the Supreme Court stated that a plaintiff had to demonstrate that an electoral arrangement that diluted its voting power was the product of discriminatory intentions on the part of the legislature. In response, Congress amended the Voting Rights Act in 1982 to read that an electoral arrangement could be challenged if it had a discriminatory impact, regardless of legislative motive.

The Court has remained divided regarding the constitutionality of the cause of action created by Congress in the 1982 amendments. The members of the Court have generally agreed that voting is a fundamental right that must be protected from infringement regardless of legislative motivations. However, the justices have divided regarding the scope of the franchise. In *Allen v. State Board of Elections,* the Court asserted that the right to vote included more than just equal access to the polls because such access would not protect minority groups from vote dilution.

Thus in *Thornburg v. Gingles,* the Court stated that a vote dilution claim needed to be based only on a showing of discriminatory impact. This was, essentially, a showing that the threshold of exclusion (the number of votes necessary to gain election) was high enough to prevent a minority group from cohering and electing a representative. The problem with this formulation became clear in *Holder v. Hall.* Justice Clarence Thomas chastised the Court for developing a jurisprudence that left virtually no electoral arrangement safe from challenge. He argued that the wisest, most manageable route for the Court to take would be to limit the scope of the franchise to equal access to the polls.

Ironically, it can be argued that the Court came full circle as a result of the *Holder* decision. Justice Thomas's concurring opinion echoes the concurrence of Justice Charles E. Whittaker back in *Gomillion v. Lightfoot.*

1

Gomillion et al. v. Lightfoot, Mayor of Tuskegee, et al., 364 U.S. 339 (1960)

Syllabus

Negro citizens sued in a Federal District Court in Alabama for a declaratory judgment that an Act [Act 140] of the State Legislature changing the boundaries of the City of Tuskegee is unconstitutional and for an injunction against its enforcement. They alleged that the Act alters the shape of Tuskegee from a square to an irregular 28-sided figure; that it would eliminate from the City all but four or five of its 400 Negro voters without eliminating any white voter; and that its effect was to deprive Negroes of their right to vote in Tuskegee elections on account of their race.

Opinion of the Court (JUSTICE FRANKFURTER).

Prior to Act 140 the City of Tuskegee was square in shape; the Act transformed it into a strangely irregular twenty-eight-sided figure. . . . The essential inevitable effect of this redefinition of Tuskegee's boundaries is to remove from the city all save only four or five of its 400 Negro voters while not removing a single white voter or resident. The result of the Act is to deprive the Negro petitioners discriminatorily of the benefits of residence in Tuskegee, including, *inter alia,* the right to vote in municipal elections. . . . Act 140 was not an ordinary geographic redistricting measure even within familiar abuses of gerrymandering. . . . [T]he legislation is solely concerned with segregating white and colored voters by fencing Negro citizens out of town so as to deprive them of their pre-existing municipal vote.

According to the allegations here made, the Alabama Legislature has not merely redrawn the Tuskegee city limits with incidental inconvenience to the petitioners; it is more accurate to say that it has deprived the petitioners of the municipal franchise and consequent rights and to that end it has incidentally changed the city's boundaries. While in form this is merely an act redefining metes and bounds, if the allegations are established, the inescapable human effect of this essay in geometry and geography is to despoil colored citizens, and only colored citizens, of their theretofore enjoyed voting rights.

JUSTICE WHITTAKER, concurring.

I concur in the Court's judgment, but not in the whole of its opinion. It seems to me that the decision should be rested not on the Fifteenth Amendment, but rather on the Equal Protection Clause of the Fourteenth Amendment to the Constitution. I am doubtful that the averments of the complaint, taken for present purposes to be true, show a purpose by Act No. 140 to abridge petitioners' "right . . . to vote," in the Fifteenth Amendment sense. It seems to me that the "right . . . to vote" that is guaranteed by the Fifteenth Amendment is but the same right to vote as is enjoyed by all others within the same election precinct, ward or other political division. And, inasmuch as no one has the right to vote in a political division, or in a local election concerning only an area in which he does not reside, it would seem to follow that one's right to vote in Division A is not abridged by a redistricting that places his residence in Division B *if* he there enjoys the same voting privileges as all others in that Division, even though the redistricting was done by the State for the purpose of placing a racial group of citizens in Division B rather than A.

In Gomillion, *the Court stated that gerrymandering was wrong, but the justices were divided regarding whether it violated the Fourteenth or the Fifteenth Amendment. As Justice Whittaker noted, black voters in Tuskegee were not really denied their right to vote. They were denied the opportunity to vote as a majority in the city of Tuskegee. Whereas Frankfurter considered this to be a virtual denial of the right to vote (and therefore a violation of the Fifteenth Amendment), Whittaker suggested that the case might have been more logically decided on Fourteenth Amendment grounds.*

This raised the question regarding the scope of the right to vote. If Frankfurter was correct, then the right to vote included more than mere access to the polls. It included as well the right to an effective *vote, one that could* ensure *a desired result. If Whittaker was right, then gerrymandering was only a denial of equal protection, electoral results notwithstanding.*

In the following case, Reynolds v. Sims, *Chief Justice Earl Warren attempt-*

ed to elaborate on the scope of the franchise. Whereas Gomillion *involved a clear attempt to gerrymander a particular group out of political power,* Reynolds *addressed* malapportionment—*the unequal weighting of individual votes.*

2

Reynolds, Judge, et al. v. Sims et al., 377 U.S. 533 (1964)

Syllabus

Charging that malapportionment of the Alabama Legislature deprived them and others similarly situated of rights under the Equal Protection Clause of the Fourteenth Amendment and the Alabama Constitution, voters in several Alabama counties brought suit against various officials having state election duties. Complainants sought a declaration that the existing state legislative apportionment provisions were unconstitutional; an injunction against future elections pending reapportionment in accordance with the State Constitution; or, absent such reapportionment, a mandatory injunction requiring holding the 1962 election for legislators at large over the entire State. The complaint alleged serious discrimination against voters in counties whose populations had grown proportionately far more than others since the 1900 census which, despite Alabama's constitutional requirements for legislative representation based on population and for decennial reapportionment, formed the basis for the existing legislative apportionment. Pursuant to the 1901 constitution the legislature consisted of 106 representatives and 35 senators for the State's 67 counties and senatorial districts; each county was entitled to at least one representative; each senate district could have only one member; and no county could be divided between two senate districts. A three-judge Federal District Court declined ordering the May 1962 primary election to be held at large, stating that it should not act before the legislature had further opportunity to take corrective measures before the general election. Finding after a hearing that neither of two apportionment plans which the legislature thereafter adopted, to become effective in 1966, would cure the gross inequality and invidious discrimination of the existing representation, which all parties generally conceded violated the Equal Protection Clause, and that the complainants' votes were unconstitutionally debased under all of the three plans at issue, the District

Court ordered temporary reapportionment for the 1962 general election by combining features of the two plans adopted by the legislature, and enjoined officials from holding future elections under any of the invalid plans. The officials appealed, claiming that the District Court erred in holding unconstitutional the existing and proposed reapportionment plans and that a federal court lacks power affirmatively to reapportion a legislature; two groups of complainants also appealed, one claiming error in the District Court's failure to reapportion the Senate according to population, the other claiming error in its failure to reapportion both houses on a population basis.

Opinion of the Court (CHIEF JUSTICE WARREN).

Legislators represent people, not trees or acres. Legislators are elected by voters, not farms or cities or economic interests. As long as ours is a representative form of government, and our legislatures are those instruments of government elected directly by and directly representative of the people, the right to elect legislators in a free and unimpaired fashion is a bedrock of our political system. It could hardly be gainsaid that a constitutional claim had been asserted by an allegation that certain otherwise qualified voters had been entirely prohibited from voting for members of their state legislature. And, if a State should provide that the votes of citizens in one part of the State should be given two times, or five times, or 10 times the weight of votes of citizens in another part of the State, it could hardly be contended that the right to vote of those residing in the disfavored areas had not been effectively diluted. It would appear extraordinary to suggest that a State could be constitutionally permitted to enact a law providing that certain of the State's voters could vote two, five, or 10 times for their legislative representatives, while voters living elsewhere could vote only once. And it is inconceivable that a state law to the effect that, in counting votes for legislators, the votes of citizens in one part of the State would be multiplied by two, five, or 10, while the votes of persons in another area would be counted only at face value, could be constitutionally sustainable. Of course, the effect of state legislative districting schemes which give the same number of representatives to unequal numbers of constituents is identical. Overweighting and overvaluation of the votes of those living here has the certain effect of dilution and undervaluation of the votes of those living there. The resulting discrimination against those individual voters living in disfavored areas is easily demonstrable mathematically. Their right to vote is simply not the same right to vote as that of those living in a favored part of the State. Two, five, or 10 of them must vote before the effect of their voting is equivalent to that of their favored neighbor. Weighting the votes of citizens differently, by any method or means, merely because of where they happen to reside, hardly seems justifiable. . . .

. . . [R]epresentative government is in essence self-government through the medium of elected representatives of the people, and each and every citizen has an inalienable right to full and effective participation in the political processes of his State's legislative bodies. Most citizens can achieve this participation only as qualified voters through the election of legislators to represent them. Full and effective participation by all citizens in state government requires, therefore, that each citizen have an equally effective voice in the election of members of his state legislature. Modern and viable state government needs, and the Constitution demands, no less.

Logically, in a society ostensibly grounded on representative government, it would seem reasonable that a majority of the people of a State could elect a majority of that State's legislators. To conclude differently, and to sanction minority control of state legislative bodies, would appear to deny majority rights in a way that far surpasses any possible denial of minority rights that might otherwise be thought to result. Since legislatures are responsible for enacting laws by which all citizens are to be governed, they should be bodies which are collectively responsive to the popular will. And the concept of equal protection has been traditionally viewed as requiring the uniform treatment of persons standing in the same relation to the governmental action questioned or challenged. With respect to the allocation of legislative representation, all voters, as citizens of a State, stand in the same relation regardless of where they live. Any suggested criteria for the differentiation of citizens are insufficient to justify any discrimination as to the weight of their votes, unless relevant to the permissible purposes of legislative apportionment. Since the achieving of fair and effective representation for all citizens is concededly the basic aim of legislative apportionment, we conclude that the Equal Protection Clause guarantees the opportunity for equal participation by all voters in the election of state legislators. Diluting the weight of votes because of place of residence impairs basic constitutional rights under the Fourteenth Amendment just as much as invidious discriminations based upon factors such as race, or economic status. Our constitutional system amply provides for the protection of minorities by means other than giving them majority control of state legislatures. And the democratic ideals of equality and majority rule, which have served this Nation so well in the past, are hardly of any less significance for the present and the future. . . .

To the extent that a citizen's right to vote is debased, he is that much less a citizen. The fact that an individual lives here or there is not a legitimate reason for overweighting or diluting the efficacy of his vote. The complexions of societies and civilizations change, often with amazing rapidity. A nation once primarily rural in character becomes predominantly urban. Representation schemes once fair and equitable become archaic and outdated. But the basic principle of representative government remains, and must remain, unchanged —the weight of a citizen's vote cannot be made to depend on where he lives.

Population is, of necessity, the starting point for consideration and the controlling criterion for judgment in legislative apportionment controversies. A citizen, a qualified voter, is no more nor no less so because he lives in the city or on the farm. This is the clear and strong command of our Constitution's Equal Protection Clause. This is an essential part of the concept of a government of laws and not men. This is at the heart of Lincoln's vision of "government of the people, by the people, [and] for the people." The Equal Protection Clause demands no less than substantially equal state legislative representation for all citizens, of all places as well as of all races. . . .

We hold that, as a basic constitutional standard, the Equal Protection Clause requires that the seats in both houses of a bicameral state legislature must be apportioned on a population basis. Simply stated, an individual's right to vote for state legislators is unconstitutionally impaired when its weight is in a substantial fashion diluted when compared with votes of citizens living in other parts of the State. . . .

History indicates, however, that many States have deviated, to a greater or lesser degree, from the equal-population principle in the apportionment of seats in at least one house of their legislatures. So long as the divergences from a strict population standard are based on legitimate considerations incident to the effectuation of a rational state policy, some deviations from the equal-population principle are constitutionally permissible with respect to the apportionment of seats in either or both of the two houses of a bicameral state legislature. But neither history alone, nor economic or other sorts of group interests, are permissible factors in attempting to justify disparities from population-based representation. Citizens, not history or economic interests, cast votes.

Chief Justice Warren's opinion pulls in two somewhat contradictory directions. On the one hand, he states that individuals have the right to have their votes counted equally. On the other, he asserts that citizens are entitled to "fair and effective representation" as well. The problem, however, is that the equally weighted votes do not necessarily ensure that voters will obtain representation. Black voters in Tuskegee, for example, still had the right to vote, but the gerrymandering of the city boundary clearly denied them representation.

In Wright v. Rockefeller, *the Court addressed this issue. New York State had drawn its congressional districts in a manner that created opportunities for minority voters to elect minority representatives. The Court struck down a Fourteenth and Fifteenth Amendment challenge to the districting scheme. This created a tension within the Court's jurisprudence: Why was it unconstitutional to gerrymander minorities out of power in* Gomillion *but constitutional to gerrymander them into power in* Wright? *In their dissent, Justices William O. Douglas and Arthur J. Goldberg chastised the Court for this inconsistency.*

3

Wright et al. v. Rockefeller, Governor of New York, et al., 376 U.S. 52 (1964)

Syllabus

Appellants, voters in the four congressional districts in Manhattan Island, brought suit before a three-judge District Court challenging the constitutionality of part of New York's 1961 congressional apportionment statute. They charged that, in violation of the Due Process and Equal Protection Clauses of the Fourteenth Amendment and in violation of the Fifteenth Amendment, irregularly shaped districts were drawn with racial considerations in mind, resulting in one district which excluded non-white citizens and those of Puerto Rican origin, who were largely concentrated in one of the other districts.

MR. JUSTICE DOUGLAS, with whom MR. JUSTICE GOLDBERG concurs, dissenting.

This case raises a question kin to that in *Gomillion v. Lightfoot*, where racial gerrymandering was used to deprive Negroes of the right to vote. Here no Negroes are deprived of the franchise. Rather, zigzag, tortuous lines are drawn to concentrate Negroes and Puerto Ricans in Manhattan's Eighteenth Congressional District and practically to exclude them from the Seventeenth Congressional District. Neighborhoods in our larger cities often contain members of only one race; and those who draw the lines of Congressional Districts cannot be expected to disregard neighborhoods in an effort to make each district a multiracial one. But where, as here, the line that is drawn can be explained only in racial terms, a different problem is presented. . . .

In 1961 the [New York State] legislature expanded the Seventeenth District by altering its boundaries in three respects: (1) it added an area on the upper East Side between 59th Street and 89th Street *of whose population Negroes and Puerto Ricans make up 2.7% of the total;* (2) it added an area on the lower East Side called Stuyvesant Town *of whose population Negroes and Puerto Ricans make up 0.5% of the total;* and (3) it dropped from the Seventeenth District and added to the Eighteenth District a two-block area from 98th Street to 100th Street between Fifth Avenue and Madison Avenue *of whose population Negroes and Puerto Ricans make up 44.5% of the total.*

To achieve this racial gerrymandering, careful manipulation of the boundaries of the Eighteenth District was necessary. The southeast corner is near the East River and from there it goes—west four blocks, north two blocks, west one block, north five blocks, west one block, north one block, west one block, north one block, west one block, north eleven blocks, west five blocks across the northern line of Central Park to Morningside, north along Morningside about twelve blocks, west one block, north along Amsterdam from 122d to 150th, east two blocks, north fifteen blocks to 165th, and east to the East River.

The record strongly suggests that these twists and turns producing an 11-sided, step-shaped boundary between the Seventeenth and Eighteenth Districts were made to bring into the Eighteenth District and keep out of the Seventeenth as many Negroes and Puerto Ricans as possible. There is to be sure no finding to this effect by the three-judge District Court. One of the three judges thought, as I do, that the uncontradicted facts establish *per se* a prima facie case of a legislative purpose to design the Seventeenth and Eighteenth Districts on racial lines, saying that: "[In *Gomillion*] . . . it was a glaring exclusion of Negroes from a municipal district. Here it is a subtle exclusion from a 'silk stocking district' (as the 17th is so frequently referred to) and a jamming in of colored and Puerto Ricans into the 18th or the kind of segregation that appeals to the intervenors." . . .

I had assumed that since *Brown v. Board of Education*, no State may segregate people by race *in the public areas*. The design of voting districts involves one important *public area*—as important as schools, parks, and courtrooms. We should uproot all vestiges of *Plessy v. Ferguson* [in which the Court upheld the use of separate but equal public facilities] from *the public area*.

The intervenors are persons who apparently have a vested interest in control of the segregated Eighteenth District. They and the State seem to support this segregation not on the "separate but equal" theory of *Plessy v. Ferguson, supra,* but on another theory. Their theory might be called the theory of "separate but better off"—a theory that has been used before. . . .

The fact that Negro political leaders find advantage in this nearly solid Negro and Puerto Rican district is irrelevant to our problem. Rotten boroughs were long a curse of democratic processes. Racial boroughs are also at war with democratic standards.

What we have in the Seventeenth and Eighteenth Districts in Manhattan is comparable to the Electoral Register System which Britain introduced into India. That system gave a separate constituency to Sikhs, Muslims, Anglo-Indians, Europeans, and Indian Christians. Religious minorities found comfort and safety in such an arrangement. A Muslim deputation made the following demand [at this point, Justice Douglas quotes from Ahsan, *Community Electorates in India* (1934)]:

> "(1) That in the whole of India the Muslims number over 62 millions or between one-fifth and one-fourth of the total population;
>
> "(2) that as their numbers exceed the entire population of any first-class European Power, except Russia, Muslims might justly claim adequate recognition as an important factor in the State;
>
> "(3) that the representation hitherto accorded to them, almost entirely by nomination, had been inadequate to their requirements and had not always carried with it the approval of those whom the nominees were selected to represent; and
>
> "(4) that while Muslims are a distinct community with additional interests of their own, which are not shared by other communities, no Muslim would ever be returned by the existing electoral bodies, unless he worked in sympathy with the Hindu majority in all matters of importance."

Lord Morley made the following reply:

> "The Muslims demand three things. I had the pleasure of receiving a deputation from them and I know very well what is in their minds. They demand an election of their own representatives to these councils in all the stages just as in Cyprus, where, I think, Muslims vote by themselves; they have nine votes and the non-Muslims have three or the other way about; so in Bohemia where the Germans vote alone and have their own register; therefore we are not without a precedent and a parallel for the idea of a separate register. Secondly, they want a number of seats in excess of their numerical strength. These two demands we are quite ready and intend to meet in full."

Hindus responded favorably. The Joint Report of 1918 stated:

> "Some persons hold that for a people, such as they deem those of India to be, so divided by race, religion and caste as to be unable to consider the interests of any but their own section, a system of communal electorates and class representation is not merely inevitable but is actually best. They maintain that it evokes and applies the principle of democracy over the widest range over which it is actually alive at all, by appealing to the instincts which are strongest; and that we must hope to develop the finer, which are also at present the weaker instincts by using the forces that really count. According to this theory communal representation is an inevitable and even a healthy stage in the development of a non-political people." . . .

Racial electoral registers, like religious ones, have no place in a society that honors the Lincoln tradition—"of the people, by the people, for the people." Here the individual is important, not his race, his creed, or his color. The principle of equality is at war with the notion that District A must be represented by a Negro, as it is with the notion that District B must be represented by a Caucasian, District C by a Jew, District D by a Catholic, and so on. The racial electoral register system weights votes along one racial line more heavily than it does other votes. That system, by whatever name it is called, is a divisive force in a community, emphasizing differences between candidates and voters that are irrelevant in the constitutional sense. Of course race, like religion, plays an important role in the choices which individual voters make from among various candidates. But government has no business designing electoral districts along racial or religious lines. . . .

When racial or religious lines are drawn by the State, the multiracial, multireligious communities that our Constitution seeks to weld together as one become separatist; antagonisms that relate to race or to religion rather than to political issues are generated; communities seek not the best representative but the best racial or religious partisan. Since that system is at war with the democratic ideal, it should find no footing here.

"Separate but equal" and "separate but better off" have no more place in voting districts than they have in schools, parks, railroad terminals, or any other facility serving the public.

Justices Douglas and Goldberg challenged the principle underpinning the creation of legislative districts that would enhance minority electoral opportunities. If the process of fencing black voters out in Gomillion *was wrong, how could the process of "fencing them in" in* Wright *be justified? In* United Jewish Organizations of Williamsburgh v. Carey (UJO), *the inherently controversial nature of race-conscious redistricting became clear. This time, a group of Hasidic Jews claimed that they had been denied their fair representational opportunity because, in order to draw black-majority districts, the State of New York had divided the Williamsburgh Hasidic community.*

What is truly troubling in this case is the Court's disregard for the Hasidic plaintiffs' assertions that they comprised a distinct community. Instead, the Court saw things literally in black and white. Since the Hasidics were white, they could not complain, because the redistricting process was not harmful to white representational opportunities. This is especially clear in Justice William J. Brennan's dismissal of the Hasidics' complaint.

4

United Jewish Organizations
of Williamsburgh, Inc., et al. v. Carey,
Governor of New York, et al.,
423 U.S. 945 (1975)

Syllabus

After New York State had submitted for the approval of the Attorney General its 1972 reapportionment statute with respect to Kings County and two other counties which were subject to §§4 and 5 of the Voting Rights Act of 1965, he concluded that as to certain districts in Kings County the State had not met its burden under §5 of demonstrating that the redistricting had neither the purpose nor the effect of abridging the right to vote by reason of race or color. In May 1974 the State submitted to the Attorney General a revision of those portions of the 1972 plan to which he had objected, including provisions for elections to the state senate and assembly from Kings County. The 1974 plan did not change the number of districts with nonwhite majorities but did change the size of the nonwhite majorities in most of those districts. To attain a nonwhite majority of 65%, which it was felt would be acceptable to the Attorney General for the assembly district in which the Hasidic Jewish community was located (which had been 61% nonwhite under the 1972 plan), a portion of the white population, including part of the Hasidic community, was reassigned to an adjoining district, and that community was also split between two senatorial districts though it had been within one such district under the 1972 plan. Petitioners, on behalf of the Hasidic community, brought this suit for injunctive and declaratory relief, alleging that the 1974 plan violated their rights under the Fourteenth and Fifteenth Amendments. Petitioners contended that the plan "would dilute the value of [their] franchise by halving its effectiveness," solely for the purpose of achieving a racial quota, and that they were assigned to electoral districts solely on the basis of race. Upon motions by the

Attorney General (who had advised the State that he did not object to the 1974 plan) and an intervenor, the District Court dismissed the complaint, holding that petitioners enjoyed no constitutional right in reapportionment to separate community recognition as Hasidic Jews; that the redistricting did not disenfranchise them; and that racial considerations were permissible to correct past discrimination. The Court of Appeals affirmed. Noting that the 1974 plan left approximately 70% of the Kings County senate and assembly districts with white majorities and that only 65% of the county was white, the court held that the plan would not underrepresent the white population. The court, relying on *Allen v. State Board of Elections,* concluded that a State could use racial considerations in an effort to secure the approval of the Attorney General under the Voting Rights Act, reasoning that the Act contemplated that he and the state legislature would have "to think in racial terms"; because the Act "necessarily deals with race or color, corrective action under it must do the same."

MR. JUSTICE BRENNAN, concurring in part.

The one starkly clear fact of this case is that an overt racial number was employed to effect petitioners' assignment to voting districts. In brief, following the Attorney General's refusal to certify the 1972 reapportionment under his §5 powers, unnamed Justice Department officials made known that satisfaction of the Voting Rights Act in Brooklyn would necessitate creation by the state legislature of 10 state assembly and senate districts with threshold nonwhite populations of 65%. Prompted by the necessity of preventing interference with the upcoming 1974 election, state officials complied. Thus, the Justice Department's unofficial instruction to state officials effectively resulted in an explicit process of assignment to voting districts pursuant to race. The result of this process was a countywide pattern of districting closely approximating proportional representation. While it is true that this demographic outcome did not "underrepresent the white population" throughout the county—indeed, the very definition of proportional representation precluded either underrepresentation or overrepresentation—these particular petitioners filed suit to complain that *they* have been subjected to a process of classification on the basis of race that adversely altered *their* status.

If we were presented here with a classification of voters motivated by racial animus, or with a classification that effectively downgraded minority participation in the franchise, we promptly would characterize the resort to race as "suspect" and prohibit its use. Under such circumstances, the tainted apportionment process would not necessarily be saved by its proportional outcome, for the segregation of voters into "separate but equal" blocs still might well have the intent or effect of diluting the voting power of minority voters. It follows, therefore, that if the racial redistricting involved here, imposed with the avowed intention of clustering together 10 viable nonwhite majorities at the expense of preexisting white groupings, is not similarly to be prohibited, the distinctiveness that avoids this prohibition must arise from either or both of two considerations: the permissibility of affording preferential treatment to disadvantaged nonwhites generally, or the particularized application of the Voting Rights Act in this instance.

The first and broader of the two plausible distinctions rests upon the general propriety of so-called benign discrimination: The challenged race assignment may be permissible because it is cast in a remedial context with respect to a disadvantaged class rather than in a setting that aims to demean or insult any racial group. Even in the absence of the Voting Rights Act, this preferential policy plausibly could find expression in a state decision to overcome nonwhite disadvantages in voter registration or turnout through redefinition of electoral districts—perhaps, as here, through the application of a numerical rule—in order to achieve a proportional distribution of voting power.

I begin with the settled principle that not every remedial use of race is forbidden. For example, we have authorized and even required race-conscious remedies in a variety of corrective settings. Once it is established that circumstances exist where race may be taken into account in fashioning affirmative policies, we must identify those circumstances, and, further, determine how substantial a reliance may be placed upon race. . . .

First, a purportedly preferential race assignment may in fact disguise a policy that perpetuates disadvantageous treatment of the plan's supposed beneficiaries. Accordingly, courts might face considerable difficulty in ascertaining whether a given race classification truly furthers benign rather than illicit objectives. An effort to achieve proportional representation, for example, might be aimed at aiding a group's participation in the political processes by guaranteeing safe political offices, or, on the other hand, might be a "contrivance to segregate" the group, thereby frustrating its potentially successful efforts at coalition building across racial lines. . . .

. . . [E]specially when interpreting the broad principles embraced by the Equal Protection Clause, we cannot well ignore the social reality that even a benign policy of assignment by race is viewed as unjust by many in our society, especially by those individuals who are adversely affected by a given classification. This impression of injustice may be heightened by the natural consequence of our governing processes that the most "discrete and insular" of whites often will be called upon to bear the immediate, direct costs of benign discrimination. . . .

Similarly, the history of the Voting Rights Act provides reassurance that, in the face of the potential for reinvigorating racial partisanship, the congressional decision to authorize the use of race-oriented remedies in this context was the product of substantial and careful deliberations. Enacted following "voluminous legislative" consideration, the Voting Rights Act represents an unequivocal and well-defined congressional consensus on the national need for "sterner and more elaborate measures" to secure the promise of the Fourteenth and Fifteenth Amendments with respect to exercise of the franchise. Insofar as the drawing of district lines is a process that intrinsically involves numerical calculations, and insofar as state officials charged with the task of defining electoral constituencies are unlikely simply to close their eyes to considerations such as race and national origin, the resort to a numerical racial criterion as a method of achieving compliance with the aims of the Voting Rights Act is, in my view, consistent with that consensus. . . .

[T]he obvious remedial nature of the Act and its enactment by an elected Congress that hardly can be viewed as dominated by nonwhite representatives belie the possibility that the decisionmaker intended a racial insult or injury to those whites who are adversely affected by the operation of the Act's provisions. [The Hasidic] petitioners have not been deprived of their right to vote, a consideration that minimizes the detrimental impact of the remedial racial policies governing the §5 reapportionment. True, petitioners are denied the opportunity to vote as a group in accordance with the earlier districting configuration, but they do not press any legal claim to a group voice as Hasidim. In terms of their voting interests, then, the burden that they claim to suffer must be attributable solely to their relegation to increased nonwhite-dominated districts. Yet, to the extent that white and nonwhite interests and sentiments are polarized in Brooklyn, the petitioners still are indirectly "protected" by the remaining white assembly and senate districts within the county, carefully preserved in accordance with the white proportion of the total county population. While these considerations obviously do not satisfy petitioners, I am persuaded that they reinforce the legitimacy of this remedy.

The differences between Justice Douglas in Wright *and Justice Brennan in* UJO *are clearly controversial because they expose the premise underlying state attempts to gerrymander for malicious or remedial reasons. Such strategic line drawing presumes that the state can not only identify salient political groups but also decide which groups "count" for purposes of allocating legislative representation and which groups do not. Thus, while a majority of the Court—as well as Congress—was willing to recognize black and Hispanic voters as salient political groups in* Wright *and* UJO, *it was not willing to acknowledge Hasidic Jews.*

Wright *established that the Court was willing to allow state legislatures to take special efforts to enhance minority representational opportunities. However, the scope of the franchise—as set forth in the Voting Rights Act—was still unclear. Did a vote dilution claim require a demonstration of legislative intent to discriminate against minority voters? In* Mobile v. Bolden, *the Court first addressed this issue.*

5

City of Mobile, Alabama, et al.
v. Bolden et al.,
446 U.S. 55 (1980)

Syllabus

Mobile, Ala., is governed by a Commission consisting of three members elected at large who jointly exercise all legislative, executive, and administrative power in the city. Appellees brought a class action in Federal District Court against the city and the incumbent Commissioners on behalf of all Negro citizens of the city, alleging, *inter alia*, that the practice of electing the City Commissioners at large unfairly diluted the voting strength of Negroes in violation of the Fourteenth and Fifteenth Amendments. Although finding that Negroes in Mobile "register and vote without hindrance," the District Court nevertheless held that the at-large electoral system violated the Fifteenth Amendment and invidiously discriminated against Negroes in violation of the Equal Protection Clause of the Fourteenth Amendment, and ordered that the Commission be disestablished and replaced by a Mayor and a Council elected from single-member districts. The Court of Appeals affirmed.

Opinion of the Court (MR. JUSTICE STEWART, joined by THE CHIEF JUSTICE, MR. JUSTICE POWELL, and MR. JUSTICE REHNQUIST).

The Court's early decisions under the Fifteenth Amendment established that it imposes but one limitation on the powers of the States. It forbids them to discriminate against Negroes in matters having to do with voting. "The Fifteenth Amendment does not confer the right of suffrage upon any one," but has "invested the citizens of the United States with a new constitutional right which is within the protecting power of Congress. That right is exemption from discrimination in the exercise of the elective franchise on account of race, color, or previous condition of servitude."

Our decisions, moreover, have made clear that action by a State that is racially neutral on its face violates the Fifteenth Amendment only if motivated by a discriminatory purpose. . . . The Court's more recent decisions confirm the principle that racially discriminatory motivation is a necessary ingredient of a Fifteenth Amendment violation. In *Gomillion v. Lightfoot*, the Court held that allegations of a racially motivated gerrymander of municipal boundaries stated a claim under the Fifteenth Amendment. The constitutional infirmity of the state law in that case, according to the allegations of the complaint, was that in drawing the municipal boundaries the legislature was "solely concerned with segregating white and colored voters by fencing Negro citizens out of town so as to deprive them of their pre-existing municipal vote." The Court made clear that in the absence of such an invidious purpose, a State is constitutionally free to redraw political boundaries in any manner it chooses. . . .

The appellees have argued in this Court that . . . the at-large system of elections in Mobile is unconstitutional, reasoning that the effect of racially polarized voting in Mobile is the same as that of a racially exclusionary primary. The only characteristic, however, of the exclusionary primaries that offended the Fifteenth Amendment was that Negroes were not permitted to vote in them. The difficult question was whether the "State [had] had a hand in" the patent discrimination practiced by a nominally private organization.

The answer to the appellees' argument is that, as the District Court expressly found, their freedom to vote has not been denied or abridged by anyone. The Fifteenth Amendment does not entail the right to have Negro candidates elected. . . . That Amendment prohibits only purposefully discriminatory denial or abridgment by government of the freedom to vote "on account of race, color, or previous condition of servitude." . . .

The claim that at-large electoral schemes unconstitutionally deny to some persons the equal protection of the laws has been advanced in numerous cases before this Court. . . . [T]he focus in such cases has been on the lack of representation multimember districts afford various elements of the voting population in a system of representative legislative democracy. "Criticism [of multimember districts] is rooted in their winner-take-all aspects, their tendency to submerge minorities, . . . a general preference for legislatures reflecting community interests as closely as possible and disenchantment with political parties and elections as devices to settle policy differences between contending interests."

Despite repeated constitutional attacks upon multimember legislative districts, the Court has consistently held that they are not unconstitutional *per se*. We have recognized, however, that such legislative apportionments could violate the Fourteenth Amendment if their purpose were invidiously to minimize or cancel out the voting potential of racial or ethnic minorities. To prove such a purpose it is not enough to show that the group allegedly discriminated against has not elected representatives in proportion to its numbers. A plaintiff must prove that the disputed plan was "conceived or operated as [a] purposeful [device] to further racial . . . discrimination." . . .

In only one case has the Court sustained a claim that multimember legislative districts unconstitutionally diluted the voting strength of a discrete group. That case was *White v. Regester*. There the Court upheld a constitutional challenge by Negroes and Mexican-Americans to parts of a legislative reapportionment plan adopted by the State of Texas. The plaintiffs alleged that the multimember districts for the two counties in which they resided minimized the effect of their votes in violation of the Fourteenth Amendment, and the Court held that the plaintiffs had been able to "produce evidence to support findings that the political processes leading to nomination and election were not equally open to participation by the [groups] in question." In so holding, the Court relied upon evidence in the record that included a long history of official discrimination against minorities as well as indifference to their needs and interests on the part of white elected officials. The Court also found in each county additional factors that restricted the access of minority groups to the political process. In one county, Negroes effectively were excluded from the process of slating candidates for the Democratic Party, while the plaintiffs in the other county were Mexican-Americans who "[suffered] a cultural and language barrier" that made "participation in community processes extremely difficult, particularly . . . with respect to the political life" of the county. . . .

We turn finally to the arguments advanced [by] MR. JUSTICE MARSHALL. . . . The theory of this dissenting opinion—a theory much more extreme than that espoused by the District Court or the Court of Appeals—appears to be that every "political group," or at least every such group that is in the minority, has a federal constitutional right to elect candidates in proportion to its numbers. Moreover, a political group's "right" to have its candidates elected is said to be a "fundamental interest," the infringement of which may be established without proof that a State has acted with the purpose of impairing anybody's access to the political process. This dissenting opinion finds the "right" infringed in the present case because no Negro has been elected to the Mobile City Commission. . . .

Whatever appeal the dissenting opinion's view may have as a matter of political theory, it is not the law. The Equal Protection Clause of the Fourteenth Amendment does not require proportional representation as an imperative of political organization. The entitlement that the dissenting opinion assumes to exist simply is not to be found in the Constitution of the United States.

It is of course true that a law that impinges upon a fundamental right explicitly or implicitly secured by the Constitution is presumptively unconstitutional. But plainly "[it] is not the province of this Court to create substantive constitutional rights in the name of guaranteeing equal protection of the laws."

Accordingly, where a state law does not impair a right or liberty protected by the Constitution, there is no occasion to depart from "the settled mode of constitutional analysis of [legislation] . . . involving questions of economic and social policy." MR. JUSTICE MARSHALL's dissenting opinion would discard these fixed principles in favor of a judicial inventiveness that would go "far toward making this Court a 'super-legislature." We are not free to do so.

More than 100 years ago the Court unanimously held that "the Constitution of the United States does not confer the right of suffrage upon any one. . . ." It is for the States "to determine the conditions under which the right of suffrage may be exercised, . . . absent of course the discrimination which the Constitution condemns." It is true, as the dissenting opinion states, that the Equal Protection Clause confers a substantive right to participate in elections on an equal basis with other qualified voters. But this right to equal participation in the electoral process does not protect any "political group," however defined, from electoral defeat.

The dissenting opinion erroneously discovers the asserted entitlement to group representation within the "one person, one vote" principle of *Reynolds v. Sims* and its progeny. Those cases established that the Equal Protection Clause guarantees the right of each voter to "have his vote weighted equally with those of all other citizens." The Court recognized that a voter's right to "have an equally effective voice" in the election of representatives is impaired where representation is not apportioned substantially on a population basis. In such cases, the votes of persons in more populous districts carry less weight than do those of persons in smaller districts. There can be, of course, no claim that the "one person, one vote" principle has been violated in this case, because the city of Mobile is a unitary electoral district and the Commission elections are conducted at large. It is therefore obvious that nobody's vote has been "diluted" in the sense in which that word was used in the *Reynolds* case.

The dissenting opinion places an extraordinary interpretation on these decisions, an interpretation not justified by *Reynolds v. Sims* itself or by any other decision of this Court. It is, of course, true that the right of a person to vote on an equal basis with other voters draws much of its significance from the political associations that its exercise reflects, but it is an altogether different matter to conclude that political groups themselves have an independent constitutional claim to representation.

MR. JUSTICE MARSHALL, dissenting.

Under the Equal Protection Clause, if a classification "impinges upon a fundamental right explicitly or implicitly protected by the Constitution, . . . strict judicial scrutiny" is required regardless of whether the infringement was intentional. As I will explain, our cases recognize a fundamental right to equal electoral participation that encompasses protection against vote dilution. Proof of discriminatory purpose is, therefore, not required to support a claim of vote dilution. The plurality's erroneous conclusion to the contrary is the result of a failure to recognize the central distinction between *White v. Regester* and *Washington v. Davis*: the former involved an infringement of a constitutionally protected right, while the latter dealt with a claim of racially discriminatory distribution of an interest to which no citizen has a constitutional entitlement. . . .

Reynolds v. Sims and its progeny focused solely on the discriminatory *effects* of malapportionment. They recognize that, when population figures for the representational districts of a legislature are not similar, the votes of citizens in larger districts do not carry as much weight in the legislature as do votes cast by citizens in smaller districts. The equal protection problem attacked by the "one person, one vote" principle is, then, one of vote dilution: under *Reynolds,* each citizen must have an "equally effective voice" in the election of representatives. In the present cases, the alleged vote dilution, though caused by the combined effects of the electoral structure and social and historical factors rather than by unequal population distribution, is analytically the same concept: the unjustified abridgment of a fundamental right. It follows, then, that a showing of discriminatory intent is just as unnecessary under the vote-dilution approach . . . as it is under our reapportionment cases. . . .

Our vote-dilution decisions . . . involve the fundamental-interest branch, rather than the antidiscrimination branch, of our jurisprudence under the Equal Protection Clause. They recognize a substantive constitutional right to participate on an equal basis in the electoral process that cannot be denied or diminished for any reason, racial or otherwise, lacking quite substantial justification. . . .

The Fifteenth Amendment does not confer an absolute right to vote. By providing that the right to vote cannot be discriminatorily "denied *or* abridged," however, the Amendment assuredly strikes down the diminution as well as the outright denial of the exercise of the franchise. An interpretation holding that the Amendment reaches only complete abrogation of the vote would render the Amendment essentially useless, since it is no difficult task to imagine schemes in which the Negro's marking of the ballot is a meaningless exercise.

The Court has long understood that the right to vote encompasses protection against vote dilution. "[The] right to have one's vote counted" is of the same importance as "the right to put a ballot in a box." The right to vote is protected against the diluting effect of ballot-box stuffing. Indeed, this Court has explicitly recognized that the Fifteenth Amendment protects against vote dilution. In *Terry v. Adams* and *Smith v. Allwright*, the Negro plaintiffs did not question their access to the ballot for general elections. Instead they argued, and the Court recognized, that the value of their votes had been diluted by their exclusion from participation in primary elections and in the slating of candidates by political parties. The Court's struggles with the concept of "state action" in those decisions were necessarily premised on the understanding that vote dilution was a claim cognizable under the Fifteenth Amendment.

Wright v. Rockefeller recognized that an allegation of vote dilution resulting from the drawing of district lines stated a claim under the Fifteenth Amendment. The plaintiffs in that case argued that congressional districting in New York violated the Fifteenth Amendment because district lines had been drawn in a racially discriminatory fashion. Each plaintiff had access to the ballot; their complaint was that because of intentional discrimination they resided in a district with population characteristics that had the effect of diluting the weight of their votes. The Court treated this claim as cognizable under the Fifteenth Amendment. More recently, in *United Jewish Organizations v. Carey*, we again treated an allegation of vote dilution arising from a redistricting scheme as stating a claim under the Fifteenth Amendment. Indeed, in that case MR. JUSTICE STEWART found no Fifteenth Amendment violation in part because the plaintiffs had failed to prove "that the redistricting scheme was employed . . . to minimize or cancel out the voting strength of a minority class or interest; or otherwise to impair or burden the opportunity of affected persons to participate in the political process." . . .

The Fifteenth Amendment prohibits a State from denying or abridging a Negro's right to vote. The Nineteenth Amendment does the same for women. If a State in a statewide election weighted the male vote more heavily than the female vote or the white vote more heavily than the Negro vote, none could successfully contend that that discrimination was allowable. Once the geographical unit for which a representative is to be chosen is designated, all who participate in the election are to have an equal vote—whatever their race, whatever their sex, whatever their occupation, whatever their income, and wherever their home may be in that geographical unit. This is required by the Equal Protection Clause of the Fourteenth Amendment. . . .

An interpretation of the Fifteenth Amendment limiting its prohibitions to the outright denial of the ballot would convert the words of the Amendment into language illusory in symbol and hollow in substance. Surely today's decision should not be read as endorsing that interpretation.

In response to the Bolden *decision, Congress amended the Voting Rights Act in 1982. Minority plaintiffs now had to demonstrate only that an electoral arrangement had discriminatory impact on minority representational opportunities—legislative intent notwithstanding. In* Thornburg v. Gingles, *the Court set forth the criteria on which it would assess a vote dilution claim.*

6

Thornburg, Attorney General of North Carolina, et al. v. Gingles et al., 478 U.S. 30 (1986)

Syllabus

In 1982, the North Carolina General Assembly enacted a legislative redistricting plan for the State's Senate and House of Representatives. Appellees, black citizens of North Carolina who are registered to vote, brought suit in Federal District Court, challenging one single-member district and six multimember districts on the ground, *inter alia*, that the redistricting plan impaired black citizens' ability to elect representatives of their choice in violation of §2 of the Voting Rights Act of 1965. After appellees brought suit, but before trial, §2 was amended, largely in response to *Mobile v. Bolden,* to make clear that a violation of §2 could be proved by showing discriminatory effect alone, rather than having to show a discriminatory purpose, and to establish as the relevant legal standard the "results test." Section 2(a), as amended, prohibits a State or political subdivision from imposing any voting qualifications or prerequisites to voting, or any standards, practices, or procedures that result in the denial or abridgment of the right of any citizen to vote on account of race or color. Section 2(b), as amended, provides that §2(a) is violated where the "totality of circumstances" reveals that "the political processes leading to nomination or election . . . are not equally open to participation by members of a [protected class] . . . in that its members have less opportunity than other members of the electorate to participate in the political process and to elect representatives of their choice," and that the extent to which members of a protected class have been elected to office is one circumstance that may be considered. The District Court applied the "totality of circumstances" test set forth in §2(b) and held that the redistricting plan violated §2(a) because it resulted in the dilution of black citizens' votes in all of the disputed districts. Appellants, the Attorney

General of North Carolina and others, took a direct appeal to this Court with respect to five of the multimember districts.

Opinion of the Court (JUSTICE BRENNAN).

In April 1982, the North Carolina General Assembly enacted a legislative redistricting plan for the State's Senate and House of Representatives. Appellees, black citizens of North Carolina who are registered to vote, challenged seven districts, one single-member and six multimember districts, alleging that the redistricting scheme impaired black citizens' ability to elect representatives of their choice in violation of the Fourteenth and Fifteenth Amendments to the United States Constitution and of §2 of the Voting Rights Act.

After appellees brought suit, but before trial, Congress amended §2. The amendment was largely a response to this Court's plurality opinion in *Mobile v. Bolden* which had declared that, in order to establish a violation either of §2 or of the Fourteenth or Fifteenth Amendments, minority voters must prove that a contested electoral mechanism was intentionally adopted or maintained by state officials for a discriminatory purpose. Congress substantially revised §2 to make clear that a violation could be proved by showing discriminatory effect alone and to establish as the relevant legal standard the "results test." . . .

Section 2 [of the Voting Rights Act], as amended, 96 Stat. 134, reads as follows:

> "(a) No voting qualification or prerequisite to voting or standard, practice, or procedure shall be imposed or applied by any State or political subdivision in a manner which results in a denial or abridgement of the right of any citizen of the United States to vote on account of race or color, or in contravention of the guarantees set forth in section 4(f)(2), as provided in subsection (b).
>
> "(b) A violation of subsection (a) is established if, based on the totality of circumstances, it is shown that the political processes leading to nomination or election in the State or political subdivision are not equally open to participation by members of a class of citizens protected by subsection (a) in that its members have less opportunity than other members of the electorate to participate in the political process and to elect representatives of their choice. The extent to which members of a protected class have been elected to office in the State or political subdivision is one circumstance which may be considered: *Provided,* That nothing in this section establishes a right to have members of a protected class elected in numbers equal to their proportion in the population." Codified at 42 U.S.C. §1973.

The Senate Judiciary Committee majority Report accompanying the bill that amended §2 elaborates on the circumstances that might be probative of a §2 violation, noting the following "typical factors":

"1. the extent of any history of official discrimination in the state or political subdivision that touched the right of the members of the minority group to register, to vote, or otherwise to participate in the democratic process;

"2. the extent to which voting in the elections of the state or political subdivision is racially polarized;

"3. the extent to which the state or political subdivision has used unusually large election districts, majority vote requirements, anti–single shot provisions, or other voting practices or procedures that may enhance the opportunity for discrimination against the minority group;

"4. if there is a candidate slating process, whether the members of the minority group have been denied access to that process;

"5. the extent to which members of the minority group in the state or political subdivision bear the effects of discrimination in such areas as education, employment and health, which hinder their ability to participate effectively in the political process;

"6. whether political campaigns have been characterized by overt or subtle racial appeals;

"7. the extent to which members of the minority group have been elected to public office in the jurisdiction.

"Additional factors that in some cases have had probative value as part of plaintiffs' evidence to establish a violation are:

"whether there is a significant lack of responsiveness on the part of elected officials to the particularized needs of the members of the minority group;

"whether the policy underlying the state or political subdivision's use of such voting qualification, prerequisite to voting, or standard, practice or procedure is tenuous." . . .

SECTION 2 AND ITS LEGISLATIVE HISTORY

Subsection 2(a) prohibits all States and political subdivisions from imposing *any* voting qualifications or prerequisites to voting, or any standards, practices, or procedures which result in the denial or abridgment of the right to vote of any citizen who is a member of a protected class of racial and language minorities. Subsection 2(b) establishes that §2 has been violated where the "totality of circumstances" reveal that "the political processes leading to nomination or election . . . are not equally open to participation by members of a [protected class] . . . in that its members have less opportunity than other members of the electorate to participate in the political process and to elect representatives of their choice." While explaining that "[the] extent to which members of a protected class have been elected to office in the State or political subdivision is one circumstance which may be considered" in evaluating an alleged violation, §2(b) cautions that "nothing in [§2] establishes a right to have members of a protected class elected in numbers equal to their proportion in the population."

The Senate Report which accompanied the 1982 amendments elaborates on the nature of §2 violations and on the proof required to establish these violations. First and foremost, the Report dispositively rejects the position of the plurality in *Mobile v. Bolden*, which required proof that the contested electoral practice or mechanism was adopted or maintained with the intent to discriminate against minority voters. The intent test was repudiated for three principal reasons—it is "unnecessarily divisive because it involves charges of racism on the part of individual officials or entire communities," it places an "inordinately difficult" burden of proof on plaintiffs, and it "asks the wrong question." The "right" question, as the Report emphasizes repeatedly, is whether "as a result of the challenged practice or structure plaintiffs do not have an equal opportunity to participate in the political processes and to elect candidates of their choice."

In order to answer this question, a court must assess the impact of the contested structure or practice on minority electoral opportunities "on the basis of objective factors." The Senate Report specifies factors which typically may be relevant to a §2 claim: the history of voting-related discrimination in the State or political subdivision; the extent to which voting in the elections of the State or political subdivision is racially polarized; the extent to which the State or political subdivision has used voting practices or procedures that tend to enhance the opportunity for discrimination against the minority group, such as unusually large election districts, majority vote requirements, and prohibitions against bullet voting; the exclusion of members of the minority group from candidate slating processes; the extent to which minority group members bear the effects of past discrimination in areas such as education, employment, and health, which hinder their ability to participate effectively in the political process; the use of overt or subtle racial appeals in political campaigns; and the extent to which members of the minority group have been elected to public office in the jurisdiction. The Report notes also that evidence demonstrating that elected officials are unresponsive to the particularized needs of the members of the minority group and that the policy underlying the State's or the political subdivision's use of the contested practice or structure is tenuous may have probative value. The Report stresses, however, that this list of typical factors is neither comprehensive nor exclusive. While the enumerated factors will often be pertinent to certain types of §2 violations, particularly to vote dilution claims, other factors may also be relevant and may be considered. Furthermore, the Senate Committee observed that "there is no requirement that any particular number of factors be proved, or that a majority of them point one way or the other." Rather, the Committee determined that "the question whether the political processes are 'equally open' depends upon a searching practical evaluation of the 'past and present reality'" and on a "functional" view of the political process. . . .

While many or all of the factors listed in the Senate Report may be relevant to a claim of vote dilution through submergence in multimember districts, unless there is a conjunction of the following circumstances, the use of multimember districts generally will not impede the ability of minority voters to elect representatives of their choice. Stated succinctly, a bloc voting majority must *usually* be able to defeat candidates supported by a politically cohesive, geographically insular minority group. These circumstances are necessary preconditions for multimember districts to operate to impair minority voters' ability to elect representatives of their choice for the following reasons. First, the minority group must be able to demonstrate that it is sufficiently large and geographically compact to constitute a majority in a single-member district. If it is not, as would be the case in a substantially integrated district, the *multimember form* of the district cannot be responsible for minority voters' inability to elect its candidates. Second, the minority group must be able to show that it is politically cohesive. If the minority group is not politically cohesive, it cannot be said that the selection of a multimember electoral structure thwarts distinctive minority group interests. Third, the minority must be able to demonstrate that the white majority votes sufficiently as a bloc to enable it—in the absence of special circumstances, such as the minority candidate running unopposed—usually to defeat the minority's preferred candidate. In establishing this last circumstance, the minority group demonstrates that submergence in a white multimember district impedes its ability to elect its chosen representatives. . . .

The reason that a minority group making such a challenge must show, as a threshold matter, that it is sufficiently large and geographically compact to constitute a majority in a single-member district is this: Unless minority voters possess the *potential* to elect representatives in the absence of the challenged structure or practice, they cannot claim to have been injured by that structure or practice. The single-member district is generally the appropriate standard against which to measure minority group potential to elect because it is the smallest political unit from which representatives are elected. Thus, if the minority group is spread evenly throughout a multimember district, or if, although geographically compact, the minority group is so small in relation to the surrounding white population that it could not constitute a majority in a single-member district, these minority voters cannot maintain that they would have been able to elect representatives of their choice in the absence of the multimember electoral structure. . . .

In sum, we would hold that the legal concept of racially polarized voting, as it relates to claims of vote dilution, refers only to the existence of a correlation between the race of voters and the selection of certain candidates. Plaintiffs need not prove causation or intent in order to prove a prima facie case of racial bloc voting and defendants may not rebut that case with evidence of causation or intent.

In Gingles *the Court provided an extended exegesis of the amended Voting Rights Act. While* Gingles *dealt with the use of multimember districts, the analysis of vote dilution and the "results test" applied as well to any electoral arrangement that could be said to discriminate against a geographically and politically cohesive minority.*

Gingles, *along with decisions such as* UJO *and* Wright, *exacerbated the uneasy tension within the Supreme Court's voting rights jurisprudence. The Court had ruled that gerrymandering was unconstitutional—unless it was done to assist those minority groups enumerated in the Voting Rights Act. In addition, it ruled that virtually any electoral system could be challenged if challengers/opponents could show that the system could be reorganized to enhance the representational opportunities of large, geographically compact minority groups.*

In arriving at these decisions, successive Court majorities left unanswered questions posed by Justices Douglas and Goldberg (in Wright*) and by the majority in* Bolden. *If we wanted to ensure fair representational opportunity for political groups, who would decide which groups ought to qualify for the benefits of remedial redistricting (blacks, Hispanics) and which would not (Hasidic Jews)? An even more problematic question arose in the wake of the* Gingles *decision: Why should representational opportunities be limited only to those groups that were geographically compact? Why should a politically cohesive yet geographically dispersed group suffer only because its members lived in different areas? This clearly conflicted with Chief Justice Warren's assertion in* Reynolds v. Sims *that "the weight of a citizen's vote cannot be made to depend on where he lives." In two subsequent cases,* Shaw v. Reno *and* Holder v. Hall, *the Court confronted these tensions in its jurisprudence.*

7

Ruth O. Shaw, et al., Appellants, v. Janet Reno, Attorney General, et al., 509 U.S. 630 (1993)

Syllabus

To comply with §5 of the Voting Rights Act of 1965—which prohibits a covered jurisdiction from implementing changes in a "standard, practice, or procedure with respect to voting" without federal authorization—North Carolina submitted to the Attorney General a congressional reapportionment plan with one majority-black district. The Attorney General objected to the plan on the ground that a second district could have been created to give effect to minority voting strength in the State's south-central to southeastern region. The State's revised plan contained a second majority-black district in the north-central region. The new district stretches approximately 160 miles along Interstate 85 and, for much of its length, is no wider than the I-85 corridor. Appellants, five North Carolina residents, filed this action against appellee state and federal officials, claiming that the State had created an unconstitutional racial gerrymander in violation of, among other things, the Fourteenth Amendment. They alleged that the two districts concentrated a majority of black voters arbitrarily without regard to considerations such as compactness, contiguousness, geographical boundaries, or political subdivisions, in order to create congressional districts along racial lines and to assure the election of two black representatives. The three-judge District Court held that it lacked subject matter jurisdiction over the federal appellees. It also dismissed the complaint against the state appellees, finding, among other things, that, under *United Jewish Organizations of Williamsburgh, Inc. v. Carey*, appellants had failed to state an equal protection claim because favoring minority voters was not discriminatory in the constitutional sense and the plan did not lead to proportional underrepresentation of white voters statewide.

Opinion of the Court (JUSTICE O'CONNOR).

"The right to vote freely for the candidate of one's choice is of the essence of
a democratic society." For much of our Nation's history, that right sadly has
been denied to many because of race. The Fifteenth Amendment, ratified in
1870 after a bloody Civil War, promised unequivocally that "the right of citizens of the United States to vote" no longer would be "denied or abridged . . .
by any State on account of race, color, or previous condition of servitude."

But "[a] number of states . . . refused to take no for an answer and continued to circumvent the fifteenth amendment's prohibition through the use of
both subtle and blunt instruments, perpetuating ugly patterns of pervasive
racial discrimination." Ostensibly race-neutral devices such as literacy tests
with "grandfather" clauses and "good character" provisos were devised to
deprive black voters of the franchise. Another of the weapons in the States'
arsenal was the racial gerrymander—"the deliberate and arbitrary distortion
of district boundaries . . . for [racial] purposes." In the 1870's, for example,
opponents of Reconstruction in Mississippi "concentrated the bulk of the
black population in a 'shoestring' Congressional district running the length of
the Mississippi River, leaving five others with white majorities." Some 90
years later, Alabama redefined the boundaries of the city of Tuskegee "from
a square to an uncouth twenty-eight-sided figure" in a manner that was
alleged to exclude black voters, and only black voters, from the city limits.

Alabama's exercise in geometry was but one example of the racial discrimination in voting that persisted in parts of this country nearly a century after
ratification of the Fifteenth Amendment. In some States, registration of eligi-
ble black voters ran 50% behind that of whites. Congress enacted the Voting
Rights Act of 1965 as a dramatic and severe response to the situation. The Act
proved immediately successful in ensuring racial minorities access to the voting booth; by the early 1970's, the spread between black and white registration
in several of the targeted Southern States had fallen to well below 10%.

But it soon became apparent that guaranteeing equal access to the polls
would not suffice to root out other racially discriminatory voting practices.
Drawing on the "one person, one vote" principle, this Court recognized that
"the right to vote can be affected by a *dilution* of voting power as well as by
an absolute prohibition on casting a ballot." Where members of a racial minority group vote as a cohesive unit, practices such as multimember or at-large
electoral systems can reduce or nullify minority voters' ability, as a group, "to
elect the candidate of their choice." Accordingly, the Court held that such
schemes violate the Fourteenth Amendment when they are adopted with a discriminatory purpose and have the effect of diluting minority voting strength.
Congress, too, responded to the problem of vote dilution. In 1982, it amended
§2 of the Voting Rights Act to prohibit legislation that *results* in the dilution of
a minority group's voting strength, regardless of the legislature's intent.

It is against this background that we confront the questions presented here. . . . Our focus is on appellants' claim that the State engaged in unconstitutional racial gerrymandering. That argument strikes a powerful historical chord: It is unsettling how closely the North Carolina plan resembles the most egregious racial gerrymanders of the past. . . . This Court never has held that race-conscious state decision-making is impermissible in *all* circumstances. What appellants object to is redistricting legislation that is so extremely irregular on its face that it rationally can be viewed only as an effort to segregate the races for purposes of voting, without regard for traditional districting principles and without sufficiently compelling justification.

The Equal Protection Clause provides that "no State shall . . . deny to any person within its jurisdiction the equal protection of the laws." Its central purpose is to prevent the States from purposefully discriminating between individuals on the basis of race. Laws that explicitly distinguish between individuals on racial grounds fall within the core of that prohibition.

No inquiry into legislative purpose is necessary when the racial classification appears on the face of the statute. Express racial classifications are immediately suspect because, "absent searching judicial inquiry, . . . there is simply no way of determining what classifications are 'benign' or 'remedial' and what classifications are in fact motivated by illegitimate notions of racial inferiority or simple racial politics."

Classifications of citizens solely on the basis of race "are by their very nature odious to a free people whose institutions are founded upon the doctrine of equality." They threaten to stigmatize individuals by reason of their membership in a racial group and to incite racial hostility.

In *Guinn v. United States*, the Court invalidated under the Fifteenth Amendment a statute that imposed a literacy requirement on voters but contained a "grandfather clause" applicable to individuals and their lineal descendants entitled to vote "on [or prior to] January 1, 1866." The determinative consideration for the Court was that the law, though ostensibly race neutral, on its face "embodied no exercise of judgment and rested upon no discernible reason" other than to circumvent the prohibitions of the Fifteenth Amendment. In other words, the statute was invalid because, on its face, it could not be explained on grounds other than race.

The Court applied the same reasoning to the "uncouth twenty-eight-sided" municipal boundary line at issue in *Gomillion*. Although the statute that redrew the city limits of Tuskegee was race neutral on its face, plaintiffs alleged that its effect was impermissibly to remove from the city virtually all black voters and no white voters. . . . The majority resolved the case under the Fifteenth Amendment. Justice Whittaker, however, concluded that the "unlawful segregation of races of citizens" into different voting districts was cognizable under the Equal Protection Clause. This Court's subsequent reliance on *Gomillion* in other Fourteenth Amendment cases suggests the correctness of

Justice Whittaker's view. *Gomillion* thus supports appellants' contention that district lines obviously drawn for the purpose of separating voters by race require careful scrutiny under the Equal Protection Clause regardless of the motivations underlying their adoption. . . .

. . . [W]e believe that reapportionment is one area in which appearances do matter. A reapportionment plan that includes in one district individuals who belong to the same race, but who are otherwise widely separated by geographical and political boundaries, and who may have little in common with one another but the color of their skin, bears an uncomfortable resemblance to political apartheid. It reinforces the perception that members of the same racial group—regardless of their age, education, economic status, or the community in which they live—think alike, share the same political interests, and will prefer the same candidates at the polls. We have rejected such perceptions elsewhere as impermissible racial stereotypes. . . . The message that such districting sends to elected representatives is equally pernicious. When a district obviously is created solely to effectuate the perceived common interests of one racial group, elected officials are more likely to believe that their primary obligation is to represent only the members of that group, rather than their constituency as a whole. This is altogether antithetical to our system of representative democracy.

. . . [W]e conclude that a plaintiff challenging a reapportionment statute under the Equal Protection Clause may state a claim by alleging that the legislation, though race neutral on its face, rationally cannot be understood as anything other than an effort to separate voters into different districts on the basis of race, and that the separation lacks sufficient justification. . . .

JUSTICE STEVENS argues that racial gerrymandering poses no constitutional difficulties when district lines are drawn to favor the minority, rather than the majority. We have made clear, however, that equal protection analysis "is not dependent on the race of those burdened or benefited by a particular classification." Indeed, racial classifications receive close scrutiny even when they may be said to burden or benefit the races equally. . . .

The state appellees suggest that a covered jurisdiction may have a compelling interest in creating majority-minority districts in order to comply with the Voting Rights Act. The States certainly have a very strong interest in complying with federal antidiscrimination laws that are constitutionally valid as interpreted and as applied. But in the context of a Fourteenth Amendment challenge, courts must bear in mind the difference between what the law permits and what it requires. . . .

Racial classifications of any sort pose the risk of lasting harm to our society. They reinforce the belief, held by too many for too much of our history, that individuals should be judged by the color of their skin. Racial classifications with respect to voting carry particular dangers. Racial gerrymandering, even for remedial purposes, may balkanize us into competing racial factions;

it threatens to carry us further from the goal of a political system in which race no longer matters—a goal that the Fourteenth and Fifteenth Amendments embody, and to which the Nation continues to aspire. It is for these reasons that race-based districting by our state legislatures demands close judicial scrutiny.

JUSTICE STEVENS, dissenting.

I believe that the Equal Protection Clause is violated when the State creates the kind of uncouth district boundaries seen in *Gomillion v. Lightfoot* and this case, for the sole purpose of making it more difficult for members of a minority group to win an election. The duty to govern impartially is abused when a group with power over the electoral process defines electoral boundaries solely to enhance its own political strength at the expense of any weaker group. That duty, however, is not violated when the majority acts to facilitate the election of a member of a group that lacks such power because it remains underrepresented in the state legislature—whether that group is defined by political affiliation, by common economic interests, or by religious, ethnic, or racial characteristics. The difference between constitutional and unconstitutional gerrymanders has nothing to do with whether they are based on assumptions about the groups they affect, but whether their purpose is to enhance the power of the group in control of the districting process at the expense of any minority group, and thereby to strengthen the unequal distribution of electoral power. When an assumption that people in a particular minority group (whether they are defined by the political party, religion, ethnic group, or race to which they belong) will vote in a particular way is used to *benefit* that group, no constitutional violation occurs.

Finally, we must ask whether otherwise permissible redistricting to benefit an underrepresented minority group becomes impermissible when the minority group is defined by its race. The Court today answers this question in the affirmative, and its answer is wrong. If it is permissible to draw boundaries to provide adequate representation for rural voters, for union members, for Hasidic Jews, for Polish Americans, or for Republicans, it necessarily follows that it is permissible to do the same thing for members of the very minority group whose history in the United States gave birth to the Equal Protection Clause.

The debate among the justices in Shaw *demonstrates the complexity of the issues underlying the voting rights cases. Justice O'Connor forcefully challenges the dissenters by pointing out that it cannot be the case that gerrymandering is justifiable when done on behalf of some groups but not others. Justice Stevens turns the tables, however, by pointing out that this principle would leave virtually no electoral scheme free from challenge since districts have always been drawn with the benefit of particular groups or candidates in mind. Thus,* Shaw *leaves us wondering: Can any districting scheme pass constitutional scrutiny?*

Ironically, Shaw *resurrected the issue of legislative motivations and intentions. Bizarrely shaped legislative districts could not be justified if they were the result of excessive racial considerations. Yet,* Gingles—*and the amended Voting Rights Act—had seemingly rendered moot the question of legislative intentions. The difference seemed to lie in the Court's decision to treat* Shaw *as a Fourteenth Amendment case while regarding vote dilution as a violation of the Fifteenth Amendment.*

In Holder v. Hall, *the Court was confronted with an extension of the logic underlying* Gingles. *Since legislative intentions were not relevant to a vote dilution inquiry, any electoral scheme that prevented a minority group from gaining representation was suspect. In* Holder, *the Bleckley County, Georgia, single-commissioner government was challenged. Since election in such a system required a majority (if not plurality) of the vote, it essentially diluted the voting power of any group that did not or could not make up a majority of the district. Accordingly, the plaintiffs in* Holder *called for a conversion to a multi-member commission in order to lower the electoral threshold.*

The Court struck down the challenge. Nonetheless, Justices Thomas and Antonin Scalia took the opportunity to write a concurring opinion in which they asserted that, under the auspices of its Fifteenth Amendment vote dilution analysis, the Supreme Court had expanded the scope of the franchise to such an extent that it was now unmanageable. They therefore rejected the Court's voting rights jurisprudence and argued for narrowing the scope of the voting right and minimizing judicial intervention in voting rights issues.

8

Jackie Holder, etc., et al., Petitioners
v. E. K. Hall, Sr., et al.,
512 U.S. 874 (1994)

Syllabus

Bleckley County, Georgia, has always had a form of government whereby a single commissioner holds all legislative and executive authority. In 1985, the state legislature authorized the county to adopt by referendum a multimember commission consisting of five members elected from single-member districts and a chair elected at large, but voters defeated the proposal, although they had previously approved a five-member district plan for the county school board. Respondents, black voters and the local chapter of the National Association for the Advancement of Colored People, filed this action. The District Court rejected their constitutional claim that the single-member commission was enacted or maintained with an intent to exclude or limit the political influence of the county's black community in violation of the Fourteenth and Fifteenth Amendments. The court also ruled against their claim that the commission's size violated §2 of the Voting Rights Act of 1965, finding that respondents satisfied only one of the three preconditions established in *Thornburg v. Gingles.* The Court of Appeals reversed on the statutory claim, holding that the totality of the circumstances supported §2 liability and remanding for a formulation of a remedy, which it suggested could be modeled after the county's school board election system.

JUSTICE THOMAS with whom JUSTICE SCALIA joins, concurring in the judgment.

As it was enforced in the years immediately following its enactment, the Voting Rights Act of 1965 was perceived primarily as legislation directed at eliminating literacy tests and similar devices that had been used to prevent black voter registration in the segregated South. . . . This focus in enforcement flowed, no doubt, from the emphasis on access to the ballot apparent in the central provision of the Act, §4, which used a mathematical formula based on voter registration and turnout in 1964 to define certain "covered" jurisdictions in which the use of literacy tests was immediately suspended. Section 6 of the Act reflected the same concern for registration as it provided that federal examiners could be dispatched to covered jurisdictions whenever the Attorney General deemed it necessary to supervise the registration of black voters. And to prevent evasion of the requirements of §4, §5 required that covered jurisdictions obtain "preclearance" from the Department of Justice before altering any "voting qualification or prerequisite to voting, or standard, practice, or procedure with respect to voting." . . .

The central difficulty in any vote dilution case, of course, is determining a point of comparison against which dilution can be measured. As Justice Frankfurter observed [in *Baker v. Carr*], "Talk of 'debasement' or 'dilution' is circular talk. One cannot speak of 'debasement' or 'dilution' of the value of a vote until there is first defined a standard of reference as to what a vote should be worth." [Later, in *Thornburg v. Gingles*, Justice O'Connor expressed a similar sentiment:] "[I]n order to decide whether an electoral system has made it harder for minority voters to elect the candidates they prefer, a court must have an idea in mind of how hard it 'should' be for minority voters to elect their preferred candidates under an acceptable system". But in setting the benchmark of what "undiluted" or fully "effective" voting strength should be, a court must necessarily make some judgments based purely on an assessment of principles of political theory. . . . The choice is inherently a political one, and depends upon the selection of a theory for defining the fully "effective" vote—at bottom, a theory for defining effective participation in representative government. In short, what a court is actually asked to do in a vote dilution case [is, as Justice Frankfurter noted in *Baker v. Carr:*] "to choose among competing bases of representation—ultimately, really, among competing theories of political philosophy."

Perhaps the most prominent feature of the philosophy that has emerged in vote dilution decisions since *Allen* has been the Court's preference for single member districting schemes, both as a benchmark for measuring undiluted minority voting strength and as a remedial mechanism for guaranteeing minorities undiluted voting power. Indeed, commentators surveying the history of voting rights litigation have concluded that it has been the objective of voting rights plaintiffs to use the Act to attack multimember districting schemes and to replace them with single member districting systems drawn with majority minority districts to ensure minority control of seats.

It should be apparent, however, that there is no principle inherent in our constitutional system, or even in the history of the Nation's electoral practices, that makes single member districts the "proper" mechanism for electing representatives to governmental bodies or for giving "undiluted" effect to the votes of a numerical minority. On the contrary, from the earliest days of the Republic, multimember districts were a common feature of our political systems. The Framers left unanswered in the Constitution the question whether congressional delegations from the several States should be elected on a general ticket from each State as a whole or under a districting scheme and left that matter to be resolved by the States or by Congress. It was not until 1842 that Congress determined that Representatives should be elected from single member districts in the States. Single member districting was no more the rule in the States themselves, for the Constitutions of most of the 13 original States provided that representatives in the state legislatures were to be elected from multimember districts. Today, although they have come under increasing attack under the Voting Rights Act, multimember district systems continue to be a feature on the American political landscape, especially in municipal governments.

The obvious advantage the Court has perceived in single member districts, of course, is their tendency to enhance the ability of any numerical minority in the electorate to gain control of seats in a representative body. But in choosing single member districting as a benchmark electoral plan on that basis the Court has made a political decision and, indeed, a decision that itself depends on a prior political choice made in answer to Justice Harlan's question in *Allen*. Justice Harlan asked whether a group's votes should be considered to be more "effective" when they provide *influence* over a greater number of seats, or *control* over a lesser number of seats. In answering that query, the Court has determined that the purpose of the vote—or of the fully "effective" vote—is controlling seats. In other words, in an effort to develop standards for assessing claims of dilution, the Court has adopted the view that members of any numerically significant minority are denied a fully effective use of the franchise unless they are able to control seats in an elected body. Under this theory, votes that do not control a representative are essentially wasted; those who cast them go unrepresented and are just as surely disenfranchised as if they had been barred from registering. Such conclusions, of course, depend upon a certain theory of the "effective" vote, a theory that is not inherent in the concept of representative democracy itself.

In fact, it should be clear that the assumptions that have guided the Court reflect only one possible understanding of effective exercise of the franchise, an understanding based on the view that voters are "represented" only when they choose a delegate who will mirror their views in the legislative halls. But it is certainly possible to construct a theory of effective political participation that would accord greater importance to voters' ability to influence, rather than control, elections. And especially in a two party system such as ours, the influence of a potential "swing" group of voters composing 10% [to] 20% of the electorate in a given district can be considerable. Even such a focus on practical influence, however, is not a necessary component of the definition of the "effective" vote. Some conceptions of representative government may primarily emphasize the formal value of the vote as a mechanism for participation in the electoral process, whether it results in control of a seat or not. Under such a theory, minorities unable to control elected posts would not be considered essentially without a vote; rather, a vote duly cast and counted would be deemed just as "effective" as any other. If a minority group is unable to control seats, that result may plausibly be attributed to the inescapable fact that, in a majoritarian system, numerical minorities lose elections.

In short, there are undoubtedly an infinite number of theories of effective suffrage, representation, and the proper apportionment of political power in a representative democracy that could be drawn upon to answer the questions posed in *Allen*. I do not pretend to have provided the most sophisticated account of the various possibilities; but such matters of political theory are beyond the ordinary sphere of federal judges. And that is precisely the point. The matters the Court has set out to resolve in vote dilution cases are questions of political philosophy, not questions of law. As such, they are not readily subjected to any judicially manageable standards that can guide courts in attempting to select between competing theories.

But the political choices the Court has had to make do not end with the determination that the primary purpose of the "effective" vote is controlling seats or with the selection of single member districting as the mechanism for providing that control. In one sense, these were not even the most critical decisions to be made in devising standards for assessing claims of dilution, for in itself, the selection of single member districting as a benchmark election plan will tell a judge little about the number of minority districts to create. Single member districting tells a court "how" members of a minority are to control seats, but not "how many" seats they should be allowed to control.

But "how many" is the critical issue. Once one accepts the proposition that the effectiveness of votes is measured in terms of the control of seats, the core of any vote dilution claim is an assertion that the group in question is unable to control the "proper" number of seats—that is, the number of seats that the minority's percentage of the population would enable it to control in the benchmark "fair" system. The claim is inherently based on ratios between the numbers of the minority in the population and the numbers of seats controlled. As Justice O'Connor has noted, "any theory of vote dilution must necessarily rely to some extent on a measure of minority voting strength that makes some reference to the proportion between the minority group and the electorate at large. As a result, only a mathematical calculation can answer the fundamental question posed by a claim of vote dilution. And once again, in selecting the proportion that will be used to define the undiluted strength of a minority—the ratio that will provide the principle for decision in a vote dilution case—a court must make a political choice.

The ratio for which this Court has opted, and thus the mathematical principle driving the results in our cases, is undoubtedly direct proportionality. Indeed, four Members of the Court candidly recognized in *Gingles* that the Court had adopted a rule of roughly proportional representation, at least to the extent proportionality was possible given the geographic dispersion of minority populations. While in itself that choice may strike us intuitively as the fairest or most just rule to apply, opting for proportionality is still a political choice, not a result required by any principle of law.

The dabbling in political theory that dilution cases have prompted, however, is hardly the worst aspect of our vote dilution jurisprudence. Far more pernicious has been the Court's willingness to accept the one underlying premise that must inform every minority vote dilution claim: the assumption that the group asserting dilution is not merely a racial or ethnic group, but a group having distinct political interests as well. Of necessity, in resolving vote dilution actions we have given credence to the view that race defines political interest. We have acted on the implicit assumption that members of racial and ethnic groups must all think alike on important matters of public policy and must have their own "minority preferred" representatives holding seats in elected bodies if they are to be considered represented at all.

It is true that in *Gingles* we stated that whether a racial group is "politically cohesive" may not be assumed, but rather must be proved in each case. But the standards we have employed for determining political cohesion have proved so insubstantial that this "precondition" does not present much of a barrier to the assertion of vote dilution claims on behalf of any racial group. Moreover, it provides no test—indeed, it is not designed to provide a test—of whether race itself determines a distinctive political community of interest. According to the rule adopted in *Gingles,* plaintiffs must show simply that members of a racial group tend to prefer the same candidates. There is no set standard defining how strong the correlation must be, and an inquiry into the cause for the correlation (to determine, for example, whether it might be the product of similar socioeconomic interests rather than some other factor related to race) is unnecessary. Thus, whenever similarities in political preferences along racial lines exist, we proclaim that the cause of the correlation is irrelevant, but we effectively rely on the fact of the correlation to assume that racial groups have unique political interests.

As a result, *Gingles'* requirement of proof of political cohesiveness, as practically applied, has proved little different from a working assumption that racial groups can be conceived of largely as political interest groups. And operating under that assumption, we have assigned federal courts the task of ensuring that minorities are assured their "just" share of seats in elected bodies throughout the Nation.

To achieve that result through the currently fashionable mechanism of drawing majority minority single member districts, we have embarked upon what has been aptly characterized as a process of "creating racially 'safe boroughs.'" We have involved the federal courts, and indeed the Nation, in the enterprise of systematically dividing the country into electoral districts along racial lines— an enterprise of segregating the races into political homelands that amounts, in truth, to nothing short of a system of "political apartheid." Blacks are drawn into "black districts" and given "black representatives"; Hispanics are drawn into Hispanic districts and given "Hispanic representatives"; and so on. Worse still, it is not only the courts that have taken up this project. In response to judicial decisions and the promptings of the Justice Department, the States themselves, in an attempt to avoid costly and disruptive Voting Rights Act litigation, have begun to gerrymander electoral districts according to race. That practice now promises to embroil the courts in a lengthy process of attempting to undo, or at least to minimize, the damage wrought by the system we created.

The assumptions upon which our vote dilution decisions have been based should be repugnant to any nation that strives for the ideal of a color blind Constitution. [As Justice Douglas stated in *Wright v. Rockefeller:*] "The principle of equality is at war with the notion that District A must be represented by a Negro, as it is with the notion that District B must be represented by a Caucasian, District C by a Jew, District D by a Catholic, and so on." Despite Justice Douglas' warning sounded 30 years ago, our voting rights decisions are rapidly progressing towards a system that is indistinguishable in principle from a scheme under which members of different racial groups are divided into separate electoral registers and allocated a proportion of political power on the basis of race. Under our jurisprudence, rather than requiring registration on racial rolls and dividing power purely on a population basis, we have simply resorted to the somewhat less precise expedient of drawing geographic district lines to capture minority populations and to ensure the existence of the "appropriate" number of "safe minority seats."

That distinction in the practical implementation of the concept, of course, is immaterial. The basic premises underlying our system of safe minority districts and those behind the racial register are the same: that members of the racial group must think alike and that their interests are so distinct that the group must be provided a separate body of representatives in the legislature to voice its unique point of view. Such a "system, by whatever name it is called, is a divisive force in a community, emphasizing differences between candidates and voters that are irrelevant." Justice Douglas correctly predicted the results of state sponsorship of such a theory of representation: "When racial or religious lines are drawn by the State, . . . antagonisms that relate to race or to religion rather than to political issues are generated; communities seek not the best representative but the best racial or religious partisan." In short, few devices could be better designed to exacerbate racial tensions than the consciously segregated districting system currently being constructed in the name of the Voting Rights Act.

As a practical political matter, our drive to segregate political districts by race can only serve to deepen racial divisions by destroying any need for voters or candidates to build bridges between racial groups or to form voting coalitions. "Black preferred" candidates are assured election in "safe black districts"; white preferred candidates are assured election in "safe white districts." Neither group needs to draw on support from the other's constituency to win on election day. As one judge described the current trend of voting rights cases: "We are bent upon polarizing political subdivisions by race. The arrangement we construct makes it unnecessary, and probably unwise, for an elected official from a white majority district to be responsive at all to the wishes of black citizens; similarly, it is politically unwise for a black official from a black majority district to be responsive at all to white citizens."

As this description suggests, the system we have instituted affirmatively encourages a racially based understanding of the representative function. The clear premise of the system is that geographic districts are merely a device to be manipulated to establish "black representatives" whose real constituencies are defined, not in terms of the voters who populate their districts, but in terms of race. The "black representative's" function, in other words, is to represent the "black interest." . . .

. . . [We] should recognize that our approach to splintering the electorate into racially designated single member districts does not by any means mark a limit on the authority federal judges may wield to rework electoral systems under our Voting Rights Act jurisprudence. On the contrary, in relying on single member districting schemes as a touchstone, our cases so far have been somewhat arbitrarily limited to addressing the interests of minority voters who are sufficiently geographically compact to form a majority in a single member district. There is no reason *a priori,* however, that our focus should be so constrained. The decision to rely on single member geographic districts as a mechanism for conducting elections is merely a political choice—and one that we might reconsider in the future. Indeed, it is a choice that has undoubtedly been influenced by the adversary process: in the cases that have come before us, plaintiffs have focused largely upon attacking multimember districts and have offered single member schemes as the benchmark of an "undiluted" alternative.

. . . [A]s the destructive effects of our current penchant for majority minority districts become more apparent, courts will undoubtedly be called upon to reconsider adherence to geographic districting as a method for ensuring minority voting power. Already, some advocates have criticized the current strategy of creating majority minority districts and have urged the adoption of other voting mechanisms—for example, cumulative voting or a system using transferable votes—that can produce proportional results without requiring division of the electorate into racially segregated districts. . . .

Such changes may seem radical departures from the electoral systems with which we are most familiar. Indeed, they may be unwanted by the people in the several States who purposely have adopted districting systems in their electoral laws. But nothing in our present understanding of the Voting Rights Act places a principled limit on the authority of federal courts that would prevent them from instituting a system of cumulative voting as a remedy under §2, or even from establishing a more elaborate mechanism for securing proportional representation based on transferable votes. As some Members of the Court have already recognized, geographic districting is not a requirement inherent in our political system. . . . Rather, districting is merely another political choice made by the citizenry in the drafting of their state constitutions. Like other political choices concerning electoral systems and models of representation, it too is presumably subject to a judicial override if it comes into conflict with the theories of representation and effective voting that we may develop under the Voting Rights Act.

Indeed, the unvarnished truth is that all that is required for districting to fall out of favor is for Members of this Court to further develop their political thinking. We should not be surprised if voting rights advocates encourage us to "revive our political imagination . . ." and to consider "innovative and nontraditional remedies" for vote dilution. . . . [F]or under our Voting Rights Act jurisprudence, it is only the limits on our "political imagination" that place restraints on the standards we may select for defining undiluted voting systems. Once we candidly recognize that geographic districting and other aspects of electoral systems that we have so far placed beyond question are merely political choices, those practices, too, may fall under suspicion of having a dilutive effect on minority voting strength. And when the time comes to put the question to the test, it may be difficult indeed for a Court that, under *Gingles,* has been bent on creating roughly proportional representation for geographically compact minorities to find a principled reason for holding that a geographically dispersed minority cannot challenge districting itself as a dilutive electoral practice. In principle, cumulative voting and other non district based methods of effecting proportional representation are simply more efficient and straightforward mechanisms for achieving what has already become our tacit objective: roughly proportional allocation of political power according to race.

At least one court, in fact, has already abandoned districting and has opted instead for cumulative voting on a county wide basis as a remedy for a Voting Rights Act violation. The District Court for the District of Maryland recently reasoned that, compared to a system that divides voters into districts according to race, "[c]umulative voting is less likely to increase polarization between different interests," and that it "will allow the voters, by the way they exercise their votes, to 'district' themselves," thereby avoiding government involvement in a process of segregating the electorate. . . . If such a system can be ordered on a county wide basis, we should recognize that there is no limiting principle under the Act that would prevent federal courts from requiring it for elections to state legislatures as well.

Such is the current state of our understanding of the Voting Rights Act. That our reading of the Act has assigned the federal judiciary the task of making the decisions I have described above should suggest to the Members of this Court that something in our jurisprudence has gone awry. We would be mighty Platonic guardians indeed if Congress had granted us the authority to determine the best form of local government for every county, city, village, and town in America. But under our constitutional system, this Court is not a centralized politburo appointed for life to dictate to the provinces the "correct" theories of democratic representation, the "best" electoral systems for securing truly "representative" government, the "fairest" proportions of minority political influence, or, as respondents would have us hold today, the "proper" sizes for local governing bodies. We should be cautious in interpreting any Act of Congress to grant us power to make such determinations.

In Bush v. Vera (1996), the Court struck down several majority-minority congressional districts in Texas. In an intriguing decision, Justice O'Connor wrote the opinion of the Court but also felt compelled to write a separate concurrence to her own opinion. She did this to set forth her understanding of the relationship between the Fourteenth Amendment and the Voting Rights Act and to state clearly her criteria for assessing the constitutionality of majority-minority districts. Insofar as Justice O'Connor has played a key role in restraining the use of majority-minority districts, her discussion is illuminating, because while she believes that the redistricting process can be perverted by "excessive" racial considerations, she also believes that the Voting Rights Act's commitment to enhance minority representation opportunities is constitutional. What follows is her attempt to reconcile these two positions.

The discussion in this book indicates that the study of voting rights and representation is fraught with tensions and contradictions. There is no one political theory or vision of democracy that allows us to sift through the many competing values and concerns that inhere in debates about voting rights and arrive at anything remotely resembling a coherent conclusion. Thus, it should come as no surprise that, after fifty years of voting rights decisions, Justice O'Connor's attempt to clarify her vision of the Court's jurisprudence falls far short of its mark.

9

Bush, Governor of Texas, et al. v. Vera et al., 517 U.S. 952 (1996)

Syllabus

Because the 1990 census revealed a population increase entitling Texas to three additional congressional seats, and in an attempt to comply with the Voting Rights Act of 1965 (VRA), the Texas Legislature promulgated a redistricting plan that, among other things, created District 30 as a new majority African American district in Dallas County and District 29 as a new majority Hispanic district in Harris County, and reconfigured District 18, which is adjacent to District 29, as a majority African American district. After the Department of Justice precleared the plan under VRA §5, the plaintiffs, six Texas voters, filed this challenge alleging that 24 of the State's 30 congressional districts constitute racial gerrymanders in violation of the Fourteenth Amendment. The three-judge District Court held Districts 18, 29, and 30 unconstitutional. The Governor of Texas, private intervenors, and the United States (as intervenor) appeal.

JUSTICE O'CONNOR, concurring.

I write separately to express my view on two points. First, compliance with the results test of §2 of the Voting Rights Act (VRA) is a compelling state interest. Second, that test can co-exist in principle and in practice with *Shaw v. Reno,* 509 U.S. 630 (1993), and its progeny, as elaborated in today's opinions.

Although I agree with the dissenters about §2's role as part of our national commitment to racial equality, I differ from them in my belief that that commitment can and must be reconciled with the complementary commitment of our Fourteenth Amendment jurisprudence to eliminate the unjustified use of racial stereotypes. At the same time that we combat the symptoms of racial polarization in politics, we must strive to eliminate unnecessary race based state action that appears to endorse the disease.

Today's decisions, in conjunction with the recognition of the compelling state interest in compliance with the reasonably perceived requirements of §2, present a workable framework for the achievement of these twin goals. I would summarize that framework, and the rules governing the States' consideration of race in the districting process, as follows.

First, so long as they do not subordinate traditional districting criteria to the use of race for its own sake or as a proxy, States may intentionally create majority minority districts, and may otherwise take race into consideration, without coming under strict scrutiny. Only if traditional districting criteria are neglected and that neglect is predominantly due to the misuse of race does strict scrutiny apply.

Second, where voting is racially polarized, §2 prohibits States from adopting districting schemes that would have the effect that minority voters "have less opportunity than other members of the electorate to . . . elect representatives of their choice." That principle may require a State to create a majority minority district where the three *Gingles* factors are present—viz., (i) the minority group "is sufficiently large and geographically compact to constitute a majority in a single member district," (ii) "it is politically cohesive," and (iii) "the white majority votes sufficiently as a bloc to enable it . . . usually to defeat the minority's preferred candidate."

Third, the state interest in avoiding liability under VRA §2 is compelling. If a State has a strong basis in evidence for concluding that the *Gingles* factors are present, it may create a majority minority district without awaiting judicial findings. Its "strong basis in evidence" need not take any particular form, although it cannot simply rely on generalized assumptions about the prevalence of racial bloc voting.

Fourth, if a State pursues that compelling interest by creating a district that "substantially addresses" the potential liability, and does not deviate substantially from a hypothetical court drawn §2 district for predominantly racial reasons, its districting plan will be deemed narrowly tailored.

Finally, however, districts that are bizarrely shaped and non-compact, and that otherwise neglect traditional districting principles and deviate substantially from the hypothetical court drawn district, for predominantly racial reasons, are unconstitutional.

Index

About the Authors

MARK E. RUSH is associate professor of politics at Washington and Lee University in Lexington, Virginia, where he teaches courses on elections and electoral reform, constitutional law, American politics, and comparative politics. He has written numerous articles on redistricting, election law, and electoral reform. He is the author of *Does Redistricting Make a Difference?* and editor of *Voting Rights and Redistricting in the United States.* He is currently chair of the Representation and Electoral Systems section of the American Political Science Association.

RICHARD L. ENGSTROM is research professor of political science at the University of New Orleans. He has written extensively on the impact of election systems on minority voters. His articles on this topic, a number of which have been cited by the U.S. Supreme Court, have appeared in the *American Political Science Review, Journal of Politics, Social Science Quarterly, Electoral Studies,* and other journals. He has served as a consultant to redistricting commissions in Pennsylvania and Illinois and as an expert witness in numerous court cases involving minority vote dilution. He is a former chair of the Representation and Electoral Systems section of the American Political Science Association.